T0319767

Fiscal Federalism and Political Decentralization

STUDIES IN FISCAL FEDERALISM AND STATE–LOCAL FINANCE

Series Editor: Wallace E. Oates, *Professor of Economics, University of Maryland, College Park and University Fellow, Resources for the Future, USA*

This important series is designed to make a significant contribution to the development of the principles and practices of state–local finance. It includes both theoretical and empirical work. International in scope, it addresses issues of current and future concern in both East and West and in developed and developing countries.

The main purpose of the series is to create a forum for the publication of high-quality work and to show how economic analysis can make a contribution to understanding the role of local finance in fiscal federalism in the twenty-first century. Titles in the series include:

State and Local Finances under Pressure
Edited by David L. Sjoquist

The Property Tax, Land Use and Land Use Regulation
Edited by Dick Netzer

Restructuring Local Government Finance in Developing Countries
Lessons from South Africa
Edited by Roy Bahl and Paul Smoke

Reforming Intergovernmental Fiscal Relations and the Rebuilding of Indonesia
The 'Big Bang' Program and its Economic Consequences
Edited by James Alm, Jorge Martínez-Vázquez and Sri Mulyani Indrawati

Competition in the Provision of Local Public Goods
Single Function Jurisdictions and Individual Choice
Alexander Petermann Reifschneider

Decentralization in Asia and Latin America
Towards a Comparative Interdisciplinary Perspective
Edited by Paul Smoke, Eduardo J. Gómez and George E. Peterson

The Politics and Economics and Regional Transfers
Decentralization, Interregional Redistribution and Income Convergence
Fabio Padovano

Fiscal Reform in Spain
Accomplishments and Challenges
Edited by Jorge Martínez-Vázquez and José Félix Sanz-Sanz

Fiscal Federalism and Political Decentralization
Lessons from Spain, Germany and Canada
Edited by Núria Bosch and José M. Durán

Fiscal Federalism and Political Decentralization

Lessons from Spain, Germany and Canada

Edited by

Núria Bosch

Professor of Public Finance, University of Barcelona and Institut d'Economia de Barcelona, Spain

José M. Durán

Lecturer of Public Finance, University of Barcelona and Institut d'Economia de Barcelona, Spain

STUDIES IN FISCAL FEDERALISM AND STATE–LOCAL FINANCE

Edward Elgar

Cheltenham, UK • Northampton, MA, USA

Published by
Edward Elgar Publishing Limited
The Lypiatts
15 Lansdown Road
Cheltenham
Glos GL50 2JA
UK

Edward Elgar Publishing, Inc.
William Pratt House
9 Dewey Court
Northampton
Massachusetts 01060
USA

Reprinted 2013

A catalogue record for this book
is available from the British Library

Library of Congress Control Number: 2008927956

MIX
Paper from
responsible sources
FSC   FSC® C013056
www.fsc.org

ISBN 978 1 84720 467 7

Printed and bound in Great Britain by T.J. International Ltd, Padstow

Contents

List of contributors   vii
Preface   ix
Editorial introduction   xi

INTRODUCTION

1   The financing system of Spanish regions: main features, weak
    points and possible reforms   3
    Núria Bosch and José M. Durán

PART I   TAX ASSIGNMENT

2   Revenue assignments in the practice of fiscal decentralization   27
    Jorge Martínez-Vázquez
3   Tax assignment and tax autonomy in OECD countries   56
    Hansjörg Blöchliger
4   Tax assignment and regional co-responsibility in Spain   74
    Juan A. Gimeno Ullastres

PART II   FISCAL EQUALIZATION

5   Fiscal equalization: the Canadian experience   109
    Robin Boadway
6   Fiscal equalization in Germany   137
    Thiess Buettner
7   Fiscal equalization in Spain   147
    Jesús Ruiz-Huerta Carbonell and Ana Herrero Alcalde

PART III   TAX ADMINISTRATION

8   Tax coordination under the Canadian tax system   169
    *Paul Berg-Dick, Michel Carreau, Deanne Field and
    Mireille Éthier*
9   The decentralization of tax administration in Germany:
    consequences   193
    Alexander Ulbricht

10   Current situation and proposals for reform of Spain's tax
     administration   209
     Alejandro Esteller Moré

Index   249

Contributors

Paul Berg-Dick, Finance Canada, Canada

Hansjörg Blöchliger, Organisation for Economic Co-operation and Development (OECD)

Robin Boadway, Queen's University, Canada

Núria Bosch, University of Barcelona and Institut d'Economia de Barcelona, Spain

Thiess Buettner, Ifo Institut and Ludwig Maximilians Universität München, Germany

Michel Carreau, Finance Canada, Canada

José M. Durán, University of Barcelona and Institut d'Economia de Barcelona, Spain

Alejandro Esteller Moré, University of Barcelona and Institut d'Economia de Barcelona, Spain

Mireille Éthier, Finance Canada, Canada

Deanne Field, Finance Canada, Canada

Juan A. Gimeno Ullastres, Universidad Nacional de Educación a Distancia (UNED), Spain

Ana Herrero Alcalde, Universidad Nacional de Educación a Distancia (UNED) and Instituto de Estudios Fiscales, Spain

Jorge Martínez-Vázquez, Georgia State University, United States

Jesús Ruiz-Huerta Carbonell, Universidad Rey Juan Carlos and Instituto de Estudios Fiscales, Spain

Alexander Ulbricht, Bavarian State Tax Service, Germany

Preface

Núria Bosch and José M. Durán

Traditionally, countries have been divided into unitary and federal countries, depending on the political system of organization. The former consist of two levels of governments, central and local, while the latter have another tier of government in between, a regional one. However, an increasing number of historically unitary countries are carrying out reforms with the aim of moving toward more decentralized governance. They are not pure federal countries, but at the same time they are not purely unitary any more, since the regional governments, often set up with decentralized purposes, take on a significant number of responsibilities previously undertaken by the central government.

A key issue in the process of good political decentralization is to find an appropriate financing system for regional governments. Regions must have adequate revenues to fund their public expenditure requirements so that they enjoy effective autonomy, but at the same time they must also take responsibility for how they raise those revenues. Therefore, the objectives are to achieve autonomy but also fiscal responsibility. But in addition, central governments must ensure that all their citizens, regardless of whether they live in a rich or a poor region, enjoy similar levels of well-being. Poor regions must also raise enough revenues to fund their responsibilities and achieve national standards. In other words, autonomy and fiscal responsibility must be combined with territorial solidarity. This book analyzes political decentralization and fiscal federalism, focusing precisely on the financing system of regions, and on the issues that are important in achieving a well-designed financing system: tax assignment, fiscal equalization and tax administration. These three issues are analyzed in depth in the book, making special reference to the experience of three developed countries: Spain, Germany and Canada.

Spain is an outstanding example of a unitary country that has engaged in a very important process of decentralization over the last 25 years. Nowadays, the Spanish regions are responsible for competences, health and education among many others, which account for about 35 per cent of all public expenditure. As far as Germany and Canada are concerned, both are historical federal countries, with well-defined financing systems for the sub-national governments, which, however, continue to be subject to periodical reforms.

Tax assignment, fiscal grants and tax administration are studied in depth in the different chapters of the book with the aim of learning about and understanding the recent experiences of Spain, Germany and Canada. The authors, from the academic world, public bodies and international organizations, offer first-hand views on national experiences, reaching some conclusions that are very useful from the perspectives of other countries. In fact, this was the aim of the 4th Symposium on Fiscal Federalism organized by the Institut d'Economia de Barcelona (IEB), which took place in Barcelona on 30–31 May 2006: 'The Experience of Federal Countries: Lessons for Spain'. The reputation of the keynote speakers and the quality of their papers led us to publish the book you now have in your hands.

To conclude, we would like to thank all authors for their contributions. We hope it is informative to researchers, policy-makers and practitioners as well to everyone interested in decentralization and fiscal federalism.

Editorial introduction

The book begins with an introductory section comprising Chapter 1 and is followed by three further parts, each one comprising three chapters. In Chapter 1, Bosch and Durán, from the University of Barcelona and the Institut d'Economia de Barcelona, offer an overview perspective of the regional financing system in Spain, pointing out the general features and the weak points that should be considered in future reform.

In the last 25 years, Spain has experienced a very important process of political and fiscal decentralization, with the creation of the so-called Autonomous Communities (ACs). The financing system first begins with the assessment of the expenditure requirements of three different areas of responsibilities: common, health and social responsibilities. To provide the corresponding resources, the financing system rests on two basic sources: taxes and equalization grants. The successive reforms have increased the weight of tax resources, raising the number of ceded taxes as well as the legal power to modify some of their parameters. With the aim of ensuring that all ACs have enough resources to carry out their responsibilities, the system envisages the sufficiency fund as the key element of fiscal equalization.

According to Bosch and Durán, in spite of the improvements introduced, the financing system of regions still suffers from significant weak points: a lack of fiscal co-responsibility, an insufficient financial autonomy and the application of a bad system of fiscal equalization. Most citizens still believe most taxes are only paid to the state. The lack of transparency behind some of the key elements of the system, which are a consequence of successive political agreements, means that there are significant differences in general resources per capita among ACs. The equalization mechanism inverts the ranking positions in favor of the ACs with less fiscal capacity.

Chapter 1 ends with an analysis of the future reforms that should be introduced to improve the system. First, an increase in the regional tax power and in the role of tax administration to enhance the fiscal co-responsibility of regions. At the same time, partial equalization, so that rich ACs should be able to retain some of the revenues exceeding the average. Finally, appropriate updating mechanisms should be introduced to provide a more flexible and valid system.

Part I deals with tax assignment, and consists of three different chapters written respectively by Jorge Martínez-Vázquez, from Georgia State

University (United States), Hansjörg Blöchliger, from the OECD and Juan A. Gimeno Ullastres, from the UNED (Spain).

In Chapter 2, Jorge Martínez-Vázquez analyzes revenue assignments in the practice of fiscal decentralization. According to Martínez-Vázquez, effective fiscal decentralization requires meaningful levels of revenue autonomy at the regional and local levels of government. However, besides adequate revenues to fund the public expenditure requirements of sub-national governments, what we most want from revenue assignments is accountability and political and fiscal responsibility for sub-national government officials. This is fundamentally achieved by granting sub-national governments a significant level of tax autonomy. Achieving a good level of tax autonomy has many other benefits including the imposition of hard budget constraints on sub-national governments.

Nonetheless, the author points out that the full financing of sub-national governments from autonomous tax sources is generally not feasible. The commonly accepted compromise is that sub-national governments need to raise their own funds at the margin and operate with hard budget constraints. Operationally, this translates into the golden rule for revenue assignment: own revenue sources should fund the expenditure requirements (net of conditional grants) of the wealthiest sub-national governments, and the revenue requirements of the relatively poorer sub-national government should be supplemented with equalization grants.

However, not all forms of tax autonomy are equally desirable. All things considered, Martínez-Vázquez believes the best way to provide sub-national governments with tax autonomy is to have a closed list of taxes for which sub-national governments can set tax rates within some minimum and maximum values that are nationally legislated. Good choices for sub-national governments include maximum use of fees and charges for excludable services under the benefit principle, plus a list of well-suited taxes such as the property tax, vehicle taxes and piggyback personal income taxes. Recent advances also make it possible to introduce a sub-national VAT in either its dual Quebec-style form, or under the CVAT (compensating VAT) or VIVAT (viable integrated VAT) forms.

The international experience clearly shows that there are no unique well-defined formulas for revenue assignments. More research is needed to understand the political economy behind some of the anomalies in the choices of revenue assignments. In particular, it is important to better understand why the wrong revenue assignments have proved so difficult to change in a significant number of countries and also why the little revenue authority provided to sub-national governments quite often goes unused even though these governments might, at the same time, demand more funding. Jorge Martínez-Vázquez concludes that future research should be more heavily focused on the political economy of revenue assignments.

In Chapter 3, Hansjörg Blöchliger, from the OECD, offers an overall picture of tax assignment and tax autonomy in OECD countries. The degree of decentralization varies greatly across these countries. We can observe that the sub-central tax share and the sub-central expenditure share have diverged over the last ten years. While the share of sub-national expenditures generally increased, local taxing power – with a few notable exceptions – remained almost stable. In fact, in most countries, sub-central government expenditures exceed tax revenue by far, and this 'fiscal gap' has widened in the last decade. The difference between responsibilities and resources points to large intergovernmental transfer schemes.

Blöchliger shows that own taxes are a more important revenue source for sub-central governments than grants. With 60 percent against 40 percent, tax revenue accounts for a larger share of revenue. Nonetheless, only a part of tax revenue allocated to sub-central governments is under their control. Often their power to set and change tax rates and the tax base is restricted. In many federal countries and some unitary ones, sub-central governments take part in tax-sharing arrangements where the tax revenue allocated to a single jurisdiction is either determined by all sub-central governments together or by central government.

It is also interesting to note, indicates Blöchliger, that in some countries, despite having the right to vary tax rates, sub-central governments set the same rate across the country, a feature also pointed out by Martínez-Vázquez in the previous chapter. Such 'unused taxing power', concludes the author, invites a deeper look into fiscal institutions and the incentives they generate for tax competition. Fiscal equalization arrangements can partly explain why sub-central jurisdictions in many countries stick to a uniform tax rate although they have the right to vary their rates.

After the international view, Chapter 4 concentrates on tax assignment and regional co-responsibility in Spain. Juan Gimeno Ullastres, from the UNED (Spain) explains the recent evolution in that country. There, the rapid decentralization of competences from the state to the so-called Autonomous Communities was not accompanied by an equally rapid gain in financial competences. As a result, Spanish academia has insisted on the idea of co-responsibility for 20 years. Defining the suitable taxes for each territorial area and giving them the maximum autonomy is an approach, according to Gimeno Ullastres, that ensures genuine co-responsibility, effective financial autonomy and greater stability in the system, rather than making proportional allocations based on statistics.

The new proposals for the next reform of the financing system seem to point to effective use of retail VAT. Gimeno Ullastres believes that this proposal is highly advisable in spite of the problems that it poses because of lack of experience and predictable EU obstacles. There are several ways to achieve the corresponding system, but it is necessary to remain clear that the final result must not rest on the value added at the retail stage but rather on the end consumption. Any participation in the total VAT collected should be based on the final bases effectively observed in taxation at the retail stage.

In addition, income, fuel, tobacco and gambling are further areas that also lend themselves to decentralization, under certain conditions. Specifically, it is assumed that all indirect taxes would fall on the retail stage, since suitability is low or very low at the other stages.

According to Gimeno Ullastres, there is no ideal solution or irrefutable alternative. But thought must be given to creating a system in which the territorial treasury offices gain autonomy and co-responsibility, thereby bringing about less complexity, more transparency and a guarantee of the principle of solidarity.

Part II comprises three chapters written, respectively, by Robin Boadway, from Queen's University (Canada), Thiess Buettner, from the Ifo Institut and Ludwig Maximilians Universität München (Germany) and Jesús Ruiz-Huerta Carbonell, from the Universidad Rey Juan Carlos and Instituto de Estudios Fiscales along with Ana Herrero Alcade, from the UNED and Instituto de Estudios Fiscales (Spain).

Robin Boadway, in Chapter 5, analyzes the Canadian experience as far as fiscal equalization is concerned. He affirms that there is no perfect equalization system. In a world in which provinces truly have discretion over their spending and taxing policies, heterogeneous outcomes are bound to occur. Indeed, according to Boadway, this is a strength of the federal system. This implies that designing an equalization system that achieves the objective of ensuring that the provinces have the fiscal capacity to provide roughly comparable levels of public services at roughly comparable levels of taxation is a difficult task.

Boadway affirms that despite the difficulties of implementation, the design of the equalization system should be guided by principles, and these principles should be reflected in a formula-based approach rather than one that relies on discretion. In the Canadian case, the emphasis on revenue equalization using a so-called representative tax system (RTS) agrees well with the principles. The main issues that arise involve conflicts between the principle of equalization and other principles. These include the provincial ownership of resources, the incentive effects of equalization, and affordability to the federal government. His view is that the issues of resources and affordability should be dealt with by adjusting the standard rather than by reducing the extent to which resource revenues determine equalization entitlements. Full equalization of all revenue sources for recipient provinces at least ensures that fiscal equity is achieved among recipient provinces, although not necessarily between recipient and non-recipient provinces. In a federation as decentralized as Canada, full equalization among all provinces would be very difficult to achieve. That is one reason why the country should be very cautious about further decentralizing revenue-raising responsibilities. That would make horizontal balance even more difficult to achieve.

Finally, Boadway emphasizes that achieving a successful equalization system involves non-economic considerations. Institutions can be important in ensuring that the integrity of the equalization process is respected. Equalization policy is part of the broader set of federal–provincial fiscal arrangements and is not placed in a vacuum. The process requires that decisions be made from a long-term perspective and that the federal government behaves in a cooperative manner with respect to the provinces. Moreover, the ability of the federal government to commit to a formula-based approach to equalization that is not compromised by discretionary changes is important to ensure that problems of soft budget constraints do not emerge. Whether that level of commitment and cooperation requires some arm's-length institution such as a grants commission, found in some federations, is an open question. At least, the importance of institutional considerations and process should not be overlooked in any discussion of reforming federal–provincial fiscal relations.

Thiess Buettner from the Ifo Institut and Ludwig Maximilians Universität München analyzes the German experience in Chapter 6. The German system of fiscal federalism puts a strong emphasis on fiscal redistribution by means of revenue-sharing and fiscal equalization among all levels of governments. At the municipal level the existence of a substantial degree of horizontal fiscal redistribution may be quite helpful in curbing local business-tax competition and providing some sort of insurance against revenue fluctuations. Nevertheless, this positive role is partly offset with disincentive effects, such as, for instance, the reluctance of municipalities to use the land tax to generate revenue.

At the state level, the role of fiscal equalization is much more problematic. The system provides the states with a substantial amount of public funds while it does not require the states to take responsibility for their policies towards the taxpayer by deciding about the tax burden. The state would rather live mainly on grants. At the same time, however, the extensive use of fiscal redistribution cannot be justified on efficiency grounds as is the case with municipalities. In fact, given tax collection at state-level, the fiscal redistribution actually provides additional disincentives that are not present at the municipal level.

Buettner considers that the German example offers some interesting conclusions for the evolving fiscal federalism in Europe. The example of the

German municipalities shows that under the protection of revenue-sharing, tax competition does not necessarily result in inefficiently low tax rates. At the same time, however, the example of the German states shows that fiscal redistribution should be used with caution, in particular in a situation where there is decentralized tax collection.

In Chapter 7, Jesús Ruiz-Huerta Carbonell, from the Universidad Rey Juan Carlos and Instituto de Estudios Fiscales, and Ana Herrero Alcade, from the UNED and Instituto de Estudios Fiscales concentrate on the Spanish equalization system, its characteristics and problems, and the main alternatives for its reform in the near future. To the authors, the search for a new equalization grant should deal with some restrictions. First of all, it should try to achieve more equitable results, responding to an explicit equity target. The central government plays the main role in deciding how much equalization should be achieved, but the regional governments should also participate in the decision process, to foster the stability of the system.

From the technical perspective, the two basic alternatives in choosing the intensity of equalization are a *net equalization*, which means that all regional differences are eliminated, and a *gross equalization* that tries to reduce, but not to eliminate, interregional differences. In the Spanish system there seems to be greater support for a net equalization scheme, although the current debate argues that equalization grants should be devoted to finance only essential, and not all devolved, public services.

The authors indicate that the equalization system should not generate great changes in the ranking of regional abilities to provide services, since its purpose must be to allow all territories to provide similar levels of public services with similar levels of fiscal effort. In addition, from a dynamic point of view, a good equalization system must address the evolution of regional fiscal capacity and expenditure requirements.

The aim is to build up a more stable regional financial system. Despite the fact that the proposals generate some costs to the central government and/or certain regions, they would achieve better results from the equity perspective. For that reason, Ruiz-Huerta Carbonell and Herrero Alcade believe that the gradualism of the reforms is a key issue.

The last three chapters of the book in Part III analyze tax administration. In Chapter 8, Paul Berg-Dick, Michel Carreau, Deanne Field and Mireille Éthier, from Finance Canada, explain how tax coordination works under the Canadian tax system. In Canada, provinces have considerable flexibility with respect to taxation. As a result of the joint occupancy of the three main tax fields (income tax, corporate tax and sales taxes), the federal government and many provincial governments have entered into administration agreements covering each of the tax fields. These administration agreements represent one of the main components of tax coordination between the federal and provincial governments.

Tax Collection Agreements are the major instrument for coordinating the income tax systems in Canada, which exist in all provinces except Quebec. The provincial tax structure is required to be harmonized to a certain degree with the federal tax structure. For instance, provinces agree to adhere to a common tax base. This is the primary reason why the federal government absorbs virtually all of the administrative costs associated with the collection of provincial taxes. According to the authors, the single administration of federal and provincial income taxes benefits both tax-payers and governments. Taxpayers benefit from a reduction in overall compliance costs and both benefit from increased simplicity in the operation of the tax system.

Regarding sales tax, there are currently two arrangements in place between the federal government and some provinces that provide for coordination. The first arrangement is the Comprehensive Integrated Tax Coordination Agreements, under which the federal government is the administrator of the tax for Newfoundland and Labrador, Nova Scotia and New Brunswick. The second arrangement is between Canada and Quebec, under which the province is the administrator of federal and provincial value-added taxes within Quebec. The other provinces except Alberta have their own retail sales tax, which increases the complexity and the cost of doing business. For that reason the federal government is inviting these provinces to engage in discussions on the harmonization of their provincial retail sales taxes with the federal general sales tax. In this context, the Canada Revenue Agency plays a key role in administering provincial taxes that are subject to the coordination agreements, being the principal revenue collector for both the federal and provincial governments. It was created in 1999 at the instigation of the federal government to provide better service to Canadians, become a more efficient and effective organization and establish a closer partnership with the provinces and territories. Eleven of the 15 members of the Board of Management are nominated by the provinces, which, for the authors, is a clear example of the willingness of the agency to serve the various client governments properly.

The German experience is studied in Chapter 9, by Alexander Ulbricht, from the Bavarian State Tax Service. The author offers a brief overview of the main features of the German tax system, and focuses on the organization of the German tax administration, analyzing the consequences of a decentralized administration in the German case. In Germany the most important taxes (VAT, income tax and corporate tax) are managed by the state offices. The *Länder* are free to choose the organization of their tax administration and there is no federal rule concerning how to administer taxes and organize the administration, regardless of a general principle of 'uniform taxation'.

Consequently, some problems may arise. The cross-state cases are sometimes difficult to control. Tax equalization is a disincentive for states to invest money and personnel in a more extensive auditing process. Due to different approaches to fighting tax evasion and encouraging compliance, and the lack of coordination in this area of tax administration, most of the measures lose their effectiveness the moment another state becomes involved.

Ulbricht believes that in order to work effectively, a centralized tax administration is not required, and is probably even more obstructive than a decentralized one. The only necessity is a superior coordinating authority with a greater influence on the way the states organize their tax administration: a federal tax office.

In Chapter 10, the final chapter, Alejandro Esteller Moré, from the University of Barcelona and the Institut d'Economia de Barcelona (Spain), concentrates on the current situation and proposals for reform of the tax administration in Spain. Over time, while assuming legal power over income tax, some Spanish regions have simultaneously begun to lay claim to a more important role in the administration of the taxes levied in their territory, at least over taxes shared with the state and administered by the AEAT (Agencia Estatal de Administración), the state's tax agency. In spite of some steps forward, certain regions call for greater involvement in tax administration, especially in income tax.

Indeed, the new Statute of Autonomy of Catalonia anticipates the creation of the Tax Agency of Catalonia (ATC; Agència Tributària de Catalunya), to encourage greater organizational flexibility and budgetary autonomy. This regional agency alongside the AEAT will set up a consortium (or equivalent entity) in which both agencies have an equal share of participation and that would take on the application of all taxes in Catalonia. Therefore, Esteller Moré affirms that the not yet fully defined formula would involve decentralizing income tax administration in Catalonia, in collaboration with the AEAT.

The author believes the reform is very positive, because, on the one hand, it guarantees a degree of uniformity in the tax processes, avoids the fragmentation of tax information generated in Catalonia that is of interest to other regions and obviously to the AEAT, and, finally, does away with any possible disincentives to efficient tax management, perhaps caused by questions of tax competence and/or horizontal equalization. This is all because membership on the consortium's board will be equally shared between the state and the regional agencies. However, the reform allows a degree of non-uniformity in the tax processes (e.g., permitting specific fraud detection filters and differing rules for taxpayer treatment). It allows for improvement to the income tax assessment procedure used locally and gives the Catalan administration much greater access to tax information. Finally, it helps to set tax collection forecasts and assess the impact of envisaged tax reforms.

According to Esteller Moré, the most serious issue to be raised by the consortium in Catalonia is the extent to which taxes may, in fact, become non-uniform because of decentralization. Certainly, the drawbacks of non-uniformity should be contrasted with the benefits that decentralization may bring in terms of effectiveness. In any case, both factors seem difficult to quantify, especially more effective administration, in resolving this dilemma. As a result, the most reasonable assumption to make is that any factors causing non-uniformity in the application of taxes that are caused by decentralization will need to be reduced, especially with regard to income tax. Even so, the author affirms that decentralization in the form of a consortium seems to be an improvement on the present institutional structure of tax administration in Spain.

INTRODUCTION

1. The financing system of Spanish regions: main features, weak points and possible reforms

Núria Bosch and José M. Durán

1 INTRODUCTION

In the last 25 years, Spain has undergone a very important process of political and fiscal decentralization. The Constitution of 1978 created an intermediate level of government, the Autonomous Communities (ACs hereafter), covering autonomous regions that have received considerable powers and responsibilities from the state. In about 30 years, Spain has gone from being a unitary, centralized country to a highly decentralized one, where ACs play an essential role in the provision of public services and take up a significant share of public revenues.

As a consequence, if we see Spain from an international perspective, its current situation is nowadays closer to the federal countries than to the unitary ones, although it is not a federal country from a legal point of view. Undoubtedly, the Spanish experience in decentralization is significant from an international perspective, since it may be a reference for a number of historically unitary countries that have started a political process of decentralization more recently, or wish to do so.

For that reason, the aim of this chapter is to describe the most outstanding features of the financing system of the Spanish ACs, with reference to the more recent reforms and paying particular attention to their problems and further possible reforms. The chapter is divided into six sections, including this introduction. The second section describes the institutional organization at territorial level and the sub-national responsibilities. The third section deals with the present financing system of the ACs. The fourth section analyzes the problems or weak points of this financing system. The fifth section describes the future trends of the financing systems of ACs. We conclude with a summary and conclusions.

2 INSTITUTIONAL ORGANIZATION AT A TERRITORIAL LEVEL AND SUB-NATIONAL RESPONSIBILITIES

The 1978 Spanish Constitution establishes that the territory of the state is divided into ACs, provinces and municipalities. It also states that all of these entities have autonomy in the administration of their own interests.

The ACs (of which there are 17) make up an intermediate level of government (regional). Their establishment introduced a decentralized political model with three levels of government, which could, in practice, develop into a federal system.

The local level of government consists of two administrative tiers: the provincial and the municipal. Currently there are 50 provinces and 8110 municipalities. The municipality is the basic local body of the national territorial organization. The provincial government (the *Diputación*) is also a local entity. The territorial extent of the province corresponds to that of several municipalities, and its representatives are indirectly elected through municipal elections.

Nevertheless, the two-tier local government does not operate in all territories of Spain because after the 1978 Constitution, seven provincial territories became ACs and had to integrate their provincial institutions and finances into the new regional powers.[1] Therefore, the former two-tier configuration only continues in eight ACs.[2] Apart from this, in the insular ACs (the Balearic and the Canary Islands), in addition to municipalities, the Constitution establishes their own local administration or councils (called *Consejos* or *Cabildos*).

In relation to the allocation of responsibilities among levels of government, the state holds legislative power only in the areas for which the state is exclusively competent, as set out in Article 149 of the Constitution: international relations; defense, administration of justice; commercial, criminal, labor and civil legislation; customs matters; currency, general finance and state debt, public health; basic legislation and general coordination.

Those matters that are not expressly vested in the state by the Constitution can be devolved to the ACs. These exercise legislative power via their assemblies, but strictly within the limits of their devolved powers. The powers of the ACs are enshrined in Article 148 of the Constitution (the list is not exclusive): organization of the institutions of autonomous government; spatial planning, town planning and housing; public works, railways and roads throughout the AC; agriculture, waterways and forestry, fisheries; expansion of economic activity, culture and research; museums, libraries and public monuments; tourism, sport and leisure activities throughout the Autonomous Community; social welfare, health and safety. Article 148 also provides for the powers of the ACs to be extended to other areas.

Likewise, ACs share responsibilities with the state: education; energy and mines; social security; labor; water; science; commerce and consumer policy; credit, banking and insurance; culture and leisure; economy and finance; industry; public security; environmental protection; communication media; public works and transportation; fisheries; health.

The responsibilities of the provinces are the autonomous management of the respective specific interests of local communities: 1) participation in the coordination of local administrations with the Autonomous Community and the state; 2) the provincial powers: coordination of municipal services in order to guarantee the provision of services that are the responsibility of the municipal authorities; assistance, legal, economic and technical cooperation with the local authorities; provision of supra-municipal services; development and administration of the specific interests of the province.

Finally, the responsibilities of the municipalities are the following: municipal powers: public safety; planning and cooperation on education; traffic control; civil defense; fire services (mandatory for any municipality with over 20 000 inhabitants); town planning; historical and artistic heritage; environmental protection (mandatory for any municipality with over 50 000 inhabitants); public health; consumer protection; social promotion and integration (mandatory for any municipality with more than 20 000 inhabitants), water supply and public lighting; cleaning and waste disposal (for any municipality with more than 5000 inhabitants); public transport (for any municipality with more than 50 000 inhabitants).

According to this allocation of responsibilities among levels of government, in 2005 the distribution of public expenditure among levels of government was the following: 52 percent central government 35 percent autonomous government and 13 percent local government (table 1.1). In spite of the fact that Spain is not a federal country, these figures show that the degree of decentralization is similar to that of federal countries. Table 1.2 contains the distribution of public expenditure by levels of government in seven federal countries (Australia, Austria, Belgium, Canada, Germany, Switzerland and the United States). We can see that the degree of Spanish decentralization is above that of Australia, Austria, Belgium and Germany. The relative weight of the Spanish central government (52 percent of total public expenditure) is below the average weight of the central governments of the above-mentioned federal countries (55 percent). Likewise, the weight of the Spanish intermediate level of government (Autonomous

Table 1.1   Distribution of public expenditure by levels of government, 2005 (% overall public expenditure)

	% of Expenditure
Central government	52
Autonomous Communities	35
Local governments	13
Total	100

Source: Ministry of Economy and Finance.

Table 1.2   Distribution of public expenditure by levels of government in federal countries (% overall public expenditure)

	Federal	States	Local Governments	Total
Australia (2004)	55	39	6	100
Austria (2003)	70	16	14	100
Belgium (2003)	65	22	13	100
Canada (2004)	38	46	16	100
Germany (2004)	63	22	15	100
Switzerland (2002)	44	34	22	100
USA (2000)	51	23	26	100
Average	55	29	16	100

Source: International Monetary Fund, *Government Finance Statistics Yearbook 2005*, Washington, DC: IMF.

Communities) (35 percent) is above that of the average of the federal countries (29 percent). On the contrary, the weight of the Spanish local level of government (13 percent) is below the average of the federal countries (16 percent).

Table 1.3 shows the distribution of Spanish public expenditure by functions and levels of government. In the case of the central government, the expenditure on social security appears separately from the rest of central expenditure. So, the principal function of the central government is social protection. The ACs devote more than 60 percent of their expenditure to health (35.5 percent) and education (28.0 percent). And, finally, the principal functions of the local governments are economic affairs (14.2 percent), recreation, culture and religion (10.9 percent), environment protection (10.1 percent) and housing and community amenities (9.5 percent).

Table 1.3   Distribution of public expenditure by functions and levels of government, 2004 (% overall public expenditure)

	Central Public Administration	Social Security (Central Government)	Autonomous Communities	Local Governments	Total Consolidated
General public services	60.1	3.1	9.9	33.4	12.3
Defense	7.1				2.8
Public order and safety	6.5		2.6	7.9	4.8
Economic affairs	13.1	3.6	12.5	14.2	13.0
Environment protection	0.4		1.5	10.1	2.2
Housing and community amenities	0.2		1.6	9.5	2.1
Health	1.6	1.5	35.5	1.3	14.2
Recreation, culture and religion	2.1		3.2	10.9	3.6
Education	1.4		28.0	4.5	11.4
Social protection	7.5	91.8	5.2	8.2	33.6
Total	100.0	100.0	100.0	100.0	100.0

Source: Ministry of Economy and Finance.

3   THE PRESENT FINANCING OF THE ACs

Two different regional financing systems coexist in Spain: the so-called common regime that covers 15 ACs, and the special foral (Comunidades Forales) regime that includes two ACs (the Basque Country and Navarre). These two ACs levy all state taxes, but in return they pay an annual quota for the public services provided by the state, which is set by an agreement with the state. A notorious aspect of this system is that there is no effective mechanism of horizontal equalization between these ACs and the common regime ACs. Despite the interest of this special regime, this chapter concentrates on the common regime of autonomous finance.

3.1 Determination of the Autonomous Expenditure Requirements

The agreement of the Fiscal and Financial Policy Council (CPFF; Consejo de Política Fiscal y Financiera) of 27 July 2001 establishes the basis for the financing system of the ACs of the common regime from the year 2002 onwards. The financing system in this agreement was meant to appear as definitive, for which reason it was given the rank of a law (Law 21/2001, of 27 December, regulation of the fiscal and administrative measures of the new system of financing of the ACs within the common regime and cities with a Statute of Autonomy).

The first step taken by the agreement is to establish the resources that the AC must receive, determining its expenditure needs. Three areas of expenditure are established: common responsibilities (to simplify we can consider that they include all the responsibilities, except those of health and of social services), health responsibilities and responsibilities in social services. Taking 1999 as the year on which to base calculation, to every block of responsibilities some resources are assigned, which are the result of adding together the financing that every Autonomous Community received in each block, in the year used as a basis from the previous system. The sum of the three blocks represents the total volume of resources guaranteed by the system, since it is guaranteed that every Autonomous Community receives, at a minimum, a quantity of financing equal to that received in the previous system.

The resources allocated to the block of common responsibilities are divided into three funds: a general fund, a fund to correct low population density and a relative income fund. The general fund, once 39.66 million euros are discounted for every community with regard to functional expenditures for the autonomous institutions, is distributed among them depending on the population (94 percent), the surface area (4.2 percent), the dispersion of the population (1.2 percent) and insularity (0.6 percent). The fund to correct low population density (endowed with 48.08 million euros), which tries to compensate for the greater cost of provision of public services in sparsely populated territories, is distributed among the communities with a population density lower than 27 inhabitants/km^2, only if they have a surface area below 50 000 km^2. Finally, the relative income fund (endowed with 150.3 million euros) is designated to those ACs with a lower than average income per capita. The communities that in the distribution of these resources received an amount lower than they received for these responsibilities in the base year, are granted the amount of the difference through what is called the 'guarantee of minimums'. Finally, once the financing requirements of each community are established for common responsibilities, a set of modulation rules are applied that establish a maximum and a minimum value to financing growth with respect to a base year, in order to avoid significant deviations among the ACs.

With regard to the block of health responsibilities, its resources are distributed between the ACs by means of two funds: the general health finance fund and the savings fund for temporary disability. The first is distributed depending on the protected population (75 percent), the elderly (≥65 years old) population (24.5 percent) and insularity (0.5 percent). The second is endowed with 240.4 million euros and is distributed between the ACs depending on the protected population. Its aim is to finance the adoption of programs and measures directed towards the control of expenditure on temporary disability and towards the improvement of the management of the medical services for this contingency. To the resources obtained by each community for these two funds, it is necessary to add the corresponding guarantee of minimums, when these resources are lower than those that were being received, and the revenues proceeding from the health cohesion fund. This additional fund has the purpose of guaranteeing equality in access to public health services in the entire national territory (replacing the displacement fund in force in the previous agreement).

Finally, the resources corresponding to the social services block are distributed between the ACs depending on the elderly population. In this case, the system also guarantees as a minimum a volume of resources equal to that received in the base year.

Therefore, the expenditure requirements of every community are the sum of the expenditure requirements calculated for common responsibilities, for health responsibilities and for responsibilities in social services.

3.2 Resources

To cover the requirements of estimated expenditure, the 2001 agreement establishes the following financial resources for the ACs:

3.2.1 Taxes

The revenue raised by most state taxes is partially or totally ceded to ACs. Therefore, they are called ceded taxes. ACs have the legal power to modify the rules for certain ceded taxes and can also be responsible for their administration, that is, management, assessment, auditing and collection. The ACs' shares of ceded taxes are summarized in Table 1.4, where we also indicate whether they have the right to introduce legal changes and to administer them.

In particular, since 2002, ACs receive 33 percent of the personal income tax (IT); 35 percent of the VAT; 40 percent of the excise taxes (taxes on fuel, tobacco and alcohol); and 100 percent of the wealth tax, inheritance and

Table 1.4   Taxes ceded to ACs since 2002

Tax	ACs' Share (%)	ACs' Legal Powers	Administration
Income tax	33	Yes	State
VAT	35	No	State
Excises (fuel, tobacco and alcohol)	40	No	State
Capital transfer tax	100	Yes	AC
Stamp duty	100	Yes	AC
Inheritance and gift tax	100	Yes	AC
Car registration	100	Yes	State/AC*
Gambling tax	100	Yes	AC
Retail fuel sales	100	Yes	State/AC*
Wealth tax	100	Yes	State/AC*
Electricity tax	100	No	State

Note: * State currently administers the tax, although it could be carried out by the AC.

gift tax, capital transfer tax and stamp duty, gambling tax, electricity tax, car registration tax and retail fuel sales tax. However, the system of territorial participation, the legal power to introduce changes and the responsibility to administer the ceded taxes may differ considerably.

The income tax law sets up two different liabilities: one for the state (67 percent) and one for the ACs (33 percent).[3] The state establishes two different tax rates, one for the state and the other for the ACs, so that taxpayers can calculate both liabilities. Nevertheless, ACs are responsible for modifying the tax rate schedule that levies the general base, that is, in general all income but that from capital. In fact, they enjoy a high degree of freedom, since there is only one legal restriction: the number of tax brackets in the rate schedule has to be the same as in the state schedule. In addition to the statutory rates, ACs can also introduce new tax credits, only deductible from the regional liability, based on personal and family circumstances and non-business investments. Furthermore, ACs can modify the general tax credit for housing. The IT revenue is distributed among ACs according to the residence of taxpayers. The state, through a national tax agency, is responsible for the general administration of the IT.

As far as VAT and excises are concerned, ACs do not have any kind of legal power to modify the tax, mainly for two reasons. First, a legal restriction due to European harmonization. Second, the configuration of taxes, which means that revenue collection does not coincide with the consumption generated in the territory. As a consequence, the tax is distributed among

ACs according to official indices of consumption. Only the state agency is also responsible for the collection and general administration of the taxes.

Regarding the totally ceded taxes, regional power is usually much greater. The basic rules of taxes on wealth, inheritance and gifts, capital transfers and stamp duty, and gambling are fixed by the state, but ACs enjoy a great deal of autonomy to change the final liability. For instance, they can modify tax rates, allowances and tax credits almost without any restriction. Furthermore, ACs are responsible for the management, assessment, auditing and collection of the taxes. The above-mentioned taxes had already been ceded to the ACs before the 2001 agreement, but in this case the outstanding matter introduced in the latest reform was the expansion of the ceded tax powers. The points of contact used to allocate revenues are residence and territory. For instance, inheritance tax is paid in the AC where the deceased had his or her residence; gift tax is paid to the AC where the donor has his or her residence just before transfer, except if he or she donates property, in which case the territorial principle is used; or capital transfer tax corresponds to the AC where the property is located.

With respect to the other three totally ceded taxes, the level of regional legal power is much lower. Spanish regions do not have any legal power in the electricity tax, and with regard to car registration tax and retail fuel sales tax they can only raise the tax rate up to a maximum. The retail fuel sales tax was introduced in the 2001 agreement. It created this new tax, with specific purposes, since the revenue is entirely ceded to ACs to finance health expenditure. In addition to the state tax rate, ACs can establish a regional rate, up to a limit, the revenue of which is earmarked for health and environment expenditures. The tax rate on car registration can be increased by ACs up to 15 percent. Although ACs could also receive the responsibility for administering the car registration tax and the retail fuel sales tax, both are currently administered by the state.

To sum up, the aim of the 2001 agreement that set the basis for the current system since 2002 followed two basic aims. First, to increase the number of ceded taxes. Second, in turn, to increase the tax power of the ACs in order to improve their fiscal responsibility.

Apart from ceded taxes, ACs can levy their own taxes, although subject to important legal constraints since ACs cannot levy any taxable event already taxed by the state or municipalities. As most important events are already taxed, the scope for their own taxation is quite restricted. Thus, ACs have introduced a range of their own taxes mainly related to environmental issues (i.e., water, emissions and waste) and gambling (i.e., bingo), which on average accounts for a small percentage of the revenue of ACs, as we later comment. More recently, a few ACs have also levied taxes on large shopping areas.

3.2.2   Grants

The Savings Fund for Temporary Disability (Fondo de Ahorro en Incapacidad Temporal) and the Sufficiency Fund (Fondo de Suficiencia) must be referred to here. The first one has already been defined previously in Section 3.1. The Sufficiency Fund is a general grant proceeding from the state. This grant covers the entire system, since it is determined by the difference between the expenditure requirements estimated for each Autonomous Community and the resources proceeding from the sources previously mentioned (taxes plus the Savings Fund for Temporary Disability). In fact, its objective is fiscal equalization. The quantity to be received from the Sufficiency Fund in each fiscal year is calculated by updating the quantity of the fund in the base year by the rate of variation of the Tax Resources of the State (Inguesos Tributanors del Estado; ITE).

3.2.3   Structure of revenues

The latest reform of autonomous financing, with the incorporation of important tax concepts into the bundle of ceded taxes, logically meant a substantial change in the structure of AC revenues. The set of ceded taxes happens to be the most important item, representing slightly more than the half of their revenues, 55.7 percent in 2006 (Table 1.5).

Table 1.5   ACs' revenues, 2006

	Millions €	%
Taxes	70 587	55.7
Own taxes	1 759	1.4
Ceded taxes	68 828	54.4
– IT	19 774	15.6
– VAT	18 178	14.4
– Capital transfer tax	8 529	6.7
– Excises	7 524	5.9
– Stamp duty	6 578	5.2
– Others	8 245	6.5
Grants	48 495	38.3
Sufficiency Fund	29 941	23.6
Grants from EU	8 608	6.8
Other grants	9 946	7.9
Other revenue	7 544	6.0
Total revenue	126 627	100.0

Source: ACs' budget.

On their own initiative, ACs can also create taxes. In 2006, they represented 1.4 percent of total resources. As we mentioned before, their weight is very low, because the ACs only have powers to levy upon tax bases not occupied by central government. In practice this means their own taxes are mainly related to environment and gambling.

In correspondence with the increase in the ceded taxes, the joint weight of grants decreases significantly, being placed at 38.3 percent of all revenues, below the total weight of the ceded taxes. The Sufficiency Fund represents 23.6 percent of all revenue, other grants, 7.9 percent, and the grants from the EU, 6.8 percent. Therefore, the general financial dependence of the ACs with regard to the state decreases significantly, because of the transfer of new taxes and the disappearance of the specific grants for the financing of health and social services. With the current system, health and the social services are financed by means of the general resources, which is now possible because of the transfer of health responsibilities to the communities. Thus, the yielded responsibilities of the ACs are now much more homogeneous.

Table 1.6 shows the structure of resources of intermediate-level governments in some federal countries, apart from the Spanish case. In these cases,

Table 1.6 Resources of the intermediate level of government (% of the total non-financial resources)

	Germany (2003)	Australia (2003)	Austria (2002)	Canada (2003)	Switzerland (2001)	USA (2000)	Spain (2002)
Total resources	100	100	100	100	100	100	100
Taxes on	71	32	29	59	48	45	53
Individual income	33	–	13	21	29	16	15
Corporate income	3	–	3	5	–	–	–
Wages	–	9	–	4	–	–	–
Wealth, property	3	12	–	3	8	2	18
Goods and services	30	11	13	26	4	24	20
Payroll taxes	6	–	6	4	–	1	–
Grants	17	48	55	17	32	22	43
Other resources	6	20	10	22	20	32	4

Source: International Monetary Fund, *Government Finance Statistics Yearbook 2005*, Washington, DC: IMF.

the share of taxes is counted as pure taxes. Thus, the country where the tax resources have most weight is Germany, where they represent 71 percent of the total of non-financial resources of the *Länder*, although the majority of them came from the share of taxes. Below this figure are Canada (59 percent), Switzerland (48 percent) and the United States (45 percent). Where the weight of the taxes is smallest is in Australia (32 percent) and Austria (32 percent). In the Spanish case the tax resources represent 53 percent of the total of non-financial resources.

Regarding the grants, which measure the degree of financial dependence, these include some grants of a general as well as a specific character. The general transfers include those of fiscal equalization. The countries where grants have greater weight are Austria (55 percent of the total non-financial resources) and Australia (48 percent), coinciding also with the countries with a lesser weight of tax resources. Switzerland and the United States are in an intermediate situation, 32 percent and 22 percent, respectively. In the case of the United States, a good part of the federal grants in the states is destined for the local governments. Where the grants have the least relative weight is in Germany and in Canada, with a weight of 17 percent. Regarding Spain, it can be ascertained that the weight of the grants stands on the high side (43 percent) in relation to the other countries, although it is decreasing in the last years. Therefore, the funding of the ACs at present still entails an important degree of financial dependence with regard to the central government.

3.3 Grants of Guarantee of a Minimum Level of Fundamental Services

The agreement of 2001 envisages the establishment of the grants foreseen in Article 15 of the LOFCA (Ley Orgánica de Financiación de las Comunidades Autónomas; Financial Act of the Autonomous Communities).[4] According to the agreement, the aim of these grants is to guarantee a minimum level for the provision of the fundamental public services in all the national territory. The services defined as fundamental are health and education. This way, when a deviation of more than three points takes place with respect to the national average in the number of compulsory education students and/or protected population from an Autonomous Community, the reasons and possible solutions will be analyzed. This is intended to examine the overall financing of the Autonomous Community, and to decide whether it is convenient or not that the community benefits from grants of guarantee.

3.4 Guarantee of Minimums

The financing agreement of 2001 did not establish any general system of guarantee that refers to the dynamics of autonomous sufficiency. The only existing guarantee refers to the health services. During the first three years that the financing system was in force the state was guaranteeing that resources devoted to health had an index of development equal to the nominal GDP at market prices. In the 2nd Conference of Community Presidents this guarantee was extended up until the existence of a new financing system.

4 WEAK POINTS OF THE CURRENT MODEL OF AUTONOMOUS FINANCING

4.1 Problems of Vertical Imbalance Between the ACs and the State

In Spain an imbalance exists between the weight that the ACs have in tax revenue as a whole and the degree of public expenditure that they manage. Though the autonomous governments manage 32 percent of the volume of public expenditure, they only dispose of 20 percent of the tax revenues. On the other hand, the central government, which manages 55 percent of the expenditure (including pensions), has 72 percent of the tax revenues. We are, therefore, facing a non-correspondence between the responsibilities of expenditure and the tax responsibilities of the autonomous governments. The problems that this generates are fundamentally a lack of fiscal co-responsibility, which (1) blocks the accountability of the autonomous governments before their citizens, reducing the incentives of the ACs to carry out an efficient management of their expenditure; (2) limits the political autonomy of the autonomous governments and (3) stimulates conflict between these and the central government.

In addition, this vertical imbalance has been worsening with time. First, because of the behavior of the revenues. In the period 2001–05 the resources of the state grew at an annual rate of 10 percent (in nominal terms), whereas those of the ACs grew at 7.2 percent, almost equal to that of GDP (7.3 percent). Second, because of the evolution of expenditure requirements. In the period 2001–05 state expenditure linked to its exclusive responsibilities grew at an annual rate of 5.1 percent, whereas that of the ACs grew at 9.7 percent. And third, because of changes in the state regulation that cause an increase in the autonomous expenditure requirements or a decrease in the autonomous revenues.

The lack of fiscal responsibility is demonstrated well by the answers given to opinion surveys about fiscal issues.[5] In 2005, 53 percent of citizens believed IT and VAT were both exclusively paid to the state, and only about 20 percent knew they were shared.

4.2   Insufficient Financial Autonomy on Taxation

Ceded taxes contribute an important volume of resources to the common regime ACs, especially since the last autonomous financing agreement in the year 2001. However, there is still an insufficient financial autonomy on taxation. The ACs have a limited normative capacity in some of the ceded taxes. Though they can take decisions on certain elements of the IT and of the so-called 'traditional ceded taxes' (i.e., wealth tax, inheritance and gift tax), their normative capacity is zero with regard to VAT and excise taxes. In fact, it is the central government that has the capacity to modify the 'great' taxes of the Spanish fiscal system (IT, VAT and corporate tax). If the distribution of the tax revenues by government levels is analyzed, 72 percent of the whole corresponds to the state, 20 percent to the ACs and 8 percent to the local governments. Also, if we exclude the taxes on which the ACs do not have legal power, the above-mentioned 20 percent diminishes to 11 percent.

In fact, for the time being, use of their legal capacity by ACs has been quite limited, which does not help to foster their fiscal responsibility. After enjoying tax power for 11 years, only one AC, Madrid, and in 2007, has modified the regional tax-rate schedule of the IT. Regarding this tax, ACs have concentrated on introducing different tax credits (8 on average in 2007). However, these have a restricted scope since they make reference to particular situations (e.g., birth of children, housing rents for young people) and are limited to very severe constraints (e.g., level of income).[6] Only fewer than 5 percent of all taxpayers enjoy some regional tax credit. Spanish ACs have been more active in other ceded taxes, but those taxes are unimportant or imperceptible, such as, tax on capital transfers or tax on retail fuel sales. ACs have indeed introduced many changes in the inheritance and gift tax, as a 'race to the bottom' process seems to have started. In five years, seven ACs have decided to give up taxation on transmissions from the deceased to the spouse or the direct descendants, which accounts for about 85 percent of all taxed transmissions. In any case, the inheritance and gift tax only account for 2.7 percent of all ceded taxes.

Furthermore, the degree of financial autonomy of the ACs worsens if tax administration is taken into account. In the current model of autonomous financing, the state agency manages all 'great' taxes (IT, VAT, excise taxes). In spite of this, a relatively important part of these taxes constitutes a financing source of the ACs. In fact, in the current fiscal Spanish system, the autonomous governments only have administrative capacity over about one-fourth of their tax revenues, which is only 5 percent of all tax revenues.

Too many resources of the autonomous governments depend on the good or bad management carried out by another administration (the state), without there being any real possibility of taking part in it somehow. This fact exacerbates at least two problems: 1) the delay in receiving the amount of the tax liquidations that correspond to the autonomous governments; 2) the lack of tax information about tax collection in their territories, which means a difficulty for the exercise of their normative capacity, as they do not have the necessary information to simulate the possible effects of a modification of any tax element.

4.3 Existence of a Bad System of Fiscal Equalization

The functioning of the Sufficiency Fund was explained in the third section of this study. This fund should be an instrument in the service of the principle of equality of resources among the autonomous governments. That is to say, the Sufficiency Fund should make it possible for the autonomous governments to gather a similar volume of revenues in order to provide the services that are attributed to them, applying a similar tax effort. This aim is not fulfilled, and this is, precisely, one of the principal weak points of the current model of autonomous financing

The reasons that explain the poor functioning of the Sufficiency Fund can be summarized as follows in points 1–5:

1. The inexistence of a definition of the criterion of inter-territorial equity that should be complied with. The criterion of equity that has to be obtained has never been made explicit. The functioning of the Sufficiency Fund is explained without reference to its aim.

2. Lack of justification of the variables and weighting that intervene in the calculation of the indicator of requirements, and the inclusion of certain funds and modulations of difficult comprehension in the allotment of the resources between the ACs in the base year.

The indicator of the expenditure requirements of the different ACs, as seen previously, refers to the population as the principal variable (weighs 94 percent in the calculation of the requirements linked to the block of common services). Therefore, it would be reasonable to expect that the resources per inhabitant that the model provides to the different autonomous governments were equal (or very similar). But this does not happen, and the explanation is to be found in the inclusion of specific funds and of the modulations. The existence of the specific funds means that the population, instead of explaining 94 percent of the distribution of the resources, explains 90.6 percent. This reduction has a different impact among the different ACs. It improves ACs' relative situation in, for example, La Rioja, Extremadura, Cantabria and Castile-León and worsens it for ACs like Madrid, Catalonia and Valencia. Likewise, the ratio between the Autonomous Community with the greatest resources and that with the least is 1.158 before specific funds are included, and 1.259 after specific funds are included.

The application of the rules of modulation initially meant a reduction of the total resources to be distributed among the group of ACs (by 1.6 percent). This reduction, like the application of the specific funds, also affected the different ACs in a very uneven way. Whereas Extremadura was the community that most benefited from the application of the modulations (meaning an increase by 4.2 percent of its resources), the Balearic Islands were most harmed (meaning a reduction by 9.5 percent of its resources). Similarly, the modulations meant an increase in the inequalities between the ACs. When this occurred, the standard deviation of the resources per capita went from 7.65 to 9.9 percent.

3. Lack of arguments that justify using an indicator for fiscal capacity as a variable to calculate the Sufficiency Fund.

The indicator used to measure the fiscal capacity of the different autonomous governments is not based on the methods recommended by the economic literature and comparable systems. The indicator used to estimate the fiscal capacity linked to the 'ceded traditional taxes' (the wealth tax, the inheritance and gift tax) was effective collection updated by means of a growth rate that has no relation to the evolution of the real fiscal capacity. Regarding the rest of the taxes (IT, VAT and excise taxes) fiscal capacity is determined by their effective collection.

4. Lack of arguments that justify the use of the selected index to compute the evolution of the Sufficiency Fund.

As previously explained, once the Sufficiency Fund corresponding to each Autonomous Community for the base year (1999) was computed, an index of development was defined to apply throughout the years (no time limit exists as a five-year review was eliminated). This index is that of the growth rate of the state tax revenues (ITE). The choice of this index was not justified. During the five-year period 1997–2001 (before the current agreement of financing), the structurally adjusted growth rate of the exact revenues of the state (ITAE; Ingresos Tributarios del Estado Ajustados Estructuralmente) was used without the limits (guarantee of the GDP and of the equivalent state expenditure), which were applied during the years 1987–96. The fact is that these changes of criteria were never justified. The application of this index to update the resources of the Sufficiency Fund generates two problems: 1) it is considered that expenditure requirements and fiscal capacity change at the same rate and also that this rate is the same for all the ACs, therefore, the possible specific behaviors that affect only one Autonomous Community are not taken into account and 2) the possibility that the global volume of the fund should change before there is a rupture of the vertical balance is not considered.

5. Inexistence of updates and adjustment mechanisms for the Sufficiency Fund.

The current model of financing does not have mechanisms that take account of the possible rupture of horizontal equity. The Sufficiency Fund corresponding to each Autonomous Community was calculated for one base year (1999). At that time it was considered that the volume corresponding to each autonomous government was that which made the equalization of the resources possible. Therefore, the equalization agreed in the year 2001 should be kept throughout time. This is very hard to maintain because it is highly probable that circumstances will occur that alter it. These circumstances can be: 1) the existence of changes in the expenditure requirements of the different ACs due to changes in the users (demographic changes) or in the costs of provision of public goods; 2) the existence of changes in the capacity of different ACs due to modifications in the behavior of its taxable bases. In fact, given these circumstances, if the model foresees them and contains mechanisms designed to adapt to the new circumstances that alter the situation of the base year, there will be no problem. We can easily verify that the current model does not have these mechanisms if we compare the evolution of the expenditure requirements of the different autonomous governments with the evolution of their revenues. If this comparison is made considering that expenditure requirements have a direct relation to the population variable, it can be observed that there is no direct relation between increases in this variable and increases in resources. In some cases there is an inverse relation.

It would be advisable for the stability of the model to update it, for example every five years. Besides, it would be necessary to foresee the possibility of carrying out exceptional updates when certain circumstances occur. When the expenditure requirements of an Autonomous Community were growing at a certain pre-established level it may be advisable not to postpone the solution until the end of the agreed period of review.

4.4   Results of Existing Fiscal Equalization

Table 1.7 shows in a very illustrative way the redistribution of resources
between the ACs that the mechanism of fiscal equalization perpetuates.
Table 1.7 shows autonomous tax revenues in the left column and the
resources of the communities proceeding from the ceded taxes and from the
Sufficiency Fund in the right. The latter are called general resources and
constitute the major part of the resources of the common regime ACs. The
information appears in homogeneous conditions (with equal responsibilities), in per capita terms, expressed as an index, considering the Spanish
average to be 100. The change in the level of resources that passing
from the first column to the second one means is due to the equalization
mechanism.

The analysis of the information in Table 1.7 allows us to affirm that the
equalization mechanism leads to an excessive redistribution. On one hand,
the Balearic Islands and Madrid have an index of tax resources of 138
(which means that they pay taxes 38 percent above the average). To those
communities corresponds a total index of resources of 85 and 87, respectively, which means that they are substantially below the average.

On the other hand, Extremadura, with an index for tax resources of 67
(pays taxes 33 percent below the average), has an index for total resources

Table 1.7   Indices per capita of tax resources and of total resources, 2004

	Tax Resources	Total General Resources
Balearic Islands	138	85
Madrid	138	87
Catalonia	123	96
Aragón	111	115
La Rioja	103	119
Cantabria	102	116
Asturias	99	113
Valencia	99	91
Castile-León	94	118
Galicia	84	113
Murcia	81	91
Castilla-La Mancha	80	109
Andalucía	80	101
Extremadura	67	123
Canary Islands	42	96
Total	100	100

Source: Ministry of Economics and Public Finance and own elaboration.

of 123 (uses resources 23 percent above the average). In the case of Catalonia, the index of tax revenues is 123 and of total resources 96. Therefore, the citizens of Catalonia pay autonomous taxes 23 percent above average. But after the equalization mechanism operates the resources of the Catalan autonomous government are 4 percent below the average. Therefore, it can be stated that the equalization mechanism inverts the initial positions in favor of the ACs with less fiscal capacity and that therefore it leads to an excessive redistribution. The majority of federal countries have powerful equalization mechanisms, but in none of them does this reversal of positions occur. The resources differential diminishes between the different sub-central governments, but the positions are not inverted. In the majority of these countries a share of the contribution that citizens make above the average in tax resources is used to increase sub-central government resources.

4.5   Lack of Transparency and of Coordination Mechanisms

The current financing model of the ACs is the fruit of successive political agreements between the state and the ACs. Quite often these agreements were made without having a few clear and pre-established rules. Neither the Fiscal and Financial Policy Council nor the Senate have facilitated a suitable model for the negotiation process. Institutional reforms are necessary that facilitate coordination between the different agents that intervene in the negotiation and in the monitoring of the financing model.

5   FUTURE TRENDS

At present, several ACs have reformed their Statutes of Autonomy (Catalonia, Valencia, Andalucia, Aragón and the Balearic Islands) and others have started the process. Catalonia was the first AC to start the process to reform its statute, but was immediately followed by other ACs. For historical reasons, Catalonia has always been one of the ACs with a greater claim to political autonomy. But its claims have a kind of 'demonstration effect', as economists would call it, and the process of reforming proliferated.

One of the aspects that the ACs' statutes regulate is the system of financing. Consequently, the central government has declared that there will be a reform of the financing system of the common regime ACs probably in 2009 in accordance with the new trends established by the ACs. We can distinguish four aspects of these new trends: percentage of share of the ceded taxes, normative capacity on ceded taxes, tax administration and fiscal equalization.

5.1 Percentage of Share of the Ceded Taxes

The new Statute of Autonomy of Catalonia enlarges the percentage of the share of the following ceded taxes: income tax (from 33 percent to 50 percent), VAT (from 35 percent to 50 percent) and excise taxes (from 40 percent to 58 percent). The other new statutes do not establish percentages of share, leaving this aspect to central regulation. They only distinguish between the partially and totally ceded taxes.

5.2 Normative Capacity on Ceded Taxes

The new Statute of Autonomy of Catalonia also enlarges the present tax power on ceded taxes. The new statute contains a commitment to expand tax powers on individual income tax and to cede tax powers in the retail phase of VAT and excise taxes, while taking into account the corresponding harmonization rules within the EU.

The other Statutes of Autonomy so far approved only establish that the ACs can have tax powers over the partially and totally ceded taxes in accordance with central regulation.

5.3 Tax Administration

Regarding tax administration, what has been established by the Catalan statute has been copied by the others. The AC creates a Taxation Agency to administer its own taxes and the totally ceded taxes. In the administration of shared taxes, the State Tax Administration (Agencia Estatal de Administración Tributaria) and the Taxation Agency of every AC will collaborate by means of a consortium in the administration of shared taxes depending on the administrative feasibility due to the nature of each tax (e.g., easier in the individual income tax than in the VAT). In particular, it has been recognized that individual income tax will be the first tax to be jointly administered by this consortium.

5.4 Fiscal Equalization

The new Statute of Autonomy of Catalonia includes several articles specifying the general traits that a new equalization grant should consider, aimed at solving the problems pointed out above. The system established is copied, basically, by the new statutes of the Balearic Islands and Aragón.

Equalization refers only to some services, for which the central government is clearly responsible for ensuring a basic equity of provision across the country. The Catalan statute specifies that these services refer to health, education and other essential social services of the welfare state. This means that equalization should be partial, in the sense that rich communities should be allowed to retain some of the revenues exceeding the average to fund services provided to the residents in the region. Of course, this requires present 'excess equalization' to be eliminated, but goes one step beyond on this by suggesting that regions with per capita revenues above average before equalization should also be above average after equalization. Of course, the Catalan statute also explicitly says that there should be tax capacity equalization and, therefore, acknowledges that the equalization grant should reduce (but not completely eliminate) inequalities in per capita revenues.

One possible explanation for only equalizing welfare state services is that it was the practical way the writers of the Catalan statute found of implementing partial equalization. In fact, actual expenditure on health, education and social services might move between 70 and 80 percent of overall regional spending, suggesting, therefore, that equalization should be limited to this amount.

The Catalan statute also introduces a detailed list of expenditure requirement indicators. The basic variable mentioned is to be the resident population, modified to take the immigrant share of the population into account, and adjusted for the differential costs of providing public services. It also mentions other possible variables, such as the demography, population density, urban influences and poverty level. The other statutes also take the population as the basic variable.

Finally, the new statutes foresee appropriate updating mechanisms for all the variables and periodical revisions of the equalization system.

6   SUMMARY AND CONCLUSIONS

In the last 25 years, Spain has experienced a very important process of political and fiscal decentralization. Spanish ACs are responsible for 35 percent of all public expenditure, a significant proportion even greater than in several historical federal countries. The current financing system first begins with the assessment of the expenditure requirements for three different areas of responsibilities: common, health and social responsibilities. To provide the corresponding resources, the financing system rests on two basic sources: taxes and equalization grants. The 2002 system increases the weight of tax resources, raising the number of ceded taxes as well as the legal power to modify some of their parameters. With the aim of ensuring that all ACs have enough resources to carry out their responsibilities, the system envisages the Sufficiency Fund as the key element of fiscal equalization.

In spite of the improvements introduced, the financing system of ACs still suffers significant weak points: a lack of fiscal co-responsibility, an insufficient financial autonomy and the application of a bad system of fiscal equalization. Most citizens still believe most taxes are only paid to the state. The lack of transparency behind some of the key elements of the system, which are a consequence of successive political agreements, gives rise to significant differences in general resources per capita among ACs. The equalization mechanism inverts the ranking positions in favor of the ACs with less fiscal capacity.

To improve the system, future reforms should enhance the fiscal co-responsibility of regions, by increasing their tax power and their role on the administration of taxes. At the same time, equalization should be partial, so that rich ACs should be able to retain some of the revenues exceeding the average. Finally, appropriate updating mechanisms should be introduced to provide a more flexible and valid system.

NOTES

1. These ACs are Asturias, Cantabria, Madrid, Murcia and La Rioja, plus the two insular ACs, the Balearic and the Canary Islands.
2. These are Andalucía, Aragón, Castile-León, Castilla-La Mancha, Catalonia, Extremadura, Galicia and Valencia.
3. In fact, the regional liability accounts for more than 33 percent of all IT liability, as a consequence of two subsequent reforms in the IT carried out by the central government (in 2003 and 2007). As both reforms represented a reduction in the effective rates of the tax, the costs of the reforms were assumed by the state, which consequently increased the weight of the regional liability.
4. These grants are foreseen in Art. 15 of the LOFCA. Up to the agreement of 2001 they had not been embodied in any other agreement.
5. The opinion surveys were conducted by the sociology department of the Instituto de Estudios Fiscales, an institute of the Ministry of Finance. See more information in Área de Socilogía Tributaria (2006), 'Opiniones y actitudes fiscales de los españoles en 2005', *Documentos* 10/2006, Instituto de Estudios Fiscales.
6. For a further study see Durán, J.M. and A. Esteller (2006): 'Exploring personal income tax diversity among Spanish regions', *Tax Notes International*, **42** (7), 645–55.

PART I

Tax assignment

2. Revenue assignments in the practice of fiscal decentralization[1]

Jorge Martínez-Vázquez

1 INTRODUCTION

Over the past two decades there has been an unprecedented move toward decentralized governance all over the world. These changes have taken special significance in many developing and transitional countries where centralized systems were perceived to have failed to deliver improved general welfare. The promise of political, administrative and fiscal decentralization is that it can strengthen democratic representative institutions, increase the overall efficiency of the public sector and lead to improved social and economic welfare for countries that decide to adopt it.

One critical assumption in expecting these benefits is that decentralized governments will generally be more accountable and responsive to citizens' needs and preferences than centralized governments were in the past. At the same time, there is general agreement among experts in decentralization that the increased accountability associated with decentralization can only be assured when sub-national governments have an adequate level of autonomy and discretion in raising their own revenues.

Thus, if effective fiscal decentralization requires meaningful revenue autonomy at the regional and local levels of government, the question is, which taxes should be allocated at these levels? This is known in the fiscal decentralization literature as the 'tax assignment problem'.[2] In a chapter like this, which is strictly focused on revenue assignments, it is important to make clear that revenue assignment is just one element in the design of the entire system of government decentralization and that if revenue autonomy is to work effectively to increase accountability it has to be within the context of other well-designed institutions in a decentralized system. Decentralization involves more than what are traditionally thought of as fiscal decentralization issues (revenue assignments, the assignments of expenditure functions, transfers, and so on); and what is thought of as political decentralization, with democratically elected officials; and what is thought of as administrative decentralization – in particular in what pertains to civil service issues. All are important in assuring good outcomes from decentralization.

A common mistake in some countries recently involved in decentralization reform has been to ignore the 'completeness' of decentralized systems and to have focused on some form of revenue decentralization alone (e.g., central government revenue-sharing with local governments). The consequences have been not only the failure to capture the benefits of decentralization, but also central government deficits and macroeconomic instability.[3] The well-known dictum that 'finance should follow function' reflects the wisdom that revenue assignments should come after the assignment of expenditure responsibilities has been completed.[4] The main goal of this chapter is to provide a policy overview and update on the problem of revenue assignments, an aspect of fiscal decentralization design with which developing countries, and also many developed countries, continue to struggle. The organization of the chapter is as follows. Section 2 reviews the perspectives that can be taken on the nature of revenue assignments. Section 3 examines what we want from revenue assignments. Section 4 reviews different forms of revenue autonomy, while Section 5 lists the fundamental principles of tax assignment. Section 6 studies the different tax instruments that are available for assignment at the sub-national level. Section 7 briefly reviews the international experience with tax assignments, with a special focus on new developments for the feasibility of sub-national VATs. Section 8 summarizes and concludes.

2   PERSPECTIVES ON REVENUE ASSIGNMENTS

The theory and practice of revenue assignments asks two fundamental questions:[5] 1) What taxes should be assigned to different levels of government? 2) How should these arrangements be implemented? These two questions are typically examined from a normative perspective using efficiency and equity criteria, as we also do in most of this chapter. However, it can be insightful to study revenue assignments from a political economy perspective, an approach taken much less frequently. This approach can be helpful in addressing several important puzzles in the practice of revenue assignments, for which the commonly used normative criteria of equity and efficiency offer little or no help.

The first puzzle is that it is common to observe in the practice of fiscal federalism significant deviations from what would be acceptable or recommended under the normative criteria. Often in the literature these deviations are brushed aside as being the product of 'the dead hand of history'.

However, in many cases what needs to be explained is not so much why certain revenue assignments came into being, since historical factors and circumstance can no doubt play a role, but why are wrong (inefficient, inequitable and so on) assignments so difficult to reform?[6] Part of the answer has to be in the unequal bargaining position sub-national governments have with respect to central powers. The counter example of the weak central powers in the history of federalism in North America is a case in point. But, this is a question that still remains to be studied fully in the literature. A second puzzle in revenue assignments is not so much in the design but in the actual implementation. Very often the revenue authority provided to sub-national governments in the law goes unused, while at the same time these sub-national governments cry out for more funding from their central government. A political economy perspective can also be of help here. Revenue assignment is just one mode of financing sub-national governments and when the incentives are right, it is to be expected that these governments will prefer to be financed by transfers from the central government as opposed to asking their residents directly to contribute to the refunds. In the absence of a hard budget constraint and adequate revenue autonomy, many behave in a fiscally irresponsible manner, asking for ever-increasing national transfers, perhaps under the erroneous collective belief that residents of other sub-national governments will foot the bill. Systems where sub-national governments can count on ever-increasing revenue-sharing and other transfers from the central government become just another manifestation of the well-known problem of the 'tragedy of the commons'.

However, as we will see below in this chapter, the theory of public finance provides helpful guidelines on the assignment problem, but these guidelines are far from being deterministic and in some cases the guidelines can conflict with each other. Thus, it should not be surprising to find significant diversity in the actual implementation of revenue assignments; it is well accepted that there is no unique or 'one-size-fits-all' tax assignment. For better or worse, the history and institutions of particular countries also matter significantly. So, in practice, the choice of assignments has to do as much with politics as with economic principles. In addition, we should expect the 'preferred' tax assignments to change over time with changes in the economy, for example in response to globalization, as well as with changes in what we could call the available 'technology' of tax assignment. For example, until recently, sub-national VATs had been considered unfeasible, but this position has changed as the result of several intellectual innovations, to be discussed later in the chapter.

3 WHAT DO WE WANT FROM REVENUE ASSIGNMENTS?

The most fundamental purpose of revenue assignments is to get adequate levels of financing so that sub-national governments can implement the functions that have been assigned to them. However, this requirement does not offer much of a guide for revenue assignments because adequate financing levels can be obtained from many different tax assignments or even without them through intergovernmental transfers.

The more critical requirement for revenue assignments is to provide revenue autonomy as the means of enhancing political accountability among sub-national officials. There are several other benefits from revenue autonomy. When all financing of sub-national governments is from revenue-sharing and other forms of transfers from higher-level governments, there is a danger that sub-national governments will become spending agents of the center becoming less interested and efficient,[7] and that imposing a hard budget constraint on sub-national governments becomes more difficult.[8]

Sub-national tax autonomy is the best way, if not the only way, to address in a permanent way the difficult problem of vertical imbalances, or mismatch of expenditure needs and revenue sources at different government levels. Adequate revenue autonomy is also a key indicator of sub-national governments' borrowing capacity and creditworthiness. There is also some evidence that more revenue autonomy at the sub-national level is associated with greater macroeconomic stability.[9]

On the other hand, greater tax autonomy can lead, depending on the geographical distribution of economic activity and tax bases, to larger horizontal fiscal disparities across sub-national governments. Richer jurisdictions can have the ability to finance their expenditure needs with little effort, while poorer communities may have to exert much greater tax effort with their residents to provide for their expenditure needs. However, these horizontal fiscal disputes can be addressed quite well through the proper design of equalization grants.

If we agree that tax autonomy is paramount, then we need to ask: how much tax autonomy is needed? Shouldn't sub-national governments be asked to finance themselves entirely from autonomous tax sources? The answer is that full own-financing by all sub-national governments is generally not feasible or even desirable. The generally accepted rule is that sub-national governments need to raise their own funds at the margin and operate with hard budget constraints, which means that revenue-sharing and grants should represent only infra-marginal funding.[10]

In reality we tend to observe low levels of tax autonomy. One reason, discussed in the previous sections, involves simple political economic forces.

Central governments may not want to devolve taxing powers for fear of competing with local governments for the same taxing base and at the same time sub-national governments do not want to take on the responsibility of making politically unpopular taxing decisions to meet their budget needs. Using intergovernmental transfers is seen as a much easier path for all concerned.

Insufficient revenue autonomy can also be the result of the lack of administrative capacity in some sub-national governments. When low capacity is combined with the desire to provide all sub-national governments (regardless of size and capacity) with the same autonomous taxing powers, low levels of tax autonomy can follow. This situation poses a dilemma in decentralization design. A uniform intergovernmental fiscal system under which all sub-national governments must operate has an important appeal. If all sub-national governments have the same expenditure responsibilities and revenue-raising powers, management of the system and evaluation of its success are made easier. Uniform treatment of all sub-national governments also seems generally fairer. On the other hand, a more effective route for effective decentralization may be the adoption of an asymmetric tax assignment providing more tax autonomy to larger sub-national governments with more capacity and according to transparent objective criteria and let the smaller ones 'grow into this role' over time.[11]

Although decentralized systems in some developed countries have high levels of tax autonomy, in reality it is quite rare, especially among developing countries to find significant taxing powers devolved to sub-national governments at the onset of decentralization. Often, there is considerable reluctance from central government to let go of part of its authority and control over taxes, which in turn is justified because of the need to facilitate attainment of proper capacity at the sub-national level. However, these stumbling blocks generally linger for many years of a decentralization program, with the side effect of a culture of dependency taking hold where sub-national governments have become accustomed to relying on central transfers for their financing needs.

Regardless of actual practice, it is undeniable that a goal for revenue assignments in all countries remains granting sub-national governments a high level of tax autonomy. However, the general principle of providing sufficient tax autonomy at the margin is not easily operationalized. In particular, what is the specific meaning of 'sufficient tax autonomy at the margin'? Here are some difficulties. Expenditure needs (and their changes) are very often hard to quantify properly. In addition, tax autonomy leads to horizontal fiscal disparities giving rise to the need for equalization grants. But then the question becomes how much are central governments willing and able to equalize?

Although there are no certain answers, it is possible to provide some guidance to policy makers responsible for the design of revenue assignments. First, quite obviously there is a need to devise some sensible way to measure the expenditure needs of sub-national governments and to keep these measurements reasonably updated. Next, the golden rule for revenue assignment should be that these assignments should be sufficient to fund the expenditure needs (net of conditional grants) of the wealthiest sub-national governments. Sometimes, however, it may be advisable to break this rule somewhat and to have even the wealthiest sub-national governments partly financed by central transfers. This may be because of vertical externalities in the use of tax bases, economies of scale in the administration of some taxes, the need to maintain the integrity (harmonized nature) of some taxes, and other considerations in tax administration, which are discussed below.

4 IMPLEMENTING REVENUE ASSIGNMENTS: WHAT FORM OF TAX AUTONOMY?

If we accept that tax autonomy for sub-national governments is the requirement in revenue assignments, then we need to address two questions: 1) What type of revenue autonomy is desirable? 2) What kind of tax instruments should be used to provide this autonomy? With respect to the form of tax autonomy, four dimensions have been identified in the literature.[12] The first is which level of government has the right to choose the taxes that this given level can impose. There are good reasons to limit the ability of sub-national governments, for example to introduce internal tariffs, as done with the interstate constitutional clause in the United States. Provided that these general restrictions are to be in place, there is a choice between an open list of taxes to be determined by the sub-national governments within general limits and restrictions, or instead a closed list of allowable taxes determined at the national level from which sub-national governments can choose. There is no clear choice between these two approaches as there are advantages and disadvantages associated with each. Overall, a closed list of sub-national taxes is preferable because it avoids the introduction of nuisance taxes in some cases or higher and inefficient distortionary taxes that can easily impede local economic development and growth.[13] But, a closed list may not be needed if, for example, all tax bases are nationally legislated and harmonized. However, this alternative may be interpreted as just another version of a closed-list choice. In the international experience, where sub-national governments are given more constitutional discretion, as in the case of some federal systems, open lists with some general restrictions are common. Closed lists are used more frequently in unitary systems of government.

Whether an open-list or closed-list approach is adopted, an additional decision needs to be made as to whether the base of specific taxes should be used exclusively by one level of government or whether these bases can be used simultaneously by several levels of government. The latter approach has the disadvantage of introducing vertical tax externalities due to the fact that one level will not typically take into account the impact its policies may have on the tax base and revenues of the other level of government.[14]

Several corrective policies can be implemented to correct for this type of externality, including separating tax bases for all levels of government providing intergovernmental grants or increasing the number of sub-national governments.[15] In practice, when an open-list approach is chosen it is generally the case that the cohabitation of bases is allowed. In contrast, it is often the case that a closed-list approach is used to eliminate the possibility of the cohabitation of tax bases. Sometimes the country Constitution, even in the case of some federal countries, is used to delineate clearly what taxes can be used at different levels of government (for example, this is the case in India, Pakistan or Switzerland). The exclusionary approach to the use of tax bases has led in some countries to cumbersome tax structures. For example, in India and Pakistan the federal governments can tax services but only the sub-national government can tax goods. These were choices made many years back and today they significantly complicate the ability to have functional VATs in those countries.

In practice, the choice between exclusive or shared tax bases comes down to weighing the advantages and disadvantages associated with each choice. As we just discussed, the main disadvantage of cohabitation is vertical externalities. The most important disadvantage of using the exclusive basis is that, typically, sub-national governments will be shut out of any opportunity to use significant (either in size or elastic over time) tax bases, thus drastically reducing any meaningful possibility of sub-national tax autonomy. The imposition of exclusive tax bases can also lead to cumbersome tax structures, as in the mentioned cases of India and Pakistan. All things considered, it appears that a choice of a closed list allowing for the cohabitation of tax bases by different levels of government and using intergovernmental transfers to correct for vertical externalities may be the preferred approach.

The second dimension of tax autonomy relates to which level of government can legislate over the structure of the tax bases and which level has discretion to set the tax rates. Of the two types of autonomy for structuring sub-national taxes, autonomy to define the tax base is generally less desirable than autonomy to set the tax rates.[16] Variations in the definition of the tax base, either through especial exclusions from tax, deductions from the tax base and credits against the tax liabilities can more easily lead to complexity and lack of harmonization across jurisdictions.

The most important unwanted consequence of the lack of harmonization and complexity is the higher tax administration cost for all the jurisdictions involved and higher compliance costs for taxpayers who have tax obligations in several jurisdictions. On the other hand, autonomy to define the tax rate generally tends to be more desirable because it is simpler to deal with across jurisdictions for both tax administrators and taxpayers. Focusing on autonomy in a tax rate setting has the additional important advantage of being perceived to generate political accountability.

It is often also argued that tax rate setting autonomy may be preferred because it has a more direct impact on revenues and spending ability of sub-national jurisdictions, because it has a more transparent impact on locational decisions and fiscal competition: both households and businesses have an easier time figuring out the fiscal exchange or net benefits provided by different jurisdictions in their tax-public-service packages when the differences in tax burdens are expressed in terms of differences in tax rates.

The third and last dimension of revenue autonomy refers to which level of government is put in charge of administering the various taxes. This dimension of sub-national tax autonomy is often overlooked and in some cases is summarily dismissed as being of no consequence. In this latter perspective, centralized tax administration is always more efficient and the discussions about decentralizing tax administration are mostly about turf and patronage issues (who can hire workers, and so on). However, there are some potentially important issues here. First, administration by sub-national governments of their own taxes is likely to enhance accountability at the sub-national level if taxpayers are more aware of sub-national taxes under this arrangement. But second, sub-national tax administration is likely to be less cost effective because of economies of scale. Thus, a useful way to approach this decision is to identify a trade-off between more efficient administration, which generally increases with more centralized administration, and enhanced accountability at the sub-national level, which generally increases with more decentralized administration. This efficiency–accountability trade-off is likely to differ for different taxes. For example, the efficiency gains from the centralized administration of sub-national piggyback personal income taxes may dominate any increase in accountability generated by decentralized administration of those taxes. In contrast, there may be no significant efficiency gains in the centralized administration of sub-national property taxes by comparison to the losses in local accountability implied by the centralization of the administration of these taxes. The administration of sub-national taxes or even shared taxes by the central administration can present a problem with low incentives even for shared taxes when the central administration's share in the revenues is relatively small. What this means is that when cost advantages make it desirable to centralize the administration, there will be a need for setting incentive-compatible arrangements between levels of government for the collection of taxes.[17]

There is one cost issue we need to discuss briefly before we leave the issue of the most desirable form of tax autonomy. It is sometimes argued that certain forms of tax revenue-sharing on a derivation basis can contribute to the revenue autonomy of sub-national governments. The more generally accepted view is that tax-sharing is not a form of revenue assignment because sub-national governments do not have a direct role in the structure and administration of the tax; in this view, revenue-sharing should be considered just another form of transfers. In the minority view, shared taxes may be considered a form of tax assignment when the shared rates are stable over a period of several years and especially when the sub-national authorities can influence the level of administration and affect the size of the tax bases. For these reasons, it is customary in many transitional countries, especially those in the former Soviet Union, to consider shared taxes as part of the own revenues of sub-national governments.[18]

There are some other cases that appear just to be another form of tax-sharing but in reality are special cases of tax assignment. For example, currently in Spain some important taxes have been partially ceded to regional governments. For example, 33 per cent of the personal income tax belongs to the regional governments, but this is not a usual form of revenue-sharing. The Spanish law divides the tax schedule for the personal income tax into a central government schedule and a regional government schedule. In general, these forms of revenue assignment tend to be less transparent, and even if they yield equivalent levels of tax autonomy, they are less likely to produce the same level of accountability in comparison to an arrangement with separate tax assignments to each level of government with the regional governments granted several forms of discretion over their share.[19]

5   WHAT KIND OF TAX INSTRUMENTS ARE BEST SUITED FOR SUB-NATIONAL GOVERNMENTS?

The principles of tax assignment or criteria that should guide the assignment of revenue sources across different government levels in a country reflect the dual role of taxes. First, taxes simply provide the means to finance the provision of public goods and services, but taxes are also used as an instrument to achieve government policy objectives, such as the redistribution of income through progressive taxation.

The classic starting point for the principles of tax assignments is Musgrave's (1959) seminal work, where he argued that the economic objectives for government are fundamentally threefold: assuring a stable economic environment, in which the market is able to function; achieving a more equitable distribution of income; and assuring a more efficient allocation of resources in case the market fails. While, generally, the knowledge of circumstances of time and place make decentralized market forces superior to a centralized allocation of economic resources, there are a number of areas where the market fails because of cost advantages as in the case of natural monopolies, the impossibility of exclusion in consumption, as in the case of public goods, or the presence of externalities.

Musgrave's (1959) 'three roles' for government activities can be used to guide the assignment of revenue sources across different government levels. After all, different tax instruments have varying impacts with respect to the three functions of the public sector: macroeconomic stabilization, redistribution of income and resource allocation. Further characteristics can be identified that make certain taxes more appropriate for assignment at the sub-national level of government. Although there continues to be some controversy on this, the general consensus among public finance economists is to agree with Musgrave that policy decisions on economic stabilization and income distribution are best assigned to the central government,[20] while some of those related to allocative efficiency (how best to use the resources available to provide goods and services) may be assigned to local governments.

Beyond the guidance provided by Musgrave's governmental roles, there are some characteristics of taxes that are commonly acknowledged as desirable regardless of whether these taxes are to be assigned at the central or sub-national levels. These include:

1. revenue buoyancy, meaning that overall, revenues should change roughly in proportion to the economic base;
2. equity, meaning that good revenue sources are 'fair' or equitable in the sense of horizontal equity under which taxpayers in similar circumstances should be treated similarly and vertical equity under which taxpayers with different incomes should pay according to their 'ability to pay';
3. efficiency, meaning that the tax should have relatively low administration and compliance costs and create a minimum of distortion in the economy; and

4. political acceptance, meaning that taxes need to be sensitive to the historical and institutional framework in a country.

There are, in addition, several other principles that are desirable for taxes that are to be assigned at the sub-national level.[21] First, the benefit principle, which relates revenue sources to the benefits being provided, should be implemented to the largest extent possible. Second, sub-national revenue sources should have a tax base that is relatively evenly distributed across jurisdictions. This helps to minimize fiscal disparities among sub-national governments and reduces the burden put on equalization grants to allow a more uniform quantity and quality of services. Third, sub-national tax sources should have immobile bases to minimize the likelihood of tax competition among jurisdictions in a 'race to the bottom'. However, not all tax competition is undesirable; a moderate tax competition gives an incentive to politicians and bureaucrats to be efficient and to provide services according to citizens' preferences in their choice of taxes. Fourth, sub-national taxes should be geographically neutral in the sense that they do not interfere with domestic or international commerce, they do not distort the location of economic activity across the national territory and they are not exported such that the taxes levied by a sub-national government are primarily borne by residents in other jurisdictions. Fifth is a requirement for administrative feasibility so that sub-national taxes can be implemented without undue costs of compliance and administration. Certain taxes may be better administered at the local level because of information advantages (e.g., property taxes), while for the same reasons local governments have a relative disadvantage in collecting other taxes (e.g., personal income tax). Sixth, sub-national grants should exhibit generally stable tax bases; revenue sources that are highly sensitive to general economic conditions (e.g., profit taxes) should be assigned to the central government, which has greater ability to deal with cyclical fluctuations in revenues through borrowing and other means. Seventh, sub-national taxes should be highly visible so that tax burdens are clearly perceived by local residents. Of course, sub-national governments are likely to think quite differently about this. Finally, sub-national tax assignments need to be stable over time. A typical problem of transitional countries has been unstable assignments, with the assignments not being established in permanent laws but instead decided in annual budgets. Ad hoc assignments decided on an annual basis may also result in a lack of uniformity, unnecessary complexity and perverse incentives toward revenue mobilization.

One thing sub-national taxes do not need to do is to attempt to redistribute income through progressive rate structures. This is not only because, as Musgrave (1959) indicated, income redistribution is a governmental function best performed at the central level, but also because the elimination of some taxes due to their assumed regressivity may do more harm than good, as for example, in recent years in Sub-Saharan Africa. In these countries, sub-national taxes that are revenue-producing and provide a meaningful degree of autonomy have been eliminated or there have been calls for their elimination because they are regressive; that is, these taxes may require lower-income taxpayers to pay a greater percentage of their income in tax than upper-income taxpayers. However, the elimination of these revenue sources typically implies a reduction of local services, which may hurt the poor more because they do not have the possibility of using alternative private services. The elimination of those tax sources also reduces political accountability at the local level. For example, although user fees are generally regressive, residents regardless of income would be better off in a community with safe public water sources funded by user fees when compared with a community where no safe drinking water is available, and all households have to rely on more expensive private provision of potable water. Nonetheless, often the regressivity of local taxes can be mitigated by provisions for relief of hardship and other measures to protect those with the lowest incomes.

6   SELECTING TAX INSTRUMENTS FOR ASSIGNMENT AT THE SUB-NATIONAL LEVEL

There are hardly any taxes that comply with all desirable criteria listed above. A compromise across criteria is generally needed. But, even though we cannot select one single best assignment, it is clear that the criteria allow us to select among better and worse tax assignments.

In practice naturally, there are disagreements on what should be in the minimum list of requirements for tax assignment at the sub-national level. One such minimum list would include revenue autonomy at the *margin,* stable assignments over time, sufficient revenues for the wealthiest sub-national government units and for taxes to be based as much as possible on the benefit principle and on less mobile tax bases. But it must be clear that the minimum list using the benefit principle where feasible is the single most important. As Bird (2000) and others have argued, sub-national governments are mostly prescribed to engage in activities ensuring a more efficient allocation of public resources, and therefore they should be assigned revenue sources for which it is easier to establish a link with the benefits received by residents from local government spending. The most obvious example of a revenue source satisfying this benefit principle is charging for specific services provided by local governments (for example, the cost of issuing driver's licenses) and for goods and services provided by public enterprises (utility charges, museum admission and so on). Besides generating revenue for local governments, user charges also provide information on demand to public sector officials.

However, often it is not feasible to use charges for a variety of services provided by sub-national governments. In these cases it may be feasible to use 'benefit taxes', or compulsory contributions to local governments that are nonetheless related in some manner to benefits received by the taxpayer. For example, the size or value of a residential property may be seen as relating to an individual taxpayer's benefits received from improvements on the street where the property is located. Relating taxes to the benefits of public spending has the major advantage of helping increase the accountability of sub-national governments to their own constituencies. The effectiveness of benefit taxes in increasing political accountability and fiscal responsibility is enhanced with the mobility of taxpayers across jurisdictions.

6.1 Better Choices of Sub-national Taxes

Although it is not possible to come up with an exact list of taxes that must be assigned to sub-national governments, it is quite possible to draft a list of taxes that would make good choices for this task:

6.1.1 Fees and user charges

The most straightforward way to raise revenue in accordance with the benefit principle is by charging user fees to cover the cost of providing specific local government services. As remarked above, besides generating revenue for local governments, user charges are able to function as a pricing mechanism, thereby ensuring that locally provided goods are only used by local residents as long as their benefits exceed the cost to the user. One feature of this source of sub-national revenues is that revenues raised from user fees and other non-tax revenue sources are generally not available for general-purpose funding of local services or infrastructure.

One general argument that is sometimes made against the reliance on user fees at the local government level is that user fees are potentially regressive. However, as we have already commented, one needs to be careful not to overstate the importance of the redistributional role of sub-national governments. In some sense, considering the regressivity of user charges does not make much more sense than considering, for example, the regressivity of food expenses. As noted earlier, equity and distributional issues are much better addressed at other levels in the overall fiscal system of the country.

To the extent that the main purpose of 'real' licenses and user fees is to recover the administrative costs of issuing the licenses or the cost of providing the public services, it is important to price the service right. Requiring sub-national governments to set the fee levels below the actual cost of provision imposes an unfunded mandate and it can easily lead to poor provision of services.

While user fees provide important efficiency benefits, it is important to balance the cost of collecting and administering user fees with the amount of revenues collected; certain types of user fees involving many small transactions may be too costly to collect. It can make good sense to bundle the collection of a variety of fees into a single payment. For example, it is possible to collect refuse collection fees or street lighting fees as a surcharge on property taxes.

6.1.2   Property taxes and betterment levies

There is ample consensus in the public finance literature identifying the property tax as one of the best mainstays at the sub-national level. Something else makes the property tax particular in the revenue assignments problem. Almost without exception, revenues from the property tax are assigned to local governments as opposed to intermediate-level or regional governments. The degree of discretion given to local governments to manipulate the tax may vary but the thinking that this tax belongs to local governments seems well entrenched.[22]

Several features make property taxes especially attractive as a sub-national tax. Most important, the property tax is a visible tax and thus conducive to political accountability. In addition, the tax, for the most part, falls on an unmovable base. The more homogeneous both the property and population, the closer the property tax comes to being a benefit tax.[23] However, depending on how the property tax is structured, it can move away from the benefit link. For example, this may be the case if the tax burden falls on just a few classes of property, such as non-residential property.

Other advantages of property taxes are their revenue potential and stability. Note also that from a vertical equity viewpoint, the property tax can be progressive in developing countries, and therefore can increase the overall vertical equity of the tax system, although in practice it can be made regressive by exemption policies that target wealthier households.[24] The property tax also has the desirable feature that much of the tax burden is quite likely borne by residents in the jurisdiction where the services financed by property taxes are provided. The property tax also has the advantage that it imposes a relatively low compliance cost on taxpayers because taxpayer intervention in terms of the determination of tax liability is minimal, except in the case of appeals. Typically the property tax poses no significant problem of tax base competition with the central government, basically because this is not a tax that central governments tend to covet.[25] Finally, a part of property tax might be thought of as a charge for land that can lead to significant improvements in the quality of land use.

The main drawback of the property tax is that, perhaps due to its visibility it is likely to be unpopular with taxpayers and, as a result, also with public officials. Other drawbacks include the fact that it can lead to liquidity problems for homeowners with valuable real estate assets but low incomes.[26] In addition, the property tax administration requires costly revaluation of property on a regular basis, and it is difficult to enforce, because the confiscation of property may be considered too extreme because of the political fallout. Finally, the property tax lacks revenue elasticity, meaning that the tax typically exhibits little automatic revenue growth.

In practice there are several forms of the property tax. For example, some countries separate the taxation of land and improvements, or structures, and a few others tax only land values or rents. Although a tax on land tends to be more efficient, it also has less revenue potential and it is generally more difficult to administer properly, for example, in terms of valuation or assessment of properties. There is another type of property tax in the form of 'betterment levies' or lump-sum payments exacted upfront by subnational governments from land and housing developers and also from homeowners as a charge for public service improvements, such as road paving, drain infrastructure, sidewalks, street lights and so on, which all have a visible benefit on property values. Betterment levies can be useful in providing sub-national governments with liquidity to invest in needed infrastructure; they also have the advantage of being more directly contractual than property taxes and therefore reinforcing the benefit principle feature in sub-national government financing.

There are different modalities for the administration of the tax, including centralized or central oversight over cadastres and re-evaluation processes, which can make this type of tax even feasible in developing countries. Note that tax autonomy is largely preserved as long as sub-national authorities are given some discretion over rate setting.[27]

6.1.3 Vehicle and transportation taxes

These are generally attractive sub-national taxes because of the strong link between the ownership of vehicles on the one hand, and the use of local services and infrastructure (particularly roads) on the other. In addition, sub-national taxes and charges on vehicles can counteract the negative externalities associated with local traffic congestion and air pollution in the local area. This is also a tax that tends to have elastic revenues. It is perhaps for this reason that the central governments in some developing countries, wrongly, tend to assign these taxes to themselves. There are, of course, some transportation taxes such as in the case of air travel, which are rightly allocated at the central level, since air traffic control and other similar services should be centrally provided.

6.1.4   Natural resource taxes (when resources are evenly distributed)

There is at least a partial link between taxes on natural resource extraction and the benefit principle at the local level. Natural resource taxes can be justified at the local level to the extent that extraction activities use local infrastructure (e.g., roads needed to transport heavy machinery and mined resources), place stress on other local infrastructure (temporary worker camps, hospital facilities required to treat injuries incurred by those working in this industry and so on), and – depending on the type of extraction – may pollute the environment or cause other negative externalities, increasing health costs of local residents. There has been growing interest in the fiscal decentralization literature in the pros and cons of the assignment of natural resource revenues to sub-national governments.[28] Notwithstanding the arguments for some form of local taxation of natural resources, there are two major arguments against it. First, in the case of geographically concentrated natural resources, local taxation could cause extensive horizontal fiscal imbalances (e.g., the recent cases of Indonesia, Nigeria and Russia). These fiscal disparities can lead to inefficient population migration and location of business. Second, given the high volatility of world commodity prices, local taxation of natural resources would not constitute a stable source of revenue.

Therefore, some balance must be reached, especially in the case of the uneven geographical distribution of resources, between first, centralized taxation of natural resources to address disparities and avoid or correct for negative economic externalities, and second, sharing some of the revenues with sub-national governments to compensate for the environmental damage of the extraction process and so on.

6.1.5   Local business taxes

Certain forms of business taxes or business license fees are justified at the sub-national level as an indirect but administratively easier way to tax income of business owners (especially non-wage incomes), and as a benefit tax for the services and infrastructure provided by sub-national governments.

Where it is not feasible to recoup costs of local government services through user charges, some form of broad-based levy on general business activity is warranted. However, to avoid economic distortions, the broad-based levy should be neutral to the factor mix, applying equally to labor (payroll) and capital (assets) used by businesses. Such a tax, which is sometimes called a business value tax (BVT) is discussed by Bird (2003). The base of the BVT would resemble that of the VAT although the two taxes function quite differently. In contrast to the destination-based VAT, the BVT would be origin-based, therefore taxing exports (not imports) because the benefits from sub-national governments' services acrue at the place of production (not consumption). In addition, while the typical VAT is calculated by the subtraction method on transactions (gross receipts minus the cost of intermediate goods and services), a BVT would be calculated by adding payroll, interest, rents and net profits on the basis of annual accounts.

The closest example of a BVT in practice was Italy's regional business tax (known as the IRAP) prior to the elimination of payroll from the tax base in 2003.[29] A potential disadvantage of a BVT is that it requires good levels of accounting and record-keeping and quite advanced tax administration capacity. These requirements make it less of an option for taxing small business and for use in countries where tax administration is not sophisticated. Another feature that may help explain its lack of popularity is its overlap in terms of the tax base with value-added taxes, and therefore the hard political sell for this tax. An alternative to business taxation at the sub-national level is to use charges that may vary by type, size or location of the business. For example, Kenya has used this form of a tax, called the single business permit, since 1999.

6.1.6 Excise taxes (subject to area size and cross-border trade and smuggling limitations)

Subject to the area size, cross-border trade and smuggling limitations, excise taxes have potential as piggyback taxes or special taxes at the sub-national level. Excises tend to be more politically acceptable, can be easily administered in coordination with national wholesalers as withholding agents and allow for rates differentiated by region. For example, some OECD countries allow sub-national government surcharges on excises.[30] Moreover, the benefit principle accords well with the assignment of (destination-based) excises on alcohol and tobacco to the sub-national level (to the extent that the latter is responsible for health care) and on vehicles and fuel (to the extent of sub-national government involvement in road construction and maintenance). The ability to charge differential rates across sub-national jurisdictions is, of course, limited by the possibility of cross-border trade and smuggling. The extent to which excise piggyback surtaxes can be used at the local level depends also on the technology of product distribution and points of sales.

An interesting aspect of excise taxation at the sub-national level is the taxation of public utility services. There is significant revenue potential in some of these services, as in the case of electricity and phone services. Besides revenue potential and administrative ease, sub-national excises on public utility services are attractive because of the benefit principle. For example, excises on electric consumption and phone services should be in most cases good proxies for the demand of local public services by both households and enterprises. Compared with other commodities, taxation of public utilities would be associated with relatively low distortions, as most utilities show relatively low price-elasticity of demand. Also, the demand for public utilities has been shown to be income elastic, which brings two additional benefits to this form of sub-national taxes: progressivity and revenue buoyancy (Linn, 1983).

6.1.7   Flat-rate piggyback income taxes

As we have discussed above, progressive income taxes are best assigned at the central government level, because income redistribution should be an objective pursued by the central governments because of the mobility of taxpayers and so on. Another reason for this assignment is that progressive income taxes tend to act as automatic economic stabilizers and macroeconomic stabilization should primarily be a function of the central government. Nevertheless, there are several possibilities for the taxation of personal income by sub-national governments. The most commonly used form of sub-national income taxation internationally is a flat-rate income tax as a surtax or 'piggyback' tax on the central government personal income tax. This type of tax is almost always collected by the central government administration and shared on a derivation basis.[31] To enhance revenue autonomy, local governments may be allowed discretion in setting the flat rate between minimum and maximum rates, which are centrally legislated.[32] A flat-rate local piggyback income tax easily satisfies the benefit principle and, being quite visible, it promotes political responsibility and accountability at the sub-national level. This is also an elastic tax with revenues increasing commensurate with income, so that as the demand for local services increases with income, so do tax revenues.

6.2   Worse Choices for Sub-national Taxes

As we have discussed, the principles of tax assignment do not provide a deterministic list of taxes, but those principles are helpful in identifying more good choices, and also likely poor choices. First, progressive personal income taxes are not a good choice for tax assignment at the sub-national level; ultimately, it would seem to make little sense to have income redistribution only within the boundaries of sub-national jurisdictions, since richer taxpayers tend to live in richer jurisdictions. In addition, the mobility of high-income taxpayers and businesses could easily lead to distortion in the location of economic activity.

Another tax that is ill-equipped for application at the sub-national level is the corporate income tax or profit tax. This is a tax more appropriately assigned to the central government level because of its link to macroeconomic stabilization and, to the extent that corporations are owned by wealthy individuals, this tax also affects income redistribution. Perhaps even more relevant, is that even when levied by the central government, the corporate income tax hardly meets sounds principles. There are no reasons to believe that incorporated businesses benefit more from public services than unincorporated ones or that the benefits received vary with profits. The main justification for a corporate income tax is to prevent avoidance of individual income tax through incorporation and to withhold tax on foreign shareholders, who otherwise only may have to pay tax in their countries of residence. Clearly, it is administratively easier to tax profits at source rather than as individual income after distribution among shareholders.

At a more practical level, the assignment of profit taxes at the central level is justified by the difficulty of apportioning well the profits of enterprises across sub-national jurisdictions where they operate. Some countries that have corporate income taxes at the sub-national level attempt to apportion the nationwide profits of enterprises among sub-national jurisdictions using a formula. These apportionment formulas generally use a weighted index of combinations of three factors: payroll, assets and sales. But, despite these formulas, the allocation of profits across jurisdictions tends to be quite arbitrary because of the imprecise link between the location of those factors and the generation of profits. In countries where no formula is used, the typical norm is to share the revenues between the central and sub-national governments on a derivation basis, that is, according to the jurisdiction where the taxes have been actually collected. This practice leads to an arbitrary distribution of revenues, since the shared revenues stay in the very few jurisdictions where companies are registered or have their headquarters. This means that the capital of the country and a few other large cities where enterprises have their headquarters tend to benefit unfairly vis-à-vis jurisdictions where the enterprises have factories and other forms of economic activity that use local resources and public services.

Another tax that traditionally has been thought a poor choice for assignment to the sub-national level is the VAT. The main difficulty lies in the fact that the debiting and crediting of the VAT is likely to take place in different sub-national jurisdictions, which generally will imply an arbitrary apportionment of VAT revenues across those jurisdictions.[33] This also makes it problematic to share VAT revenues with sub-national governments on a derivation basis. However, it is perfectly feasible to share VAT revenues with sub-national units using a formula. For example, the VAT can be shared on the basis of population (as in Germany and Belarus), or on the basis of the regional shares in aggregate consumption (as in Canada's Maritime Provinces, Japan or Spain).[34] But, of course, this form of revenue-sharing does little to enhance revenue autonomy or accountability among sub-national governments. Nevertheless, in more recent years, there have been a series of developments in practice and at theoretical levels that clearly demonstrate that sub-national VATs on a destination basis using the invoice-credit method are quite feasible. We review those developments next.

6.3   The Feasibility of Sub-national VATs

Broad-based indirect taxes are attractive to sub-national governments because of their revenue potential. Although retail final sales taxes are still used in some countries, for example at the state level in the United States, the current consensus is that a destination-based VAT is preferable to a retail sales tax as a sub-national tax option especially when a national VAT already exists (which, of course, is not the case in the United States).[35]

However, the introduction of sub-national VATs is among the most complex issues in the theory and practice of revenue assignments. Basically, only three large federal countries have introduced sub-national VATs: Brazil, Canada and India. The mixed experience from these countries has served for many years as an example of the difficulties facing any other country contemplating the introduction of a sub-national VAT. The best experience so far is, no doubt, the Quebec Sales Tax (QST). This tax is structured as a deferred-payment plus destination-based system and in combination with Canada's federal GST (goods and services tax) consti-tutes a truly operational 'dual VAT'.[36] On the other hand, Brazil's state-level VAT, known by its initials in Portuguese as ICMS (Imposto Sobre Circulação de Mercadorias e Serviços), is an origin-based consumption tax that falls on manufacturing goods and some services with different rates for different goods in intra-state transactions and either of two rates used for inter-state transactions (a lower rate for exports to less-developed states). The tax on interstate sales is fully creditable at the expense of the import-ing state. The ICMS is a complex system that so far has not worked well.[37] The introduction of a functional VAT in India has been complicated by constitutional provisions regarding the taxation of goods and services at the federal and state levels.[38]

What type of VAT would be desirable at the sub-national level? There is now wide consensus that the preferable form of a sub-national VAT is a destination-based (as opposed to an origin-based) tax, not only because it relates more directly to the benefit principle, but because it is less likely to distort the location of economic activity and because it does not lend itself to undesirable practices, such as transfer pricing manipulations.[39] Using the destination principle has two important implications (McLure, 2006). First, the sub-national jurisdiction of destination gets the revenues. Second, the same final rate of tax applies to consumption of a given commodity in the sub-national jurisdiction of destination regardless of where it is produced. Other desirable features of a sub-national VAT besides being destination-based include some discretion to set rates, similar compliance requirements for intra- and inter-jurisdiction trades, and proper collection incentives.

There are several approaches to implementing a destination-based sub-national VAT. The most immediate one, as practiced by national governments in the case of international trade, is border tax adjustments. However, it is clear that this approach is neither feasible nor desirable for internal trade among sub-national jurisdictions. The second approach is a clearing-house arrangement. Here all sales (intra- and inter-jurisdiction) are treated the same and registered importers in other jurisdictions can reclaim a credit from their own authorities for taxed inputs; periodically all jurisdictions settle up and clear net claims. The clearing-house arrangement can be cumbersome but it is actually practiced in Israel and the West Bank and Gaza Strip. The main problem with the clearing-house arrangement is that there are no incentives within the system to verify that the claims for refunds are legitimate. The third is the zero-rating/deferred payment approach; here the sales to registered taxpayers in other states are zero-rated and the tax on imports is deferred until the importer pays tax but, at the same time, he also gets the credit for the tax on imports. This is the basic mechanism used under the QST and it is also the 'interim' solution that has been in use in the European Union for cross-member country transactions.

The essence of the Quebec dual VAT (the provincial QST and the federal GST) is to handle interstate sales on a zero-rated, deferred payment basis (Bird and Gendron, 1998). This dual VAT is administered by Quebec's provincial authorities. There is, however, an important role played by the federal authorities. This tax requires a well-functioning national VAT with joint audits and a high level of information exchange to work well. For example, even though Quebec cannot monitor a zero-rated export to another province, the normal process of the federal audit serves as a check that Quebec VAT has not been evaded. The institutional set-up provides incentives for enforcement of the provincial and federal taxes; in particular, the QST is charged on a price inclusive of the federal GST basis.

The administrative problem of imposing a destination-based sub-national VAT has attracted several recent contributions in the literature seeking creative solutions to sub-national VATs. The first of these contributions is known as the 'compensating VAT' or CVAT, first proposed by Varsano (1995, 1999) for Brazil and expanded by McLure (2000b). The CVAT preserves the zero rating of sales between the sub-national jurisdictions but maintains the VAT chain by instead charging a compensating VAT on all cross-border sales. This compensating VAT is fully creditable to the importer, so that no jurisdiction would collect any net revenue from the tax on interstate sales to registered traders. In addition, the administration of the CVAT is to be combined into the federal VAT; that is, the CVAT would be paid to the federal government and then the importer would credit it against federal VAT due – or get a refund. A significant advantage of the CVAT is that it requires a fairly low level of administrative capacity. However, it has the disadvantage of the asymmetric treatment given to the in-state and out-of-state buyers.

The second contribution to the implementation of a destination-based sub-national VAT is the 'viable integrated VAT' or VIVAT, initially proposed by Keen and Smith (1996) as a solution for the European Union. The VIVAT charges a VAT tax at a common rate on all transactions between all registered traders, inside of and outside of the jurisdiction, while sales to final consumers and non-registered traders are taxed at the rate of the jurisdiction where the seller is located. A conspicuous advantage of the VIVAT is that it does not require the existence of a federal VAT. However, it requires the asymmetric treatment of registered traders and final consumers.

In summary, there are currently three viable options for a destination-based sub-national VAT. While the dual VAT has been working in Quebec, Canada, the CVAT and the VIVAT options have yet to be implemented. Each of the three options presents advantages and disadvantages in terms of generally desirable traits of a destination-based sub-national VAT. It is desirable, for example, that sellers do not need to identify the destination jurisdiction or the type of buyer in order to charge the tax. Or it is also desirable that the tax can be implemented without the need for a central agency administering the process. When these and other desirable properties are tallied, none of the options for a sub-national VAT is inherently better than the others. The choice of the sub-national VAT will need to be made according to existing constraints and most desirable objectives.[40]

7　THE INTERNATIONAL EXPERIENCE WITH TAX ASSIGNMENTS

The international experience with revenue assignments shows great diversity of approaches and, therefore, is not easily summarized. A useful way to view this international experience is along two main dimensions: first, the form of legislation and effective use of tax autonomy; and second, the level of decentralization in tax administration arrangements. According to these dimensions, we can identify three main types of tax assignment models in the world practice.

The first is what we could call the 'tax autonomy' model, prevalent in Canada and the United States. These countries exhibit revenue assignments with a great deal of tax autonomy and independent legislation, and decentralized tax administrations at the sub-national levels. In these two countries, the same revenue bases are generally taxed by different levels of government. This international model does not present harmonized tax bases across sub-national jurisdictions, which results in relatively higher taxpayer compliance costs and administration costs.

The second model we could call the 'tax sharing/transfer' model. This is prevalent in a large number of countries including Australia, Germany, Russia and Spain. This model of revenue assignment is characterized by low tax autonomy and heavier reliance on tax-sharing and transfers. This would also offer a variety of tax administration arrangements, mostly centralized (Australia, Russia, Spain) but also exceptionally decentralized (Germany).

The third model is the 'piggyback taxes' model, and it is prevalent in the Scandinavian and other Northern and Central European countries. Here a significant degree of tax autonomy is achieved through surcharges or piggyback taxes on central taxes, while this autonomy comes mostly in the form of determining a flat surcharge rate. In this model the administration of taxes at all levels remains highly centralized.

8 SUMMARY AND CONCLUSIONS

Effective fiscal decentralization requires meaningful levels of revenue autonomy at the regional and local levels of government. These conference notes review the theory and practice of tax assignments, seeking to answer the question of which taxes are better allocated to sub-national jurisdictions.

Besides adequate revenues to fund the public expenditure needs of sub-national governments, what we most want from revenue assignments is accountability and political and fiscal responsibility for sub-national government officials. This is fundamentally achieved by granting sub-national governments a significant level of tax autonomy. Achieving a good level of tax autonomy has many other benefits including the imposition of a hard budget constraint on sub-national governments.

However, the full financing of sub-national governments from auto-nomous tax sources is generally not feasible. The commonly accepted com-promise is that sub-national governments need to raise their own funds at the margin and operate with hard budget constraints; this means that revenue-sharing and grants should represent only infra-marginal funding. Operationally, this translates into the golden rule for revenue assignment: own revenue sources should fund the expenditure needs (net of conditional grants) of the wealthiest sub-national governments, and the revenue needs of the relatively poorer sub-national government should be supplemented with equalization grants.

However, not all forms of tax autonomy are equally desirable. All things considered, the best way to provide sub-national governments with tax autonomy is to have a closed list of taxes for which sub-national govern-ments can set tax rates within some minimum and maximum values that are nationally legislated. Good choices for sub-national governments include maximum use of fees and charges for excludable services under the benefit principle, plus a list of well-suited taxes such as the property tax, vehicle taxes and piggyback personal income taxes. Recent advances also make it possible to introduce a sub-national VAT in either its dual Quebec-style form, or under the CVAT or VIVAT forms.

The international experience clearly shows that there are no unique well-defined formulas for revenue assignments. While there is ample revenue auton-omy in North America and countries in Scandinavia and in Central Europe, many other decentralized countries around the world rely very heavily on revenue-sharing and transfers to finance sub-national governments.

This latter situation continues to be puzzling. More research is needed to understand the political economy behind some of the anomalies in the choices of revenue assignments. In particular, it is important to better understand why the wrong revenue assignments have proved so difficult to change in a significant number of countries and also why the little revenue authority provided to sub-national governments quite often goes unused even though these governments might, at the same time, demand more funding. Future research should be more heavily focused on the political economy of revenue assignments.

NOTES

1. This chapter is based on the notes presented at the 4th Symposium on Fiscal Federalism organized by IEB, at the University of Barcelona in May 2006. Some parts of this chapter draw on joint work with Andrey Timofeev and I am grateful for his input. I would like to express my gratitude to Núria Bosch and José Mariá Durán for the invita-tion to the IEB, 2006 conference.

2. See, for example, Martínez-Vázquez, McLure and Vaillancourt (2006).
3. See Burki, Perry and Dillinger (1999) for the experience of some Latin American countries.
4. See Bahl and Linn (1992). Prior knowledge of expenditure assignments can also help to better design revenue assignments because different services may call for different forms of financing. Some services (public utilities, bus transportation) can be financed by user charges while other services characterized by significant externalities, should be financed from region-wide taxes and intergovernmental transfers.
5. See McLure (1998) and Bird (2000).
6. See McLure (2001) for the role of history in revenue assignments.
7. A number of recent studies (e.g., Ter-Minassian, 1997; Ebel and Yilmaz, 2002) suggest that outcomes of decentralized spending depend on the form of financing used for these expenditures, with a crucial aspect being the extent of control that local governments can exercise over the sources of their revenue.
8. A hard budget constraint implies that those local governments given autonomy will be asked to balance their budgets without recourse to any end-of-year assistance from the central government and a clear understanding that there will be 'no bailout' at year-end or in the case of debt default. See Rodden, Eskel and Litvack (2003).
9. Traditionally it has been thought that greater sub-national revenue autonomy may compromise the ability of the center to implement stabilization policies; in reality, the reverse seems to happen. It could be that greater sub-national revenue autonomy leads to more conservative budget policies and lower deficits at all levels of government. See Martínez-Vázquez and McNab (2006).
10. This argument is made very clearly in McLure (1998).
11. See Bird and Ebel (2007) on the possibilities and problems with asymmetric fiscal federalism.
12. See Musgrave (1983); Boadway (1997); Norregard (1997); McLure (1998 and 2000a) and Bird (2000).
13. The international experience shows that providing sub-national governments with freedom to select their own taxes (the open-list approach) can easily backfire when sub-national governments introduce highly inefficient (distortionary) forms of taxation. A recent example is provided by Indonesia, which adopted an open-list approach in the 2001 decentralization reform. See Alm, Martínez-Vázquez and Indrawati (2004).
14. See Dahlby and Wilson (1996, 2003); Keen (1998) and Boadway, Marchand and Vigneault (1998).
15. See, for example, Flowers (1988); Dahlby (1996); Boadway et al. (1998) and Keen (1998).
16. The ability to change either base or rate opens up the possibility of fiscal competition among sub-national governments (Wilson, 1999). Inter-jurisdictional fiscal competition can have both good aspects, such as offering choices to taxpayers and keeping public officials more accountable, and also bad aspects, such as a 'run to the bottom' type of behavior actually taking place in countries with a significant degree of sub-national tax autonomy. In addition, the ability to change tax base or rate can give rise to 'horizontal' fiscal externalities, whereby the policies of one jurisdiction (for example, raising tax rates) can have an effect on the tax bases of other jurisdictions (raising their tax bases related to mobile taxpayers). Intergovernmental grants and other policies can be implemented by the central government to correct horizontal fiscal externalities. See, for example, Arnott and Grieson (1981); Gordon (1983) and Wildasin (1983, 1989).
17. See Martínez-Vázquez and Timofeev (2005).
18. See, for example, Martínez-Vázquez and Boex (2001) and Martínez-Vázquez, Timofeev and Boex (2006).
19. The regional governments may keep the centrally designed tax schedule, in which case they will receive 33 per cent of the total tax take, or they may increase or reduce the rates but with the requirement that the rate schedule be a progressive tax with the same number of brackets as in the central government's income tax. In addition, the regional governments may also establish their own tax credits, which would only affect their

differential tax take. In practice, regional governments have changed tax credits and not the tax rate schedule. See López-Laborda, Martínez-Vázquez and Monasterio (2007).

20. Otherwise, when decisions on economic stabilization and income distribution are left to the local governments, wrong incentives and conflicts may arise, and policies may be ineffective and unsustainable.

21. See, for example, McLure (1998).

22. However, despite the wide agreement on the advantages of the property tax as a sub-national tax, sub-national governments in developing and transitional countries make relatively little use of the property tax. On average, transitional and developing countries raise property tax revenues that are equivalent to only about 0.6 percent of GDP. See Bahl and Martínez-Vázquez (2007) for an investigation of this puzzle.

23. The balance between the services received by property owners and the property taxes they pay on their real estate typically can be capitalized into property values. That is, property taxes do not have to reduce the market value of dwellings if the general perception is that the quality of services provided by the local government is good.

24. See Bahl and Linn (1992) and Sennoga, Sjoquist and Wallace (2007).

25. Of course, low interest may also reflect the perception that the property tax is complex and has low revenue potential vis-à-vis its associated political costs, although there are exceptions (for example, China, Indonesia and Jamaica).

26. Being 'house rich and income poor' can be a problem for elderly people. Some countries use special exemption schemes ('homestead exemptions' or 'circuit breakers') to increase equity in the implementation of property taxes.

27. For international experience with the property tax see Bird and Slack (2004) and Bahl and Martínez-Vázquez (2007).

28. See, for example, McLure (1996) and Bahl and Tumennasan (2004).

29. See Keen (2003). The IRAP (Imposta Regionale sulle Activià Produttive) is payable by businesses on the amount their sales exceed the sum of their material purchases and depreciation. This is an origin-based income-type (no full deduction for investment) VAT administered by the subtraction method centrally. Regions have discretion on rates. Although it has many good features of a benefit tax, it has proven to be quite unpopular with taxpayers.

30. For example, in the Netherlands, provinces impose a surcharge on the motor vehicle tax levied by the central government. Provinces are free to set the rate of the surcharge, subject to a ceiling imposed by the central government.

31. Generally speaking, a local income tax should be levied at the place of residence because it is there where most taxpayers consume sub-national government services. However, because of administrative convenience, sub-national piggyback taxes are often withheld at source at the place of work by employees. However, it is quite feasible to distribute the funds according to where workers reside.

32. Other forms of tax autonomy are practiced, such as the ability to modify the base of the tax by providing more or less deductions, exemptions and so on.

33. Revenue-sharing on a derivation basis for the VAT also means that, as in the case for the sharing of corporate income taxes, the tax tends to be paid according to the place of registration or the location of the headquarters of business firms.

34. In the case of Canada's harmonized sales tax for the Maritime Provinces, all three provinces have a uniform rate that piggybacks on the federal VAT.

35. See Fox and Luna (2003) for a discussion of the issues.

36. See Bird and Gendron (1998).

37. See Varsano (1995, 1999).

38. See Bahl et al. (2005).

39. A destination-based VAT is a tax on consumption in the taxing jurisdiction (it taxes imports but not exports), while an origin-based tax is a tax on production in the taxing jurisdiction (it taxes exports but not imports).

40. See Bird and Gendron (2000); Keen (2000), Keen and Smith (2000) and McLure (2006) for an animated discussion of the advantages and disadvantages of the dual VAT, CVAT and VIVAT.

REFERENCES

Alm, James, Jorge Martínez-Vázquez and Sri Mulyani Indrawati (2004), *Reforming Intergovernmental Fiscal Relations and the Rebuilding of Indonesia: The 'Big Bang' Program and its Economic Consequences*, Cheltenham, UK and Northampton, MA, USA: Edward Elgar Publishing.

Arnott, Richard and Ronald E. Grieson (1981), 'Optimal fiscal policy for a state or local government', *Journal of Urban Economics*, 9 (1), 23–48.

Bahl, Roy and Johannes F. Linn (1992), *Urban Public Finance in Developing Countries*, Washington, DC: Oxford University Press.

Bahl, Roy and Jorge Martínez-Vázquez (2007), 'Property Taxes in Developing Countries: Where Will We Be in 2015?', in Roy Bahl, Jorge Martínez-Vázquez and Joan Youngman (eds), *Making the Property Tax Work in the Developing World*, Cambridge, Lincoln Institute.

Bahl, Roy and Bayar Tumennasan (2004), 'How Should Revenues from Natural Resources be Shared in Indonesia?', in James Alm, Jorge Martínez-Vázquez and Sri Mulyani Indrawati (eds), *Reforming Intergovernmental Fiscal Relations and the Rebuilding of Indonesia – The 'Big Bang' Program and its Economic Consequences*, Cheltenham, UK and Northampton, MA, USA: Edward Elgar Publishing.

Bahl, Roy, Eunice Heredia-Ortiz, Jorge Martínez-Vázquez and Mark Rider (2005), 'India: An Assessment of the Fiscal Condition of the States and their Relations with the Union Government', Working Paper 05-22, International Studies Program, Andrew Young School of Policy Studies, Georgia State University.

Bird, Richard M. (2000), 'Rethinking subnational taxes: a new look at tax assignment', *Tax Notes International*, 8 (5), 2069–96.

Bird, R.M. (2003), 'A new look at local business taxes', *Tax Notes International*, 30 (7), 695–711.

Bird, Richard and Robert Ebel (eds) (2007), *Fiscal Fragmentation in Decentralized Countries: Subsidiarity, Solidarity and Asymmetry*, Cheltenham, UK and Northampton, MA, USA: Edward Elgar.

Bird, Richard M. and Pierre-Pascal Gendron (1998), 'Dual VAT and cross-border trade: two problems, one solution?', *International Tax and Public Finance*, 5 (3), 429–42.

Bird, Richard M. and Pierre-Pascal Gendron (2000), 'CVAT, VIVAT and dual VAT: vertical "sharing" and interstate trade', *International Tax and Public Finance*, 7 (6), 753–61.

Bird, Richard and Enid Slack (2004), *International Handbook of Land and Property Taxation*, Cheltenham, UK and Northampton, MA, USA: Edward Elgar Publishing.

Boadway, Robin (1997), 'Tax Assignment in the Canadian Federal System', in Neil A. Warren (ed.), *Reshaping Fiscal Federalism in Australia*, Sidney: Australian Tax Foundation, pp. 61–90.

Boadway, Robin, Maurice Marchand and Marianne Vigneault (1998), 'The consequences of overlapping tax bases for redistribution and public spending in a federation', *Journal of Public Economics*, 68 (3), 453–78.

Burki, S., G. Perry and W. Dillinger (1999), 'Beyond the Center: Decentralizing the State', Working Paper, World Bank Latin America and Caribbean Studies, Washington, DC: World Bank.

Dahlby, B. (1996), 'Fiscal externalities and the design of intergovernmental grants', *International Tax and Public Finance*, **3** (3), 397–412.

Dahlby, Bev and L.S. Wilson (1996), 'Tax Assignment and Fiscal Externalities in a Federal State', in Paul M. Boothe (ed.), *Reforming Fiscal Federalism for Global Competition*, Edmonton, Canada: The University of Alberta Press.

Dahlby, Bev and L.S. Wilson (2003), 'Vertical fiscal externalities in a federation', *Journal of Public Economics*, **87** (5/6), 917–30.

Ebel, Robert D. and Serdar Yilmaz (2002), 'On the Measurement and Impact of Fiscal Decentralization', World Bank Policy Research Working Paper No. 2809.

Flowers, Marilyn R. (1988), 'Shared tax sources in a Leviathan model of federalism', *Public Finance Quarterly*, **16** (1), 67–77.

Fox, William and LeAnn Luna, (2003), 'Subnational taxing options: which is preferred, a retail sales tax or a VAT?', *Journal of State Taxation*, Winter, 1–22.

Gordon, Roger H. (1983), 'An optimal taxation approach to fiscal federalism', *The Quarterly Journal of Economics*, **98** (4), 567–86.

Keen, Michael (1998), 'Vertical tax externalities in the theory of fiscal federalism,' *IMF Staff Papers*, **45** (3), 454–85.

Keen, Michael (2000), 'VIVAT, CVAT and all that: new forms of value-added tax for federal systems', *Canadian Tax Journal*, **48** (2), 409–24.

Keen, Michael (2003), 'Tax reform in Italy', *Tax Notes International*, **29** (7), 665–82.

Keen, Michael and Stephen Smith (1996), 'The future of the value-added tax in the European Union,' *Economic Policy*, **11** (23), 375–411.

Keen, Michael and Stephen Smith (2000), 'Viva VIVAT!', *International Tax and Public Finance*, **6** (2), 741–51.

Linn, Johannes F. (1983), *Cities in the Developing World: Policies for Their Equitable and Efficient Growth*, Oxford: Oxford University Press.

López-Laborda, J., Jorge Martínez-Vázquez and C. Monasterio (2007), 'The Practice of Fiscal Federalism in Spain', in A. Shah (ed.), *The Practice of Fiscal Federalism: Comparative Perspectives*, Quebec: The Forum of Federations/ McGill-Queen's University Press.

Martínez-Vázquez and Jameson Boex (2001), *Russia's Transition to a New Federalism*, World Bank Institute Learning Resources Series, Washington, DC: The World Bank.

Martínez-Vázquez, Jorge and Robert McNab (2006), 'Fiscal decentralization, macroeconomic stability, and economic growth', *Hacienda Pública Española-Revista de Economía Publica*, **179** (4), 25–49.

Martínez-Vázquez, Jorge and Andrey Timofeev (2005), 'Choosing Between Centralized and Decentralized Models of Tax Administration', in N. Bosch and J.M. Duran (eds), *Financiación, Solidaridad Interterritorial y Políticas Tributarias de las Comunidades Autónomas*, Edicions I Publicacions de la Universitat de Barcelona: Barcelona (in Spanish) and International Studies Working Paper #05-2, Andrew Young School of Policy Studies, Georgia State University, Atlanta (in English).

Martínez-Vázquez, Jorge, Charles E. McLure Jr and Francois Vaillancourt (2006), 'Revenues and Expenditures in an Intergovernmental Framework', in R. Bird and F. Vaillancourt (eds), *Perspectives on Fiscal Federalism*, Washington, DC: World Bank.

Martínez-Vázquez, Andrey Timofeev and Jameson Boex (2006), *Reforming Regional-Local Finance in Russia*, World Bank Institute Learning Resources Series, Washington, DC: The World Bank.

McLure, Charles E. Jr (1996), 'The Sharing of Taxes on Natural Resources and the Future of the Russian Federation', in Christine I. Wallich (ed.), *Russia and the Challenge of Fiscal Federalism*, Washington, DC: World Bank.

McLure, Charles E. Jr (1998), 'The tax assignment problem: ends, means, and constraints', *Public Budgeting and Financial Management*, 9 (4), 652–83.

McLure, Charles E. Jr (2000a), 'Tax assignment and subnational fiscal autonomy', *Bulletin for International Fiscal Documentation*, December, 54 (12), 626–35.

McLure, Charles E. Jr (2000b), 'Implementing subnational VATs on internal trade: the compensating VAT (CVAT)', *International Tax and Public Finance*, 7 (6), 723–40.

McLure, Charles E. Jr (2001), 'The tax assignment problem: ruminations on how theory and practice depend on history', *National Tax Journal*, LIV (2), 339–63.

McLure, Charles E. Jr (2006), 'The Long Shadow of History: Sovereignty, Tax Assignment, Legislation and Judicial Decisions on Corporate Income Taxes in the U.S. and the E.U., Mimeo: Hoover Institution, Stanford University.

Musgrave, Richard A. (1959), *The Theory of Public Finance*, New York: McGraw-Hill.

Musgrave, Richard A. (1983), 'Who Should Tax, Where, and What?', in Charles E. McLure Jr. (ed.), *Tax Assignment in Federal Countries*, Canberra: Center for Research on Federal Financial Relations, pp. 2–19.

Norregard, John (1997), 'Tax Assignment', in Teresa Ter-Minassian (ed.), *Fiscal Federalism in Theory and Practice*, Washington, DC: International Monetary Fund, pp. 49–72.

Rodden, Jonathon A., Gunnar Eskel and Jennie Litvack (2003), *Fiscal Decentralization and the Challenge of Hard Budget Constraints*, Cambridge, MA: MIT.

Sennoga, Edward, David Sjoquist and Sally Wallace (2007), 'Incidence and Economic Impacts of Property Taxes in Developing and Transitional Countries', in Roy Bahl, Jorge Martínez-Vázquez and Joan Youngman (eds), *Making the Property Tax Work in the Developing World*, Cambridge, MA: Lincoln Institute.

Ter-Minassian, Teresa (1997), *Fiscal Federalism in Theory and Practice*, Washington, DC: International Monetary Fund.

Varsano, Ricardo (1995), 'A Tributacao de Comercio Interstadua: ICMS versus ICMS Partilhado', Discussion Paper No. 382, Brazil: Instituto de Pesquisa Economica Aplicade.

Varsano, Ricardo (1999), 'Subnational Taxation and the Treatment of Interstate Trade in Brazil: Problems and a Proposed Solution', Paper presented to the ABCD-LAC Conference, Valdivia, Chile, July 1999.

Wildasin, David E. (1983), 'The welfare effects of intergovernmental grants in an economy with independent jurisdictions', *Journal of Urban Economics*, 13 (2), 147–64.

Wildasin, David E. (1989), 'Interjurisdictional capital mobility: fiscal externality and a corrective subsidy', *Journal of Urban Economics*, 25 (2), 193–212.

Wilson, John Douglas (1999), 'Theories of tax competition', *National Tax Journal*, 52 (2), 269–304.

3. Tax assignment and tax autonomy in OECD countries[1]

Hansjörg Blöchliger

1 INTRODUCTION

Tax autonomy is part of the institutional arrangement – such as responsibility and revenue assignment – in which the different levels of government operate. A common way to compare and assess tax autonomy is the extent to which resources and responsibilities are under the control of local and regional governments. Sub-central governments' (SCGs) tax and expenditure indicators (or 'decentralization ratios') can help to assess fiscal decentralization and its evolution over time, and give a first impression of how much power SCGs enjoy. The following figures show the current state of financial decentralization as measured by sub-central government shares of total tax revenue and expenditure in OECD countries (Figure 3.1) and the evolution of these indicators over the last decade (Figure 3.2).

The stylized facts shown by these figures can be summarized as follows:

- The degree of decentralization varies greatly across OECD countries. While the sub-central share of total government expenditures varies from less than 6 per cent to more than 60 per cent, taxes accruing to sub-central governments extend between 3 and 50 per cent. The constitutional background of a country – whether it is federal or unitary – says little about actual fiscal autonomy. Local governments in some unitary countries have a higher share in public spending than local and regional governments together in federal countries.
- The sub-central tax share and the sub-central expenditure share have diverged over the last ten years. While the share of sub-national expenditures generally increased, local taxing power – with a few notable exceptions – remained almost stable. The rising expenditure share partly reflects new responsibilities assigned to sub-central governments such as health care and/or non-university education. On the other hand, local taxing power was reduced in many countries, and replaced by intergovernmental transfers.

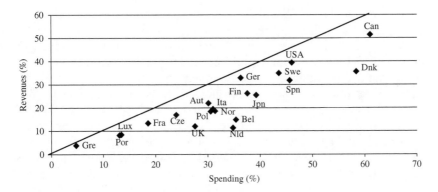

Source: OECD (2005).

Figure 3.1   Decentralization ratios in OECD countries, 2004

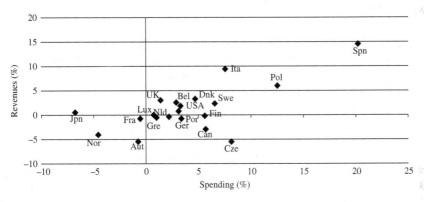

Source: OECD (2005).

Figure 3.2   Decentralization ratios, evolution 1995–2004

- In most countries, sub-central government expenditures by far exceed tax revenue, and this 'fiscal gap' has widened in the last decade. The difference between responsibilities and resources points to large intergovernmental transfer schemes. In general, the fiscal gap tends to be larger in countries with high sub-central fiscal autonomy, that is, local and regional jurisdictions with a large tax share depend more heavily on transfers; somewhat paradoxically, more decentralization can go hand in hand with more dependency on central government resources. Size and structure of intergovernmental grants thus become a particular issue in a decentralized environment.

A serious problem with these simple ratios, however, is that they only poorly measure the true degree of autonomy that SCGs enjoy in practice. On the revenue side, limits to setting own local tax bases, rates and reliefs reduce local fiscal autonomy. On the expenditure side, local spending may be strongly influenced by upper-level government regulation, thereby reducing discretion over various expenditure items. In some countries, the transfer of financial responsibility for education or health care was hardly more than a change in accounting procedures, while essential regulatory responsibilities remained with the central government. Moreover, the various strings and conditions attached to intergovernmental transfers may further influence the spending pattern of sub-central governments. To obtain a more accurate picture of sub-central fiscal autonomy, a more detailed set of indicators is required.

2   HOW SHOULD 'TAX AUTONOMY' BE MEASURED?

The term 'tax autonomy' captures various aspects of freedom that sub-central governments have over their own taxes. It encompasses features such as sub-central governments' right to introduce or to abolish a tax, to set tax rates, to define the tax base, or to grant tax allowances or reliefs to individuals and firms. In a number of countries taxes are not assigned to one specific government level but shared between the central and sub-central governments. Such tax-sharing arrangements deny a single SCG any control on tax rates and bases, but collectively SCGs may negotiate the sharing formula with central government. The wealth of explicit and implicit, statutory and common, institutional arrangements has to be encompassed by a set of indicators that are simultaneously appropriate (they capture the relevant aspects of tax autonomy), accurate (they measure those aspects correctly) and reliable (the indicator set remains stable over time).

The tax autonomy indicator set consists of five main categories of autonomy (Table 3.1). Categories are ranked in decreasing order from highest to lowest taxing power. Category 'a' represents full power over tax rates and bases, 'b' power over tax rates (essentially representing the 'piggybacking' type of tax), 'c' power over the tax base, 'd' tax-sharing arrangements, and 'e' no power on rates and bases at all. Category 'f' represents non-allocable taxes. In order to better capture the more refined institutional details, the five categories were further divided into subcategories: two for the 'a' and 'b' categories, and three for the 'c' category. Special attention was paid to tax-sharing arrangements, where the four 'd' subcategories are thought to represent the many different rules and institutions for governments to determine and

Table 3.1   Taxonomy of taxing power

Category	Level of Autonomy
a.1	The recipient SCG sets the tax rate and any tax reliefs without needing to consult a higher-level government
a.2	The recipient SCG sets the rate and any reliefs after consulting a higher-level government
b.1	The recipient SCG sets the tax rate, and a higher-level government does not set upper or lower limits on the rate chosen
b.2	The recipient SCG sets the tax rate, and a higher-level government set upper and/or lower limits on the rate chosen
c.1	The recipient SCG sets tax reliefs – but it sets tax allowances only
c.2	The recipient SCG sets tax reliefs – but it sets tax credits only
c.3	The recipient SCG sets tax reliefs – and it sets both tax allowances and tax credits
d.1	There is a tax-sharing arrangement in which the SCGs determine the revenue split
d.2	There is a tax-sharing arrangement in which the revenue split can be changed only with the consent of SCGs
d.3	There is a tax-sharing arrangement in which the revenue split is determined in legislation, and where it may be changed unilaterally by a higher-level government, but less frequently than once a year
d.4	There is a tax-sharing arrangement in which the revenue split is determined annually by a higher-level government
e	Other cases in which the central government sets the rate and base of the SCG tax
f	None of the above categories a, b, c, d or e applies

change their own share. Altogether 13 categories were established to capture the various tax autonomy arrangements in OECD countries. Where applicable, countries were asked to send separate data for both the state/regional and the local level. Twenty-four countries responded to the questionnaire, five more than in 1999. Since category f, 'non allocable' was hardly used, the taxing power universe seems to be well reflected in this taxonomy.

3   TAX ASSIGNMENT AND TAX AUTONOMY OF SUB-CENTRAL GOVERNMENTS

The stylized facts on taxing power of state and local governments in 2002 can be summarized as follows (Table 3.2):[2]

Table 3.2 *Taxing power of sub-central governments, 2002*

	Sub-central tax revenue as % of total tax revenues	Discretion on rates and reliefs (a)	Discretion on rates (b) Full	Discretion on rates (b) Restricted	Discretion on reliefs (c)	Tax-sharing arrangements (d) Revenue split set by SCG	Revenue split set with SCG consent	Revenue split set by CG, pluriannual	Revenue split set by CG, annual	Rates and reliefs set by CG (e)	Other (f)	Total
Australia	31.4											
States	28.4	54.4	–	–	–	–	45.6	–	–	–	–	100.0
Local	3.0	100.0	–	–	–	–	–	–	–	–	–	100.0
Austria	18.4											
States	8.8	7.0	–	–	–	–	82.7	–	–	9.6	0.8	100.0
Local	9.6	2.7	–	5.4	–	–	66.5	–	–	20.0	5.5	100.0
Belgium	27.8											
States	22.8	63.8	–	–	–	–	36.2	–	–	–	–	100.0
Local	5.0	10.0	–	86.4	–	–	–	–	–	3.6	–	100.0
Canada	44.1											
Provinces	35.5	98.4	–	–	–	–	1.6	–	–	–	–	100.0
Local	8.6	1.8	95.6	–	–	–	–	–	–	2.3	0.3	100.0
Czech Republic	12.5											
Local	12.5	5.5	–	4.1	–	–	–	88.8	–	1.5	0.1	100.0
Denmark	35.6											
Local	35.6	–	86.0	4.7	–	–	–	2.9	–	6.4	–	100.0
Finland	21.5											
Local	21.5	–	85.3	4.6	–	–	–	–	9.9	–	0.1	100.0

Column group heading: *As Share of Sub-central Tax Revenues (%)*

	C1	C2	C3	C4	C5	C6	C7	C8	C9	C10	Total
France	10.0	–	–	–	–	–	–	–	–	–	–
Local	10.0	72.1	–	8.5	9.1	–	–	–	3.6	6.6	100.0
Germany	28.7	–	–	–	–	–	–	–	–	–	–
Länder	21.8	–	–	2.4	–	86.3	–	–	11.2	–	100.0
Local	7.0	17.6	–	33.6	–	47.6	–	–	1.1	0.2	100.0
Greece	0.9	–	–	–	–	–	–	–	–	–	–
Local	0.9	–	–	64.6	35.4	–	–	–	–	–	100.0
Iceland	25.2	–	–	–	–	–	–	–	–	–	–
Local	25.2	–	–	91.2	–	–	–	–	–	8.8	100.0
Italy	16.4	–	–	–	–	–	–	–	–	–	–
Regional	11.3	27.1	–	58.8	–	23.7	17.6	–	9.3	–	100.0
Local	5.2	–	–	50.4	–	–	13.1	–	–	–	100.0
Japan	26.0	–	–	–	–	–	–	–	–	–	–
Local	26.0	0.1	79.7	–	–	–	–	–	20.2	–	100.0
Korea	18.9	–	–	–	–	–	–	–	–	–	–
Local	18.9	–	–	64.3	–	–	–	–	35.7	–	100.0
Mexico	3.4	–	–	–	–	–	–	–	–	–	–
States	2.4	100.0	–	–	–	–	–	–	–	–	100.0
Local	1.0	100.0	–	–	–	–	–	–	–	–	100.0
Netherlands	3.6	–	–	–	–	–	–	–	–	–	–
Local	3.6	–	99.2	–	–	–	–	–	0.8	–	100.0
Norway	12.9	–	–	–	–	–	–	–	–	–	–
Local	12.9	3.3	–	96.7	–	–	–	–	–	–	100.0
Poland	17.5	–	–	–	–	–	–	–	–	–	–
Local	17.5	–	–	23.2	–	–	76.4	–	0.4	–	100.0
Portugal	6.0	–	–	–	–	–	–	–	–	–	–
Local	6.0	–	–	44.0	–	–	18.5	–	37.3	0.2	100.0
Spain	26.6	–	–	–	–	–	–	–	–	–	–
Regions	18.1	58.3	–	0.1	–	41.6	–	–	–	0.0	100.0
Local	8.5	27.2	–	51.4	–	21.4	–	–	–	0.0	100.0

Table 3.2 (continued)

	Sub-central tax revenue as % of total tax revenues	Discretion on rates and reliefs (a)	Discretion on rates (b)		Discretion on reliefs (c)	Tax-sharing arrangements (d)				Rates and reliefs set by CG (e)	Other (f)	Total
			Full	Restricted		Revenue split set by SCG	Revenue split set with SCG consent	Revenue split set by CG, pluriannual	Revenue split set by CG, annual			
Sweden												
Local	32.1	–	100.0	–	–	–	–	–	–	–	–	100.0
Switzerland	43.1											
States	27.0	90.4	–	–	–	–	9.6	–	–	–	–	100.0
Local	18.2	2.9	–	97.1	–	–	–	–	–	–	–	100.0
Turkey	6.5											
Local	6.5	–	–	–	–	–	–	–	–	–	100.0	100.0
United	4.5											
Kingdom												
Local	4.5	–	–	100.0	–	–	–	–	–	–	–	100.0
Unweighted Average												
States	19.6	52.5	–	6.8	–	1.5	36.4	2.0	–	2.3	0.1	100.0
Local	12.4	15.4	22.7	34.6	0.4	–	5.6	8.3	0.4	5.9	5.1	100.0

As Share of Sub-central Tax Revenues (%)

Source: National source and OECD (2005), *Revenue Statistics 1965–2004.*

- First, although tax autonomy varies widely across countries, most sub-central governments have considerable discretion over their own taxes. At the average, the tax revenue share with full or partial discretion (categories a, b and c) amounts to almost 60 per cent for state and more than 70 per cent for local government. In many countries (not shown in the table), permitted maximum tax rates are often double minimum rate.
- Second, categories a, b and c put together, state and regional governments have less discretion over their tax revenue than local governments, since their tax revenue is often embedded in tax-sharing arrangements. On the other hand, with 51 per cent of SCG tax revenue, the state level has a higher share in high-powered autonomous taxes (category a), while local governments are often allowed to levy a supplement on selected regional or central taxes only (category b or 'piggybacking' tax).
- Third, the c category (representing control over the tax base but not the tax rate) plays a very small role in OECD countries. This probably points to a policy of gradually banning tax reliefs and abatements as a tool for local and regional economic development, particularly in the European Union.

In some countries, SCGs have the right to vary tax rates but actually set the same rate across the country. Such 'unused taxing power' invites a deeper look into fiscal institutions and the incentives they generate for tax competition. Fiscal equalization arrangements can partly explain why sub-central jurisdictions in many countries stick to a uniform tax rate although they have the right to vary their rates (Blöchliger et al., 2007).

Tax-sharing agreements account for a large part of sub-central tax revenue in most constitutionally federal countries (Austria, Belgium, Germany, Mexico, Italy), in constitutionally non-federal Spain, in the Czech Republic and in Poland. Tax sharing is often considered as providing a balance between granting local/regional fiscal autonomy and keeping the overall fiscal framework stable. In such an arrangement a single SCG cannot set tax rates and bases, but SCGs together may have the power to negotiate their common share. This power varies considerably across countries, from arrangements where sub-central governments are in full control over their share, to arrangements where the share is unilaterally set and modified by the central government. Often the distribution formula is enshrined in the Constitution and can only be changed with the consent of all or a majority of sub-central governments. In other countries amendments to the sharing formula are easier to obtain, either with or without prior negotiation involving sub-central governments. In some cases the institutional set-up makes it difficult to decide whether an arrangement is tax sharing or intergovernmental transfer; this issue will be dealt with in the next section.

4   EVOLUTION OF TAX AUTONOMY 1995–2002

While the share of SCG tax revenue remained almost stable, taxing power increased from 1995 to 2002 (Table 3.3) . For the 17 countries where time series is available, tax revenue share rose by 0.6 percentage points for the state level and remained stable for local governments. In Spain and Poland SCG tax revenue increased by more than ten percentage points, while it decreased considerably in Mexico and Japan. But, interestingly, the share of tax revenue over which SCGs have full or partial discretion rose. States and regions gained more tax autonomy than local governments, revealed by the increase of category a tax revenue. Tax-sharing agreements lost significance in countries such as Austria, Belgium, Germany, Mexico or Spain, mostly in favour of taxes with more autonomy. In Norway, local governments gained some autonomy over income taxes, while in Austria and Germany, they lost. In some countries (e.g., France and Sweden) the central government is required to compensate the loss of sub-central tax revenue through additional transfers; this effect is not shown in Table 3.3.

The forces shaping the evolution of SCG tax revenue and tax autonomy are political, fiscal and economic in nature:

- First and probably most important are policy reforms such as a reassignment of taxes to another government level, a change in tax autonomy or a swap between local/regional taxes and intergovernmental grants. Constitutional and legislative amendments largely account for the rapid change in countries such as Belgium or Spain that are involved in a secular decentralization process.
- Second, fiscal reasons such as a relative change in tax rates or bases can also affect the pattern of taxing power, for example, if one government level changes its tax rate or base while another government level does not. In many countries, rates and base of local property taxes remain unchanged over long periods of time, while the bases of central government income taxes or goods and services taxes are regularly updated.
- Third, different taxes react differently to the business cycle or to structural change, and this may affect tax revenue of different government levels. A local profit tax reacts more swiftly to an economic downturn than a central government income tax, and a local sales tax

Table 3.3 Evolution of tax autonomy of sub-central governments (change in 1995–2002)

	Sub-central tax revenues as % of total tax revenues	Discretion on rates and reliefs (a)	Discretion on rates (b) Full	Discretion on rates (b) Restricted	Discretion on reliefs (c)	Revenue split set by SCG	Revenue split set with SCG consent	Revenue split set by CG, pluriannual	Revenue split set by CG, annual	Rates and reliefs set by CG (e)	Other (f)
						As a Share of Sub-central Tax Revenues (%)					
						Tax-sharing arrangements (d)					
Austria	–0.1										
Länder	–1.2	5.0	–	–	–	–	–15.3	–	–	9.6	0.8
Local	1.1	–5.8	–5.9	–	–	–	–14.0	–	–	20.0	5.5
Belgium	–0.2										
States	0.3	59.8	–47.5	–	–	–	–12.3	–	–	–	–
Local	–0.5	–2.5	2.4	–	–	–	–	–2.5	–1.0	3.6	–
Czech Republic	–0.5										
Local	–0.5	3.5	–0.9	–	–3.0	–	–	–1.2	–	1.5	0.1
Denmark	4.6										
Local	4.6	–	–3.8	–	–	–	–	0.9	–	2.9	–
Finland	–0.5										
Local	–0.5	–	0.9	–	–	–	–	–11.0	9.0	–	0.1
Germany	–0.3										
Länder	–0.2	–	2.4	–	–	–	–13.7	–	–	11.2	–
Local	0.0	16.6	–18.4	–	–	–	0.6	–	–	1.1	0.2

Table 3.3 (continued)

	As a Share of Sub-central Tax Revenues (%)										
	Sub-central tax revenues as % of total tax revenues	Discretion on rates and reliefs (a)	Discretion on rates (b) Full	Discretion on rates (b) Restricted	Discretion on reliefs (c)	Tax-sharing arrangements (d) Revenue split set by SCG	Revenue split set with SCG consent	Revenue split set by CG, pluriannual	Revenue split set by CG, annual	Rates and reliefs set by CG (e)	Other (f)
Iceland	5.2										
Local	5.2	−8.0	−0.8			–	–	–	–	–	8.8
Japan	2.0										
Local	2.0	0.1	−8.8			–	–	–	–	8.7	–
Mexico	−16.6										
States	−13.6	86.0				–	−86.0	–	–	–	–
Local	−3.0	100.0				–	–	−74.0	–	−26.0	–
Netherlands	1.1										
Local	1.1	–	−0.8			–	–	–	–	–	–
Norway	−7.1										
Local	−7.1	3.3	94.2			–	–	−0.5	–	−97.0	0.8
Poland	10.5										
Local	10.5	–	−21.8		−1.0	–	–	22.4	–	0.4	–
Portugal	0.8										
Local	0.8	–	0.2			–	–	−4.3	–	3.8	0.2

Spain	13.3								
Regions	13.3	44.0	−0.5	−	31.7	−	−	−	−75.2
Local	0.0	−1.5	−2.8	−	6.1	−	−	−	−1.8
Sweden	0.1								
Local	0.1	−2.0	2.0	−	−	−	−	−	−
Switzerland	5.1								
States	5.0	1.4	−	−	3.6	−5.0	−	−	−
Local	0.2	2.9	0.1	−	−	−3.0	−	−	−
United Kingdom	0.5								
Local	0.5	−	−	−	−	−	−	−	−
Unweighted Average									
States	0.6	32.7	−7.6	−	−15.3	−0.8	−	3.5	−12.4
Local	0.9	7.9	0.4	−0.2	−0.4	−3.5	0.5	−5.4	0.8

Source: National source and OECD (1999) and OECD (2005) *Revenue Statistics 1995–2004.*

on goods reacts more slowly to the rise of the service sector than a central value-added tax.

Altogether, the net effect of the three forces during the 1995 to 2002 period tended to favour sub-central governments' tax base slightly. For most of them no tax erosion could be detected, either in terms of the revenue share or in terms of discretion. However, the tax share must be set against the expenditure share, which increased in the same period (Figure 3.2).

5   TAX-SHARING ARRANGEMENTS

Tax sharing is an arrangement where tax revenue is divided vertically between the central and sub-central governments as well as horizontally across sub-central governments. In a tax-sharing arrangement, the individual SCG has no power to set tax rates or bases. However, SCGs may collectively negotiate policy reforms such as change to the sharing formula or to the tax rates. Often, tax-sharing arrangements contain an element of horizontal fiscal equalization. Tax sharing has become a means to provide fiscal resources to sub-central governments while maintaining central control over fiscal aggregates. Tax sharing typically involves less autonomy on the part of sub-central governments than autonomous taxes, and it may also change SCGs' fiscal behaviour. By turning SCG tax revenue into a common pool resource for all government levels, tax sharing may change fiscal incentives and the resulting fiscal outcomes. For both statistical and analytical reasons, a careful distinction between both forms of sub-central tax revenue allocation is therefore necessary.

Tax-sharing arrangements can be analysed on various grounds: the type of tax that is shared, the legal procedures involved in changing the formula, the frequency of an adjustment to the formula and whether the sharing formula contributes to an equalizing objective (Table 3.4).

Most tax-sharing arrangements cover major taxes such as personal income taxes, corporate income taxes or value-added taxes. Their high yield makes them attractive for SCGs, and the pooling tackles potential drawbacks of purely local taxation. The procedure for changing the sharing formula is mostly laid down in laws on tax sharing, fiscal equalization or the like. For the countries under scrutiny, decisions on the tax-sharing arrangements seem to be taken at the parliamentary level; in some countries the share is defined in the Constitution and adjustments require a qualified majority in parliament. Consultation of SCGs is quite frequent, but their explicit consent for adjustments is needed in some federal countries only. The frequency and regularity of formula adjustment varies across countries, from irregular to

Table 3.4   Tax-sharing arrangements

Country	Tax Type Shared	Procedure for Formula Changes	Frequency of Formula Changes	Horizontal Equalization Objective
Austria	PIT, CIT, property tax, VAT	Parliament, law on fiscal equalization	Every four years	Yes
Czech Republic	PIT, CIT, VAT	Government, law on tax assignment	Irregularly	Yes
Denmark	PIT, CIT	Government, law on tax sharing	Very rarely	No
Finland	CIT	Government, law on tax sharing		No
Germany	PIT, CIT, VAT	Both parliaments (Bundestag and Bundesrat)	13 changes since 1970	Yes
Greece	Transaction and specific service taxes	Central government	Rarely	No
Spain	VAT, excise duties	Parliament	Rarely	No
Switzerland	PIT	Parliament, law on fiscal equalization	Never since 1959	Yes

Note: PIT = personal income tax, CIT = corporate income tax, VAT = value-added tax.

never, but it appears that tax-sharing arrangements are a comparatively stable item in national fiscal policy. Finally, some countries redistribute tax revenue from affluent to poorer jurisdictions; hence those countries combine tax sharing and fiscal equalization in one single arrangement.

6   TAX AUTONOMY ACROSS TAX CATEGORY

The data on tax autonomy by tax type defy the beliefs on optimal local taxation (Table 3.5). While fiscal federal theory asserts that mobile taxes should be allocated to higher levels of government, in practice the largest single tax assigned to local and regional governments is the highly mobile income tax on individuals, with more than 36 per cent of total SCG tax revenue. If local corporate taxes are added, the share rises to more than 41 per cent. Taxes on goods account for 21 per cent of total SCG tax revenue. Taxes on immovable

Table 3.5   Tax autonomy of sub-central governments by type of tax

	Discretion on rates and reliefs (a)	Discretion on rates (b)		Discretion on reliefs (c)	Tax-sharing arrangements (d)				Rates and reliefs set by CG (e)	Other (f)	Total
		Full	Restricted		Revenue split set by SCG	Revenue split set with SCG consent	Revenue split set by CG, pluriannual	Revenue split set by CG, annual			
1000 Taxes on income, profits and capital gains	5.9	9.9	10.3	2.8	–	0.8	9.9	0.3	1.5	0.3	41.7
1100 Of individuals	5.2	9.3	8.1	2.8	–	0.8	8.2	–	1.1	–	35.5
1200 Corporate	0.7	0.6	2.2	–	–	–	1.4	0.3	0.4	0.3	5.9
1300 Unallocable between 1100 and 1200	–	–	–	–	–	–	0.3	–	–	0.0	0.3
2000 Social security contributions	0.1	–	–	–	–	–	–	–	0.0	0.1	0.3
2100 Employees	0.1	–	–	–	–	–	–	–	–	0.1	0.2
2200 Employers	–	–	–	–	–	–	–	–	–	0.0	0.0
2300 Self-employed or non-employed	–	–	–	–	–	–	–	–	–	–	

As Share of Sub-central Tax Revenues(%)

2400 Unallocable between 2100, 2200 and 2300	–	–	–	–	–	–	–	–	–	–	–
3000 Taxes on payroll and workforce	2.4	–	0.2	–	–	–	–	–	0.7	–	3.3
4000 Taxes on property	11.5	5.5	9.0	0.3	0.2	–	0.2	–	0.8	–	27.3
4100 Recurrent taxes on immovable property	6.4	5.3	6.4	–	–	–	0.0	–	0.5	–	18.6
4200 Recurrent taxes on net wealth	0.4	–	1.1	–	–	–	–	–	0.0	–	1.5
4300 Estate, inheritance and gift taxes	0.3	–	0.0	–	–	–	0.0	–	0.1	–	0.4
4400 Taxes on financial and capital transactions	2.5	0.0	1.3	0.3	0.2	–	0.1	–	0.2	–	4.6
4500 Non-recurrent taxes	0.1	0.2	0.2	–	–	–	–	–	–	–	0.5
4600 Other recurrent taxes on property	–	–	–	–	–	–	–	–	–	–	–
5000 Taxes on goods and services	3.4	1.5	1.3	0.0	0.9	4.2	5.2	–	4.5	0.3	21.4
5100 Taxes on production, sale, transfer, etc	2.2	0.1	0.2	0.0	0.9	2.8	5.0	–	3.4	0.3	14.9

Table 3.5 (continued)

	Discretion on rates and reliefs (a)	Discretion on rates (b) Full	Discretion on rates (b) Restricted	Discretion on reliefs (c)	Tax-sharing arrangements (d) Revenue split set by SCG	Revenue split set with SCG consent	Revenue split set by CG, pluriannual	Revenue split set by CG, annual	Rates and reliefs set by CG (e)	Other (f)	Total
5200 Taxes on use of goods and perform activities	1.2	1.5	1.2	–	–	–	0.1	–	1.1	–	5.1
5300 Unallocable between 5100 and 5200	–	–	–	–	–	–	–	–	–	0.0	0.0
6000 Other taxes	2.1	0.1	1.4	–	–	–	0.4	–	1.2	0.6	5.9
6100 Paid solely by business	0.9	0.1	1.4	–	–	–	–	–	0.0	0.2	2.7
6200 Other	1.2	–	–	–	–	–	0.4	–	1.1	–	2.8
Total	25.5	17.1	22.3	3.0	1.1	5.0	15.6	0.3	8.7	1.4	100.0

Note: Unweighted average, Countries included are: Australia, Austria, Belgium, Canada, the Czech Republic, Denmark, Finland, France, Germany, Greece, Iceland, Italy, Japan, Korea, Mexico, the Netherlands, Norway, Poland, Portugal, Spain, Sweden, Switzerland and Turkey.

Source: National sources and OECD (2005), Revenue Statistics 1965–2004.

property account for 19 per cent only. Although most OECD countries apply some sub-central property taxation, its yield is often limited and supplemented or even replaced by other taxes such as a local income tax. In more decentralized countries, local income tax revenue largely exceeds local property tax revenue. While income taxes may have general negative impacts on labour supply, it appears that government succeeded in tackling the specific drawbacks for local government – for example, their mobility – using policies such as tax-sharing arrangements or fiscal equalization schemes.

A closer look at Table 3.5 reveals that autonomy varies according to tax type. Property taxes are usually assigned more discretion than other taxes, with almost all tax revenue in categories a and b. Around a fourth of income tax revenue is embedded in tax-sharing systems, which restrict a single SCG's control over this tax. Since many income tax-sharing arrangements include fiscal equalization, they counteract potential drawbacks, such as excessive tax competition, of local income taxation. The right to set tax rates and bases does not mean that SCGs actually make use of this right; in some countries tax rates appear to vary very little or not at all across regions. Currently no data is available on the actual range of SCG tax rates, however. It could therefore be rewarding to have data on actual tax rate variations, to have a closer look at how fiscal design actually shapes sub-central behaviour with respect to tax rates and how fiscal policy can preserve local taxing powers and at the same time reduce fiscal disparities.

NOTES

1. Based on Hansjörg Blöchliger (OECD), David King, Stirling University (UK) (2006), 'Less than you thought: The fiscal autonomy of sub-central governments', *OECD Economic Studies 43*, Paris: OECD, pp. 155–188.
2. Since for some categories no or very small numbers were reported, some categories were merged and their number reduced from 13 to 10.

REFERENCES

Blöchliger, H. and D. King (2006), 'Less than you thought: The fiscal autonomy of sub-central governments', *OECD Economic Studies 43*, Paris: OECD, pp. 155–188.
Blöchliger, H., O. Merk, C. Charbit and L. Mizell (2007) *Fiscal Equalisation in OECD Countries*, Working Paper 3, Network of Fiscal Relations across Levels of Government, Paris: OECD.
OECD (1999), *Taxing Powers of State and Local Government*, Tax Policy Studies No 1, Paris: OECD.
OECD (2005), *National Accounts of OECD Countries 1993–2004*, Paris: OECD.

4. Tax assignment and regional co-responsibility in Spain

Juan A. Gimeno Ullastres

1 INTRODUCTION – PRESENT SITUATION

1.1 Co-responsibility, Sufficiency and Solidarity

The most prominent characteristic of the evolution of the Spanish system of autonomic financing is the speed with which the process of fiscal federalization has occurred. At the end of the 1970s, an extremely centralized structure was inherited in which the central administration managed 85 per cent of public expenditure, while the remaining 15 per cent was in the hands of the local administrations (town halls and county councils or mixed bodies). The 1978 Constitution sets up what is known as the autonomic state, in which the Autonomous Communities (ACs) are intermediate administration entities for regions or nationalities. In subsequent years, it was viewed as desirable to aim for an assignment among the three cited levels of government (i.e., central, autonomous and local) of 50, 25 and 25 percent, respectively.

In only a quarter of a century the assignment percentages have become 50, 35 and 15 per cent, which are 30, 50 and 20 per cent if we exclude social security. The headline numbers serve to underline that there has been a very rapid transfer of competences from the state to the Autonomous Communities, whereas the relative weight of the local administrations has scarcely changed. Although we will center on autonomic financing, we deliberately include in the whole analysis constant references to the local administrations. This is because any ideal solution needs to take into consideration all the actors simultaneously. Ultimately, the taxpayer is always the same and we must look for the formula that allows the most efficient financing of all levels of government.

The quick decentralization of competences was not accompanied by an equally quick gain in financial competences. As a result, for 20 years, Spanish academia has insisted on the idea of co-responsibility. This concept, we might say, involves all the conditions that any efficient model requires, but we can summarize them as follows:

- The provision of basic public services is a responsibility shared by the different levels of government.
- Specific administration competence is assigned to the most efficient level in every case.
- Every territorial administration must have full autonomy, involving sufficient financial resources and power to determine their level and composition.
- Every government is responsible for spending and revenues.
- Autonomy is accompanied by a cooperative system across the various levels.

Any system must guarantee that the exchequer has sufficient revenues at any of its levels in order to fulfill the competences assigned to it. The sufficiency of revenues bears a clear relationship to the estimated level of necessary spending and to the general principle that all citizens have equal access to public services. In our case, equality relates to location, so that residence in one part of the country must not mean a priori markedly differentiated services. Finally, sufficiency has to be guaranteed dynamically: the system must have enough flexibility to allow resources to keep pace with needs and to adapt to changing priorities at any given moment.

Every administration must have sufficient instruments and the degree of autonomy necessary to determine at any moment what level of services it wants to offer its citizens and, consequently, what tax burden it considers suitable and what instruments it will use. As summarized in Table 4.1, the extent of autonomy in tax administration may range from the simple utilization of collection to potential normative changes of greater or lesser importance. The higher the number of crosses that can be put in the

Table 4.1   Tax power

Degree	Exclusive (100%)	High	Medium	Low	None (0%)
Basic legislation					
Rates and allowances					
Administration					
Auditing					
Collection					

Source: Adapted from Giménez Montero (2003).

left-hand column (or nearer to it), the greater the tax power exercised by the corresponding administration.

In the analysis that follows, we start from the fact that co-responsibility demands that the basic level of budget revenue should correspond to the authority that drafts and manages the budget in question. That is to say, a significant portion of revenues are to be set by the affected administration, subject to individual differences that may arise in each case. However, that does not prevent a portion of the resources coming from another administration, provided that the quantity is set objectively and automatically. A fundamental principle of political and economic autonomy is that spending requirements are not determined exogenously.

Whatever the regulated financing mechanism, these two principles are to be balanced by the need for the wealthiest areas to compensate for the financial shortfalls of the poorest areas (in relative terms). With any system, the more advanced the sense of co-responsibility is, the greater the significance of own taxes in wealthy ACs and municipalities and the less their significance in less affluent ACs and town halls. Therefore, where co-responsibility is at an advanced level, there will be ACs that can probably cover all their spending needs with their own revenues (the Balearic Islands, Catalonia and Madrid might manage to be self-sufficient), whereas other ACs with the same tax system but lower collection capacity (Extremadura, Andalucía, Galicia and so on) will need 40 or 50 percent of their expenditure to be covered by some supplementary system of sufficiency. Therefore:

1. The system must guarantee sufficient resources to ACs to fulfill their assumed competences, irrespective of their levels of income.
2. The kinds of taxes assigned to the territorial administrations must fall within the relevant geography and benefit from certain raising stability.
3. Most of the revenues of each level of government must leave tax burden and related competences of a tax basically in the hands of the administration to which most of the obtained resources correspond.

This does not mean ignoring the set of incentives and disincentives that could be generated by the overall interplay of tax autonomy and the equalization grants from the central government, which has warranted significant attention for some years now (see, for example, Köthenbürger's work, 2002 and Baretti, Huber and Lichtblau, 2002). The aim is to avoid the situation that policies to correct territorial inequalities also enhance behaviors that are indifferent to their own tax collection levels.

The Autonomous Communities already have a degree of financial autonomy (though, curiously, less than what the town halls enjoy), but only a small part of their financial resources lie within their autonomy. The greater part of financing comes, in one way or another, from transfers received from the central government, which exercises tax power and administrates the principal taxes.

The system brings obvious incentives with it. The ability to raise taxes involves an obvious political cost but causes a small increase in total revenues. This is the case especially when the normative room for maneuver is concentrated in direct taxes (quite visible), but it is less so for indirect taxes, where the room is extremely small. By contrast, to claim against the central government the greater part of revenues not only does not exact political costs but may also bring some electoral advantage. Thus, the system favors victimhood and discourages the use of recognized normative power.

Also, central politicians have felt comfortable with this way of working: giving up taxes and their corresponding collection is to lose power. They would no longer control the ACs if the ACs relied on their own resources. Co-responsibility can also generate administration problems and lack of coordination. It is much easier for a single administration to run everything than it is to share competences, which, in turn, makes administration more difficult.

Further, popular support does not exist for a decentralized model of shared responsibility because there are concerns that it would bring an increase in taxation (direct and indirect). Curiously, the opposite concern also exists: that freedom will initiate irresponsible competition towards lower tax levels and/or lead to differences in the tax burden between different parts of Spain.

It is obvious that autonomy inevitably involves differences. But this last argument, besides being paternalistic, also clashes with the autonomy that town halls have already exercised without particular problems. On the contrary, we predict a very stable result from any autonomic solution, based on available international experience and looking at the oligopolistic behaviors that such postulated autonomic competition would potentially resemble. (Referring to Figure 4.1, for example, let's assume a starting base of 100, a rate of 25 per cent and a collection rate of 25 monetary units. Let's also assume that the bases may increase or decrease and also shift from one administration to another. Facing a decrease in rates under another administration, the 'competitors' also reduce their own rates in order to avoid the loss of bases (dashed line). However, raising rates may not be copied by the other administrations, with an elastic response from the bases (dotted line). A dashed reaction line like the one described above implies collection expectations (continuous line) that decrease drastically if every AC decides to decrease its rates simultaneously. Moreover, a unilateral increase without a response from the rest of the ACs may possibly

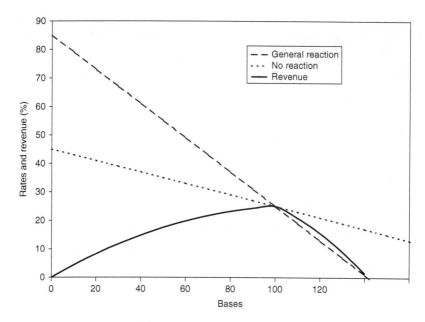

Figure 4.1   Autonomic competition

not contribute to collecting many more additional revenues (if, in fact, it does not lower them), because the bases may easily move elsewhere. This supports a policy of stable rates, unless the 'oligopolistic competitors' agree to move the rates simultaneously. If the bases are not so elastic, the analysis could be extended to a possible electoral loss, with similar conclusions.)

Therefore, the most likely outcome is an explicit or implicit agreement among the various AC treasury offices that opts for some separation only where an AC has a differentiating feature that needs to be compensated. This has, for example, been the experience of the various states of the United States, where there are different tax rates, even on income.

The constraints established by the European Union (EU) law might be acting as additional brakes. The autonomic and foral (relating to the Comunidades Forales) competences for establishing tax benefits are limited by the prohibition of state aid under EU treaty. In the same way, the fundamental freedoms (individual freedom of movement, freedom of establishment, the right to provide services, unrestricted movement of capital and free movement of trade and commerce) constitute another very important constraint. The Court of Luxembourg has been firm in defense of these freedoms.

The directives for tax harmonization are another important restriction. Thus, the EU Commission's opinion concerning the transfer of indirect taxes to the ACs (reflected in the *Report on the Reform of the System of Autonomic Financing* prepared by the Lasarte Commission; Lasarte et al., 2001) rejected giving the ACs legal powers to modify VAT rates and set significant limitations on taxes relating to some specific products.

The debate over the financing system is necessarily influenced by the coexistence of the foral regime and the common regime. The former gives more favorable treatment to the foral provinces than to the other ACs, because, in part, the Basque Country and Navarre do not participate in the general system of interregional solidarity. As an aggravating factor, they are also outside the system of useful information exchanged by tax agencies, and that causes loss of efficiency in the administration of the system. This underlines the possible coordination or assimilation problem between one regime and the other. The problem is not so much related to formulation and functioning as it is to results. This very important aspect, however, will not be pursued in this analysis.

1.2 Tax Assignment

The current system is the result of an agreement reached by the Fiscal and Financial Policy Council (CPFF – Consejo de Política Fiscal y Financiera) on 27 July 2001. The provisions of the agreement are enacted almost in their entirety in Organic Law 7/2001 of 27 December, which modified Organic Law 8/1980 of 22 September on the Financing of the Autonomous Communities (LOFCA; Ley Orgánica de Financiación de las Comunidades Autonómas), and in Law 21/2001, also of 27 December, which regulates the fiscal and administrative measures of the new financing system for ACs under the common regime. The two laws went into effect on 1 January 2002.

The estimated needs of the ACs are financed by:

- fees related to transferred services;
- ceded taxes, under expanded normative competences that we will see later on, covering:
  - wealth;
  - capital transfers and stamp duty;
  - inheritance and gifts;
  - car registration;
  - retail fuel sales, and;
  - gambling;
- revenues derived from the autonomic share of income tax, equivalent to 33 percent, with normative competence over rates and tax credits;

- thirty-five percent of VAT collected, according to the territorial indexes of consumption certified by Spain's National Institute of Statistics (INE; Instituto Nacional de Estadística);
- forty percent of excise duties on the manufacture of beer, wine and fermented drinks, intermediate products, alcohol and derivative drinks, according to the territorial indexes of consumption certified by the INE;
- forty percent of tobacco taxes collected, in accordance with the tobacco retail sales indexes for tobacconists, certified by the Tobacco Commissioner and weighted by the corresponding tax rates;
- forty percent of the fuel tax collected, in accordance with the delivery indexes for petrol, diesel and fuel oils (according to information from the Economics Ministry) weighted by the corresponding tax rates;
- a 100 percent of the collected tax on electricity, in accordance with the index of net consumption of electric power, according to information from the Economics Ministry;
- the Sufficiency Fund, which is the system's stopgap mechanism, covering the difference between the expenditure needs of each AC and its tax ability.

The established quantities increase annually in line with the rate of growth experienced by the ITE (Impuesto Tráfico de Empresas – the state's tax revenues at the national level), which is the state's tax revenues from income tax, VAT, excise duties on the manufacture on beer, on wine and fermented drinks, on intermediate products, on alcohol and derivative drinks, on fuel and on tobacco.

Equally, as additional resources outside the financing system, the following will be available:

- Inter-territorial Equalization Fund. Under the fund, up to 25 percent of operating expenditures associated with new investments may be granted during the first two years of the investments' implementation.
- Special equalization assignments when an Autonomous Community cannot provide a minimum level of public services in health or education, using ordinary financial resources. Based on relevant research clearly undertaken for the purpose, a supplemental allocation may be established to guarantee the minimum levels mentioned above in relation to the overall national average.

The description of AC resources made in the agreement does not mention AC taxes, because they arise only from the LOFCA. Nor does it modify or affect this agreement between the state and the ACs. It seems to be clear that the use of this autonomic tax ability must not affect either the ceding of taxes or the grants received from the state. Furthermore, AC taxes have a very limited scope because they can neither fall on goods and persons of other ACs nor can they come into being if a state tax already exists. Taxes that the ACs can set are exclusively either symbolic or of lesser importance. That is to say, they do not seek to collect taxes as much as correct unwanted behaviors. In any case, collection will be very limited and rather marginal.

Undoubtedly, the fundamental instrument that the Constitution and the LOFCA envisaged for fiscal co-responsibility was the use of surcharges. The Autonomous Communities can establish surcharges on income tax and on ceded taxes in general. To some extent, the possibility of surcharges is the argument made by some against co-responsibility. There is nevertheless an important distinction between a system that has an overwhelming predominance of transfer payments from the state exchequer and almost no territorial tax capacity and, on the other hand, a system that closes the door on centrally allocated resources and instead must have its own tax capacity to solve all its financial problems. Recall the perverse incentives of the system set out above. In addition, the topic of surcharges got off to a bad start with an unsuccessful attempt made by an Autonomous Community, Madrid. Nevertheless, the possibility remains that the ACs may establish surcharges on already mentioned state taxes that may be ceded, except on retail fuel sales. As for VAT and excise duties, surcharges can only be established when an AC has normative competence over the taxes in question.

The system that came into force on 1 January 2002 significantly increases tax autonomy for the ACs and paves the way for indirect taxation, almost completely absent from the previous system. In Table 4.2, we summarize the characteristics and the scope of the various transferred taxes.

However, individualizing participation in the revenues of another level of government, based on indirect statistical criteria without any legislative power, presents more disadvantages than advantages. The major innovation of the reform goes precisely along the lines that are criticized here: it involves arbitrating tax participation to be distributed later in terms of statistical indicators that can supposedly approximate collection figures on territorial terms. The negative assessment lies in reasons such as the following:

- The system still involves participation in the collection of the state exchequer, only calculated tax by tax according to specific rules for

Table 4.2 Autonomous taxes (ceded)

Tax Type	% Aut.	Administration	Calculation Criteria	Normative Capacity
Capital transfers and stamp duty	100	Autonomous	Territorial collection	Majority of the rates; allowances and tax credits
Inheritance and gifts	100	AC	Collection by residence	Tax rates, especial coefficients, allowances and tax credits
Car registration	100	AC	Territorial collection	Increase of rate up to 10%
Retail fuel sales	100	AC	Territorial collection	Implementation and tax rate
Gambling	100	AC	Territorial collection	Total
Wealth	100	Central	Residents collection	Threshold, tax rates, deductions and tax credits
Income tax	33	Central	Residents collection	Autonomic tax rates and tax credits
VAT	35	Central	% Statistical consumption	None
Beer	40	Central	% Statistical consumption	None
Other alcohol-related	40	Central	% Statistical consumption	None
Tobacco	40	Central	Weighted tobacconist sales index	None
Fuel	40	Central	Weighted sales index for petrol, diesel and fuel oils	None
Electricity	100	Central	Index of net consumption of electric energy	None

Source: Own elaboration.

each of them, but without any noticeable change in AC latitude for autonomy.

- The system is highly complex. It requires a different index for each tax as well as estimates of the corresponding percentages.
- The system rests on data that does not generate confidence. The information on which the allocation is based is normally vague, uncertain and shifting. The little experience available shows that the INE has modified some of them several times while the autonomic system has been in operation.
- It jeopardizes fulfillment of the aims of financing. Grants from the state exchequer (and participation in revenues where normative capacity is lacking, which is only another variant) aim to cover the differences between estimated needs and taxes collected. However, having estimated the revenues derived from supposedly ceded taxes based on statistical variables, it is not easy to make sure that the quantities that correspond in the end coincide with the aims sought from a normative point of view.
- The system's instability increases. The danger indicated in the previous point will tend to get worse over time, when the revenues received by each AC change as a function of the numbers estimated for various kinds of consumption or utilities. The poorer a region grows, the fewer resources it will receive, thus aggravating the predictable fall in the amount of taxes collected and managed directly. Any asymmetric problem with the economy, unfortunately, gets reinforced in this system.
- It provides no benefit from the perspective of co-responsibility. No difference whatsoever exists between receiving a part of the state's whole tax revenues and receiving many small portions of the revenues from each of the state's taxes, except that, in the second case, both volatility and instability can rise.

Consequently, it seems preferable to arbitrate a system in which the territorial entities are, as fully as possible, given the resources and taxes over which they exercise normative and/or administration capacity. The remaining needs are to be covered by transfers or participation in the state's general revenues. And this participation, obviously, must be as clear and automatic as possible. Therefore, the laudable inclusion of indirect taxation in the model is quite an insufficient advance from the perspective of co-responsibility. As a result, we will analyze what other possibilities exist to push forward the use of varying kinds of taxes.

2   USING CONSUMPTION TAXES

When assessing the suitability of a given tax for use in a decentralized setting, account must be taken first of the criteria required by Article 9 of Organic Law 8/1980, on the Financing of the Autonomous Communities (LOFCA), concerning establishment of AC taxes. This is not because the criteria impose constraints (because we are not talking about AC taxes and because the law can be modified in any case) but because the article incorporates elements of rationality that are perfectly applicable to our assumptions. Such basic criteria are as follows:

a) No wealth, income or expense arising outside the territory of an autonomous community shall be subject to taxation by said autonomous community.
b) No business, act or fact celebrated or realized outside the territory of the levying autonomous community shall incur tax. Neither shall the transfer or exercise of goods, rights or obligations that have not arisen or had to be fulfilled in said territory or whose buyer does not reside in the said territory.
c) No hindrance may be put on the free movement of individuals, commerce or capital, nor can the residence of an individual or the location of companies or capital be, in effect, compelled within the Spanish territory, nor can they attract charges from other autonomous communities.

To these criteria we might add other aspects in order to evaluate each type of tax equally and to determine what level of decentralization, if any, is most appropriate:

- Raising power, as a way of contributing effectively to sufficiency and autonomy. This condition is required for the set of taxes that are finally selected: the 'basket of taxes' as a whole, rather than for each and every one individually. But it implies that there exists at least one tax that has significant weight in terms of collection.
- Raising stability, to ensure sufficiency and to free local revenues from swings that would jeopardize balanced budgets in recessionary periods.
- A logical relationship is desirable between the tax and the competences assumed by the administration involved, to the extent that such a circumstance would add additional coherence.
- The greatest possible revenue homogeneity among the different territories. In this way, differences in payment ability would be diminished and the need for compensating state action matching expenditure and revenue would be less also, as seen above.

Generally speaking, consumption tax presents a number of especially positive characteristics from the perspective of the above criteria (Gimeno, 1997):

1. It fits the principle of territorial benefit because it falls on consumers of goods and services in the corresponding territory, whether they are residents or not. Income tax only contemplates residents, which considerably harms those territories that receive a high number of visitors, consumers of public services, and that therefore frequently require significant autonomic spending.
2. Wide bases and high buoyancy potential. Having several taxes makes it possible to combine several of them to obtain the most suitable allocation among the different administrations.
3. Consumption presents a more balanced distribution than income, so that revenue disparities between the different territorial treasury offices will be less significant. Consequently, as we indicated before, equalization grants will be reduced so that those with less capacity can reach the level of normative expenditure.
4. Territorial tax can be perfectly visible to citizens, thus contributing to greater public awareness of fiscal co-responsibility.
5. At the same time, taxpayers are less averse in comparison to income tax because consumption tax is built into the price of goods and services and payment is divided across multiple acts of purchasing. Though it could seem to contradict the previous point, it is necessary to highlight that differentiation (which allows visibility) is not contrary to the notion that a tax on every act of consumption carries a blow, psychological and budgetary, and that the blow is dampened because it occurs in small quantities on every occasion the tax is levied.

The important advantages mentioned above, together with evidence that co-responsibility could only move forward based on the interplay of taxes on the different possible bases (income, spending and wealth) have led to the defense of these taxes as part of the so-called 'basket of taxes' that must underpin the autonomic financing system. That would allow greater flexibility, an increase in collection capacity for all the ACs and, potentially, their individual self-sufficiency. Depending on the margin of freedom allowed, it would also allow an increase in the relative importance of the different taxes in each AC's treasury. As we have seen, this is how it was done in the last reform, though as a simple share in collection.

The most important difficulties for application will be connected to the taxes that are subject to harmonization within the European Union (EU) and to the related EU constraints. In some cases, we will be able to find another more economic or administration-related problem, depending on the degree of autonomy that is sought.

Of less importance here are the criticisms arising from the traditional claim that indirect taxes are more regressive. First, this is because direct taxation has lost a large part of its theoretical advantages: issues of fraud and evasion, as well as capital mobility problems that create a doubtful progressive effect. As a result, indirect taxation has garnered less negative attention than it did decades ago. Second, it is because we are only speaking now of how to distribute the existing revenue among the different public administrations without changing a priori the current distribution of the tax burden. Any potential debate in this direction would affect the system as a whole but not the specific relative weight of the territorial administrations.

The use of consumption taxes by the territorial administrations, applied habitually to retailing to avoid the tax burden falling outside the territory in question, is considered normal by literature. In fact, it has great significance and tradition in cases like Canada and the United States. In Canada there is a general principle of 'tax competence' between the states and the federation, which also affects sales taxes and taxes on special consumption. The revenues make up more than a third of the revenues of the sub-national public purse.

In the United States, the retail sales tax is the most significant tax in the states' tax systems as it represents practically half of their total revenues. The federal government still lacks a general sales tax, though it levies excise duties on tobacco, alcoholic drinks and derivatives of oil (that only represent percentages lower than 10 per cent of federal revenue).

In countries with a federal structure in which the sales tax takes the form of a value-added tax (VAT), as in Germany or Austria, the solution tends to be a single, identical, uniform tax for the whole national territory, which then leads to an allocation system between the different levels of government (in which the part destined for the regions is 30 percent of total revenues).

It does not matter whether the administration of the tax falls to the federal level or to the regional one. Though it may theoretically be possible for a surcharge to devolve on certain levels of government, no experience exists in the case of VAT. As for the EU, any action on a sales tax runs into the specific problem of the rigid rules surrounding tax harmonization that, as is known, have made more progress in this field than in any other.

The last steps of this nearly 30-year-long process include Directive 91/680/CEE, of 16 December 1991 and the supplementary Directive 92/77/CEE of 19 October 1992, which together move towards the general application of tax at source and eliminate border adjustments between member countries, without prejudice to maintaining the principle of assigning revenue to the country where end consumption occurs. As a result, in addition to the uniform definition of the VAT base, which has been highlighted above, and to the explicit prohibition of taxes on business turnover other than VAT, they have emphasized reduction in the variety of tax rates and in their homogenization.

Only two possible rates fall within this framework: the normal one, which cannot go lower than 15 percent, and the reduced one authorized for very specific goods, which in any case must be equal or superior to 5 percent (with the possible additional transitional exception of a severely reduced rate).

From a theoretical perspective, the system will tend to favor the existence of a tax at source in all countries, with a possible trend towards the obligatory minimum as a result of competition. But latitude for national autonomy should not be incompatible with major differences in the tax on goods and services that go directly to end consumers, as we will debate later on.

In conclusion, it is not strange in the comparative analysis to resort to consumption taxes at sub-central levels of government, though they seem to find more difficulties, introducing margins of co-responsibility concerning VAT because of lack of experience and predictable EU obstacles. Nor is it odd, by analogy, to resort to excise duties on manufacturing that, as we have seen, enjoy similar levels of harmonization.

3   ANALYZING THE DIFFERENT ALTERNATIVES[1]

3.1   Value-added Tax

Undoubtedly, VAT takes centre stage if we intend to study the possibilities of using various consumption taxes. Because of its broad scope and its revenue weight, it is without doubt the principal tax. Let us look at the different theoretical possibilities of its use in the system of AC financing. To clarify, we will start from the inalterable fact of state VAT with strong revenues, and this study asks only to what extent measurement systems – whether internal or supplementary – can be arbitrated to allow the ACs to take part actively in VAT revenue and, hopefully, in potentially altering the tax burden on consumers in an AC.

3.1.1   Revenue participation

In this option the regulation of the tax is unitary throughout the state, administration corresponds to a single government (either central or autonomic) and the total obtained revenue is distributed in proportion to 'territorialized' consumption, in accordance with data from statistical sources. As we have seen, this is (under centralized administration) the current option in operation.

The principal advantage of the solution is its ease of application since no legal or EU obstacles present themselves, nor any political resistance. In fact, it cannot really be considered a step forward in co-responsibility because it supposes simply that a portion of the grant share in state revenues is linked to the theoretical base on which the tax falls, starting from a hypothetical correlation between the base and the corresponding revenue on the consumers in each region.

One of the first criticisms that should be made of this solution is that the estimations on regional consumption are not necessarily trustworthy. In any case, these estimations ignore important revenue differences that can arise both from different consumption patterns and existing fraud, which diverge significantly between the various ACs. That is to say, the figures that are assigned will coincide only somewhat with the effective tax burden in each case. From the perspective of co-responsibility, citizens do not perceive any difference between this system of participation and the general one that includes VAT. Also, the Autonomous Communities do not see their latitude for action increased at all.

On the positive side, the option corresponds with developments envisaged by the process of European harmonization. As said above, the aim is to obtain revenue at source then adjust it later, depending on the territorial consumption estimated statistically. Therefore, there would be total coherence among the systems applied at the two levels.

It may be concluded that this solution does not seem ideal from the perspective of co-responsibility (except that it would abandon linking the revenue share to consumption, as in a different option that will be mentioned later on). However, it undoubtedly yields advantages from the point of view of administration.

3.1.2   Transferring retail VAT

This proposal, the literal application of an idea contemplated in the LOFCA, would involve the administration and collection of retail VAT being transferred to the ACs as if it were any other ceded tax. Strictly speaking, this solution would be unacceptable. As is well-known, VAT is equivalent theoretically to a tax on the final price of a good or service, with the special feature that it is collected piecemeal, in each stage and as the part of the final value that is added in that stage.

It involves effective collection in a given stage depending especially on the greater or lesser degree of vertical integration and therefore on a well-known mismatch between retail collection on a regional basis, and the burden supported effectively by consumers. Moreover, any differential attempt, if it were possible, would change the incentives and disincentives for vertical integration and affect the most efficient organization of the process. It would attract the same criticism deservedly made of the old 'cascading' tax.

Moreover, the administration problems stemming from an option like this would be considerable. The fragmentation of the tax by stage causes a significant increase in the difficulties of controlling crossing invoices and increases the chance of fraud in comparison to the system currently in effect. Deciding which taxpayers and operations should correspond to each administration would be a sizeable problem since the various options would obviously have a significant effect on the revenues of each one. For these reasons, this alternative can clearly be ruled out, a view that is shared unanimously by the literature.

3.1.3 Putting a territorial surcharge on the retail base for VAT

This option would involve adding to the normal VAT rate a differentiated surcharge levied by a territorial administration. At least to begin with, the surcharge may well be identical for everybody: the process of European harmonization is headed towards the standardization of rates and any possible differentiation by ACs would face resistance similar to that facing retail taxation. As in that case, however, there are also favorable arguments because the surcharge is tied to the retail stage and, therefore, not necessarily requiring border adjustments. The corresponding amount collected might be imputed directly to the territorial administration.

The surcharge, it should be underlined, would fall on the VAT base so as to take advantage of the 'tax credit' option applied in the European Union. The base of retail VAT would be taken as nothing other than the final sales price to the consumer, net of tax, and the surcharge would, in fact, be equivalent to a retail sales tax. It is obvious that the option of using the base as a reference for the surcharge avoids the problem of determining value added in the retail stage, as indicated above.

The existence of the surcharge would probably make it advisable to see the retail sales price as necessarily inclusive of state VAT. Then any autonomic surcharge would be differentiated so that the consumer could see that it had been added. This would avoid the problems of double taxation, compliance would be made easier for taxpayers and the decentralized tax would gain in visibility, which has to be considered positive from the perspective of co-responsibility.

One of the key aspects in the debate lies in how to approach the administration of the surcharge. In principle, the following three options would appear to be acceptable:

- Keeping complete administration of VAT centralized, including the surcharge, though the amount collected from the surcharge would be transferred automatically to the administrations charging it.

- Keeping the whole tax centralized, except for the local surcharge. This option would, in practice, be similar to the arbitrated retail fuel tax.
- Transferring the administration of both retail VAT and the VAT surcharge. To a large extent, this possibility can be seen to fit under the alternative looked at in the last subsection, where its advantages and disadvantages are analyzed.

The aversion of AC political leaders to the term surcharge is, obviously, a minor problem since it would not be difficult to come up with a less harsh designation such as, for example, 'the autonomic portion of VAT', as in the solution used for income tax.

As noted already, any solution involving an increase in VAT revenue ought to occasion a parallel reduction in another tax so that there is no increase in the overall burden on the taxpayer. Such an aim is not easy for the AC portion of VAT and a reasonable option might be a parallel reduction in business contributions to social security. Germany's experience may be a useful test case for this notion. But that discussion would take us too far from the focus of the present work.

The most important question raised by this option is whether the European Union will consider a surcharge acceptable if it differentiates rates not by products but by stages. We reiterate the above arguments stated to the effect that, when the tax is applied in the retail stage, it does not significantly affect the movement of commerce within the EU, and that, provided that the surcharges are limited in size, the final rates can be kept perfectly within harmonization limits since current rates in Spain are in the lowest allowed band. It would be more complicated to open the way for differentiated rates in terms of territorial normative limits, because here the European barriers appear to be more difficult to overstep. In addition, this alternative is hardly likely to promote enthusiasm among consumers or political leaders, given that it would have the 'appearance' of raising taxes and the responsibility for doing so would be clear.

3.1.4   Establishing a territorial retail sales tax

This option would create a tax on retail sales. The tax would be levied on all sales made directly to end consumers and it would be collected precisely at the point of sale, on the base of the total sales price. In principle, regulation should be standard throughout the Spanish territory (the common and foral systems might converge on this aspect) but administration and collection should be decentralized, either on the autonomic level or on the municipal level. In practice, this option coincides with the previous one, especially with the second form of administration suggested for the surcharge on VAT.

From a theoretical perspective, the tax would be beyond reproach since it draws together all the favorable circumstances of high raising potential, high visibility, comparative experiences, strong increase in co-responsibility and consistency with the principle of benefit (relationship between effective taxpayers and actual beneficiaries of the spending being financed). It completes the territorial tax picture and expands the array of tax decisions left in the hands of the territorial treasury offices. Nevertheless it is sensible to recall the possible constraints arising from European harmonization, as noted above. Such constraints affect not only the differentiation of rates but, more seriously, the very existence of the tax itself.

The prohibition of any tax on 'business turnover' seems to hit this tax squarely. Let us remember the literal text of Paragraph 1 of Article 33 of the Sixth Directive:

> Without prejudice to other Community provisions, in particular those laid down in the Community provisions in force relating to the general arrangements for the holding, movement and monitoring of products subject to excise duty, this Directive shall not prevent a Member State from maintaining or introducing taxes on insurance contracts, taxes on betting and gambling, excise duties, stamp duties and, more generally, any taxes, duties or charges which cannot be characterized as turnover taxes, provided however that those taxes, duties or charges do not, in trade between Member States, give rise to formalities connected with the crossing of frontiers.

The exclusive effect on the retail stage might permit its defense on the basis that it neither interferes significantly with EU exchanges nor gives rise to formalities related to the crossing of a border. The problem comes in defining a single market, which must equalize the tax burden on the goods and services in terms of neutral competition. If the whole territory of the European Union is thereby implied, it is obvious that the VAT rate must be unitary and identical in all countries. But this interpretation clashes with current reality (which would make the transitional process of adjustment more difficult) and it also probably clashes with the desires of governments who will refuse to accept undermining their power to determine the characteristics of their own tax systems.

As a result, it would seem to be logical to admit that uniformity should go as far as the retail stage but leave considerable latitude for autonomy. Going a bit farther, if country rates can be differentiated, then can differentiation be banned on a regional level? When borders are suppressed, do not territories deserve similar consideration, such as the Balearic Islands or Galicia? What reasons can justify autonomy in this area of competence for Luxembourg or Denmark but not for Castile or Catalonia? The cited experiences of Canada and the United States reinforce the possibility of differentiation within the same country without breaking up the unity of the market.

'Nevertheless in the contacts held in this regard, both the central Spanish administration and the EU administration have proven to be reticent or openly opposed to the idea' (Monasterio et al., 1995). Resistance is not surprising since it is the usual reaction of any administration confronted by new proposals that would alter the status quo. It must be recalled that the same commentary could be heard 10 or 15 years ago when the central Spanish administration was faced with the pros and cons of moving in the direction of autonomic co-responsibility. Consequently, European constraints make this alternative difficult to implement, though not impossible.

Later on, some other implementation problems will appear, such as the political difficulties of implementation (neither AC political leaders nor the taxpayers would welcome the creation of a new tax) or of administration, given that the tax would fall on some taxpayers mostly outside of tax control, there is a supposedly high level of fraud, and there would be additional administrative costs for the exchequer and the affected taxpayers.

Tax competition would lead to solutions of broken demand, as explained in Figure 4.1, along with a reasonable stability of tax rates. In any case, the most optimal final solution would probably be as close as possible to this option. Whatever form were adopted, its effects would be almost identical to a retail sales tax.

This tax is not proposed as an alternative to VAT, but as a complementary mechanism for autonomic financing, as much for the revenues that it would contribute directly as for the indirect effect caused by improving the control of revenues and possibly serving as an objective index for the assignment of VAT collected.

3.1.5   Transferring retail VAT as a base for participation

In some sense, this alternative involves many aspects of the previous solutions. The idea would be to transfer the administration of retail VAT to the Autonomous Communities, and the obtained revenue would have the character of an 'on account' payment against the definitive participation. It would be calculated as a proportion of the retail bases effectively observed.

Though the final result seems to be equivalent to the participation in the tax collection across the whole state across all its stages, there are two important differences from the above solution: 1) decentralized administration supposes direct involvement in the control of this important stage of the distribution process; and 2) participation is not distributed on theoretical criteria, but using real information on tax effort. The advantage of this option lies in the fact that it simultaneously takes into account both the degree of compliance in each AC and each AC's efficiency of administration. This creates incentives for the ACs. The solution does not raise any problem with European regulation because it does not enter into the controversy of possible regional tax differences mentioned above.

Advancing the aim of co-responsibility turns out to be clear from the perspective of AC treasury involvement, though it might be less clear from the perspective of consumers, since the final price would not undergo any change in principle. On the other hand, this could be considered one of its political advantages since it neither changes the tax burden nor the tax structure, nor would there be a sensation of increasing taxation or the need to compensate by making reductions in other taxes.

It is clear that the principal difficulty here lies in the deficient control of the retail sector, which is reflected in the 'equivalent special regime of surcharge' currently in effect in the wholesale stage. The practical exclusion from VAT obligations of a large part of potential taxpayers has significant negative consequences for this alternative:

- Strong sector resistance is predictable in the face of any increase in control, and this in turn involves a predictable reluctance on the part of AC leaders to take such an unpopular decision.
- The lack of tradition and the anticipated level of evasion in the sector could make the Autonomous Communities doubt the real revenue potential of transferring the tax. In other words, it might lead them to consider the cost/benefit ratio extremely unattractive.
- In any case, taking on administration of the tax brings necessary growth to the government in charge, along with an increase in expenditure and a decrease in net returns from the tax.

But the cited factors can be viewed in another way as well. One of the strongest arguments in favor of this solution comes precisely from the convenience – indeed the necessity – of our tax system to improve control on the broad taxpayer sector that retail goods and services represent. That is true not only for VAT but also for practically all related taxes. While the incentive for the state exchequer to gain greater knowledge of this taxpayer group may be considered minor in relative terms, the AC treasury offices would, by contrast, gain significantly and immediately. The most effective AC would win a double prize: it would see its net revenues increased automatically without needing to wait for grants tied to the final settlement. In addition, the final settlement would grow in absolute terms (because the general amount of the tax collected would also have grown in its entirety) and in relative terms (to the extent that better administration would allow it to increase its share at the cost of the least active ACs).

To be exact, the low starting level makes improvement easier in the short term since experience indicates that the efforts of control in similar cases are usually accompanied by big initial successes that, logically, tend to diminish as the process goes forward. These improvements would lead predictably to a general increase in the amount collected for other taxes in which the AC has participation, such as income tax.

Together all this constitutes an important set of incentives that, if the previous forecasts were fulfilled, would generate some additional resources above and beyond the cost increases, which would tend to be canceled out in net terms. Though not directly related to the problem of tax co-responsibility, this process would involve a notable improvement in the general equity of Spain's tax system and an increase in tax revenue without needing to increase the formal tax burden. It even leaves open the possibly of lowering taxes.

A more skeptical perspective would point to the administration problems caused by separating out one of the stages of the tax for which the government is responsible for collection both from the other stages and from the taxes that appear theoretically to benefit from greater administration control. This difficulty, which might be acceptable from a theoretical perspective, loses force when it is observed that, in fact, this stage already escapes central control when the similar widespread application of the equivalent special regime of surcharge in the previous stage is selected.

Doubts concerning collaboration among the levels of government can be partly minimized when it becomes necessary for ACs to adopt a relationship between taxpayers specified in terms of their bases and accrued and deducted payments as the only reliable formula to calculate the general participation afterwards. Even with only this information, the state tax administration would already have better information than it has today in a good number of cases.

It would be necessary to study carefully the treatment of invoices attracting VAT. In spite of the fact that an increase in local tax revenues is always attractive, some ACs might fall into the temptation of putting the stress more on bases than on revenues (given that the possible loss in revenues will be compensated by an increase in the participation derived from the bases). This supposes that the electoral cost is especially tied to cash income more than to any other aspect. If that were so, the control of invoices might be relaxed and thereby encourage the already known phenomenon of false invoices. Taking into consideration the effective increases in taxes collected when calculating the participation could be a sufficient incentive.

Some other details would need additional thought, such as the growing phenomenon of sales by post or electronically. Probably in such cases the 'territorialization' of the addressees would not be difficult, but doing so might make the centralized administration of this type of services more advisable.

Something similar might happen with the better part of the services provided to individuals located in other Autonomous Communities, in those cases in which it seemed valid to change the general criterion of the charge to where the supplier of the goods or services resides. Nevertheless, this type of service more often relates to business clients than to end consumers, so that it may be less relevant in practice than it might seem theoretically.

Exceptional assumptions like the ones outlined in the last two paragraphs are the only ones in which the identification of the consumer and the corresponding territory would be necessary. In the remaining cases all the sales realized by a retailer are situated in a territorial base depending on the location of the services, irrespective of the residence of the consumer. Let us remember that it is precisely this 'use of the territory' on the part of non-residents that is one of the arguments in favor of the use of consumption taxes as an instrument for financing the Autonomous Communities.

This solution would require a review of VAT regulation, which would be a disadvantage, although apparently not a serious one with regard to European harmonization since it would be in line with reducing special schemes progressively over time toward the general regime. In this sense, the design of a process of gradual adjustment is a potential approach (initially a forfeit system might be accepted, for example, in some sectors), with an autonomic margin of freedom to fix the dates for the different stages in the different sectors.

Both an advantage and a disadvantage simultaneously is the fact that the transfer might force a small adjustment in the criteria of base imputation (points of contact) with regard to the foral communities. As long as the problem affected only them vis-à-vis the state exchequer, any solution was an agreement in which each party ceded what was considered suitable. But once all the ACs are involved, it is necessary to adopt criteria balanced among all the territories. This aims to lower any sense of relative harm but it introduces into the negotiation a few ACs not involved in the other solutions.

What will happen if, as envisaged, Europe moves from the principle of destination to that of source in the administration of taxation? First, the new draft of the LOFCA already anticipates in the last paragraph of Article 19.2 that 'the competencies that the autonomous communities assume in relation to the ceded taxes will be exercised by the state when that becomes necessary to fulfill regulation on fiscal harmonization in the

European Union'. Therefore, if necessary, the general principle of reversibility would be applicable in this case in the same way as in any other. However, it must be highlighted that in the assumption noted above, when the charge falls within the retail stage, the two principles of source and destination coincide, making this one of the assumptions least affected by the hypothetical change. Table 4.3 summarizes the advantages and disadvantages of the various alternatives for using VAT as an instrument for AC financing.

3.2   Excise Duties and Other Taxes

The analysis of the possible alternatives turns out to be simpler now, because the available options are the general ones from a theoretical point of view and they have the following basic aspects:

- uniform regulation or possible differentiation of tax rates;
- centralized or ceded administration;
- complete revenue by the central administration, by the AC or by some split between the two.

The excise duties in question are:

- the tax on alcohol and derivative drinks;
- the fuel tax;
- the tobacco tax;
- the tax on electricity;
- the tax on car registration; and
- the tax on insurance premiums.

The first four taxes raise the initial problem of being taxes on manufacture. This involves any taxation collected at source reaching consumers located outside of each corresponding Autonomous Community. As we have seen, the better part of the revenue has been ceded to the ACs (40 percent in the first three, 100 percent in the fourth case) as a function of statistically calculated consumption (in the first case) and based on objective distribution information (in the three remaining cases).

It is true that the traditional excise duties are largely justified by the consumption of related public goods and services, that is, public roads justifying the fuel tax or health care expenditure justifying the two remaining taxes. With regard to competences transferred to a large extent, the parallel transfer of the corresponding revenues could be fully justified theoretically.

Table 4.3 The different alternatives for using VAT as an instrument for AC financing

Alternative	Description	Assessment
Participation in revenue	A proportional share of the total VAT revenue is distributed among the ACs, reflecting 'territorialized' consumption	No co-responsibility. Simple participation in revenues Easy administration and fulfills EU regulations
Transferring retail VAT	The administration and collection of retail VAT is transferred to the ACs	Lack of correspondence between tax revenue and the effectively supported charge Can be ruled out
Autonomic surcharge on retail VAT base	In addition to the normal rate, a differentiated territorial retail surcharge is added, with central administration and territorial collection	Difficult fit with the criteria of European harmonization Political difficulties for AC and taxpayers
Territorial tax on retail sales	It is a retail sales tax under common rules but territorial administration and collection	Difficult fit with the criteria of European harmonization Political difficulties for tax offices and taxpayers
Transferring retail VAT as base for participation	Administration of retail VAT is ceded to the ACs. Collection is 'on account' against proportional participation based on retail base (end consumption)	Fit with European regulation and LOFCA Co-responsibility and low cost Retail tax control Probable political resistance

Source: Own elaboration.

As has been argued, simply territorializing participation does not result in and of itself in a sizeable advance in terms of co-responsibility. Finding more attractive solutions would require substituting the current taxes on manufacture with retail sales taxes, which is practically unthinkable today from a European perspective. And leaving aside this important condition, it would still be hard to accept in the case of alcohol and alcoholic drinks and it would be hard to apply in the case of tobacco, the distribution of which is increasingly scattered. The only viable proposal in this respect is the fuel tax since payment is easily controllable. Gimeno (1997) has already put forward the mutual existence of a state tax on manufacturing and an autonomic retail tax.

This option, as noted already, would bring together practically all the advantages of an ideal decentralized tax on consumption and it would have very few disadvantages. The effect might appear to be a border effect generating potential disparities between neighboring ACs, but only if the disparities were considerable. But tax competition is one of the rules of the game when looking at financial autonomy, and experience shows that the consequences are not especially harmful.

The tax on electricity is somewhat different from the other three. On the one hand, it is not subject to European rules and that gives rise to greater regulatory flexibility. On the other, personalized supply would allow for the perfect differentiation of users according to where consumption took place. In other words, the transfer of this tax would be possible, including potential differentiation of tax rates among the different territorial administrations. However, an obstacle arises in collection in the production stage when production is separate from distribution. Given that the number of companies affected by one option or the other does not differ appreciably, this option would appear to argue for moving taxpayers in this direction. Regarding administration, it might be desirable to support a centralized tax in order to avoid companies facing any additional processing and differentiation cost in each of the affected administrations. But there seems to be no great difficulty in levying it regionally.

One might repeat the analysis for the tax on insurance premiums. As in the previous case, there is neither inflexibility owing to European directives nor are there problems with territorialized apportionment. Nor would the option have to be rejected in favor of a decentralized option. In both cases, a problem might appear for some company services that cannot be broken down conveniently on a geographical basis. But this would probably only affect a limited part of total business.

The car registration tax presents a different case since it is already a tax collected at the retail stage, currently by provincial delegations. Here there does not seem to be any further obstacle other than the fact that the tax could disappear within the European framework. However, from a theoretical perspective and from a concern for co-responsibility, there is no negative argument of any importance. Almost all the arguments are positive and support decentralization of the tax.

Nevertheless, the margin of normative autonomy raises some problems worthy of attention. This is because differentiated rates among territories might cause the easy delocalization of a purchase when treated as a single act of a relatively significant size. The problem worsens when speaking about big fleets that can register in any place, then operate across the length and breadth of the whole territory. Study should be given to whether, in the latter case, any exception should be made to the general principle of territorialization. Table 4.4 summarizes the advantages and disadvantages of these special taxes discussed above.

We have left customs duties out of the current discussion of consumption taxes. Customs duties are, typically centralized charges outside of the debates on territorial financing. The existence of a common external border and the dispersed destinations of most imports lead to the unanimous view that it is a tax that should be assigned to the central government.

Corporation tax is probably the most clear-cut example of a centralized tax, which is what generally happens in tax systems. It is clear that the benefits are generated in the widest territory and that the tax falls on resident taxpayers in any of its territories, whatever hypothesis of tax shifting is in operation. Moreover, establishing a fictitious location is particularly easy in the corporation tax case, making tax competition especially attractive. In fact, the European Union is especially vigilant in watching for possible favoritism, including concealed preferential treatment.

Capital taxes are usually ceded to the AC treasury offices. In the Spanish system it was precisely these taxes that were the first to be considered capable of transfer to the ACs. The unequivocal location of property can make the territorialization of property taxes appear straightforward. Nevertheless, this initial judgment is complicated when looking at personal taxes. In fact, the wealth tax is especially useful as an instrument of control because of its relation to income tax. Assigning revenue to the autonomic level, however, can involve the state tax agency losing interest in its suitable control. On the other hand, capital is not only made up of property. Capital is mobile by its very nature, especially when we are talking about financial assets. Therefore, the assignment criterion is more personal than real and the location argument loses force, evidently.

In the case of capital transfers, we are really looking at a tax that is very similar to a consumption tax. In fact, the application of VAT or a tax on capital transfers can be more affected by the nature of the seller than by the

Table 4.4   Special taxes and territorial financing

	Advantages	Disadvantages
Tax on alcohol and derivative drinks	Relation to health care spending Easy acceptance	Tax on producers: impossible transfer and extraterritorial shifting Infeasible transfer Territorialization merely statistical Normative with limited margin of freedom
Tax on tobacco	Relation to health care spending Easy acceptance	Tax on producers: impossible transfer and extraterritorial shifting Infeasible transfer. Possible territorialization Normative with limited margin of freedom
Fuel tax	Relation to use of public infrastructure Easy acceptance Likely retail application, with theoretical normative margin	Tax on producers: impossible transfer and extraterritorial shifting Infeasible transfer Possible territorialization Normative with limited margin of freedom Retail tax: possible transfer (including base of assignment)
Tax on electricity	Easy acceptance Theoretical normative margin Possible decentralization	Tax on producers: impossible transfer Possible territorialization Problem with centralized company services
Car registration tax	Relation to use of public infrastructure Theoretical normative margin Retail application	Danger of future abolition Tax competition and border effect
Tax on insurance premiums	Easy acceptance Theoretical normative margin Possible decentralization	Inadvisable transfer Possible territorialization Problem with centralized company services

Source: Our own data.

operation at issue. As a result, the ideal solution might well involve applying both taxes in the same system.

Stamp duty is yet another case. Here we are addressing certain acts that generate an identical right across the whole territory. Therefore, it is not logical to have different rates in some territories as opposed to other territories. Moreover, delocalization is easy in a good number of cases. Therefore, in my opinion, it is not a tax that is very suitable for decentralization and co-responsibility.

Inheritance and gift taxes deserve similar consideration. Because they involve significant sums, any difference of tax burden between two territories would create a serious incentive to make location decisions based on tax considerations.

In addition to the above characteristics, it is necessary to analyze the revenue behavior of the cited taxes. We are interested in finding out the raising power of each tax in order to be able to determine the size of the assignment needed to guarantee sufficient revenues for each level of administration in question. A dynamic perspective forces comparison of the tax's evolution over time, the growth of its revenue and its relation to GDP.

After income tax and VAT, the largest yielding power lies in corporation tax and fuel tax. Other collection figures worthy of attention (above 5 euros for 1000 euros of GDP) are the tobacco tax and the tax on capital transfers, which we separate here from stamp duty. Stamp duty, along with a gambling and a car registration tax would figure in the following group, with numbers of 3 euros per 1000 euros of GDP. The remaining taxes average between 1 and 2 euros for every 1000 euros of GDP.

In summary form, Table 4.5 shows each tax, its raising power and trend over the last few years and its degree of stability. There is additional information on the possible shifting of decisions taken in a sub-central treasury office onto taxpayers who do not fall within the territory. The last column reflects a subjective overall assessment, taking into consideration all the analyzed aspects. It shows the suitability of transferring each tax, including the normative aspects, to the territorial treasury offices. Retail VAT, under the conditions noted above, would appear to be ideal for supporting a decentralized financing system. Income, fuel, tobacco and gambling are further areas that also lend themselves to decentralization, under certain conditions. Specifically, it is assumed that all indirect taxes would fall on the retail stage, since suitability is low or very low in the other stages. Neither inheritance nor capital transfers nor stamp duty merit a positive assessment, basically because of the trans-territorial effects and strong displacement that any normative differentiation among the different territories would cause.

As has already been shown above, corporation tax is the least advisable tax to be decentralized. The vast majority of the literature is in agreement

Table 4.5 Incidence and revenue yield

	Power		Stability	Shifting	Suitability
	% GDP	Trend			
Income	6.28	=	Medium	Medium	High
Wealth	0.17	+	Low	Medium	Medium
Inheritance and gift	0.13	+	Medium	High	Low
Corporate	2.84	=	Medium	High	Very high
VAT	5.77	+	High	Low in retail stage, high otherwise	Very high in retail
Fuel	1.54	=	Medium	Low in retail stage, high otherwise	High in retail
Beer	0.03	–	Medium	Low in retail stage, high otherwise	Low
Alcohol and alcoholic drinks	0.12	+	Medium	Low in retail stage, high otherwise	Medium in retail
Tobacco	0.67	+	High	Low in retail stage, high otherwise	High in retail
Car registration	0.25	–	Medium	Low in retail stage, high otherwise	Medium in retail
Electricity	0.10	=	Medium	Low in retail stage, high otherwise	Medium in retail
Insurance premiums	0.13	+	Low	Low in retail stage, high otherwise	Medium in retail
Capital transfers	0.61	+	Medium	Medium	Medium–Low
Stamp duty	0.31	=	Medium	Medium	Medium–Low
Gambling	0.25	–	High	Low	High

Source: Our own data.

on the matter. The lack of clarity concerning where the actual payers of the tax are and the easy delocalization of company headquarters urge centralized maintenance.

4 PROPOSALS AND CONCLUSIONS

As a part of the unfolding debate on the reform of Catalonia's Statute of Autonomy, a number of likely reforms of the current system have been outlined. It seems sensible to avoid a bilateral solution, whereas, in fact, the need for a multilateral negotiation has been reaffirmed. As we have seen, we have a large shared pie, namely the tax revenue from the entirety of the tax system, and the portion assigned to each territorial administration is not neutral with respect to the others (either politically or financially).

A growing consensus seems to be emerging for the need to assign greater normative capacity to the ACs, but the initial extra-official agreements that have been made public seem to insist more on changing the percentages of participation than on significantly increasing sought-after co-responsibility. In particular, talk has been of raising the autonomic percentages as follows:

- for income tax, from 33 to 50 percent;
- for VAT, from 35 to 50 percent
- for excise duties, from 40 to 58 percent.

It is not worth insisting again that it appears that the best option is to set taxes rather than making proportional allocations. Statistically based assignments complicate the system and reduce its fairness. An agreement on percentages drives a permanent dynamic of negotiation in search of a slightly bigger percentage year after year. Defining the suitable taxes for each territorial area and giving them the maximum autonomy is an approach that ensures genuine co-responsibility, effective financial autonomy and greater stability in the system. According to the previous analysis, it seems that, for example, it would be preferable to transfer all those taxes on special consumption that are especially suitable for decentralization, and to keep in the state coffers others that can only be applied through forfeit.

The new proposals seem to point to effective use of retail VAT. Above, it has been made clear that this opportunity is highly advisable in spite of the problems that it poses. There are several ways of arbitrating the corresponding system but it is necessary to remain clear, in any case, that the final result must not rest on the value-added in the retail stage but rather on the end consumption. Any participation in the total VAT collected should be based on the final bases effectively observed in taxation on the retail stage.

Another of the most relevant debates has revolved around the administration of the taxes and the definition and scope of an autonomic tax agency. It seems unarguably desirable that the competences relating to a tax be entrusted to the administration to which the resources that are obtained basically correspond, in the interest of the operational effectiveness and good functioning of the system.

First, administration and auditing must correspond to whoever is going to benefit later from the basic results. It is an elementary rule of the incentives game that whoever has to obtain the maximum revenue has a reasonable interest in effective administration. This is because if the costs of the control activity are greater than its results, no great effort in the corresponding administration could be expected. The exception to this principle would be a hypothetical entity for whom the specific revenues contributed a considerable amount of its budget, although the part that corresponded to it was minor in the whole of the relevant tax.

The second rule of administration would support the need for information not to be fragmented because that would favor evasion and fraud. Therefore, if there are diverse tax administrations, it is a critical condition of efficiency that the entire database of information and taxpayers is accessible automatically throughout the entirety of the system.

The third desirable rule is that the way administration is organized remains a problem internal to the government and is not allowed to cause additional complexity for the taxpayer. The system cannot entail double audits, double obligations, repeated negotiations or inconveniences. 'One-stop shopping' is a desirable aim, though not always easy to apply in its totality.

Based on these general principles, there is no solution that is either technically irrefutable or defensible as a universal option. One option might be to unify administration in a single agency actively participated in by the territorial treasury offices, in line with the approach advocated in Monasterio et al. (1995). But if diverse administration agencies exist at each level of government (as at present and as seems inevitable) the above rules have to be followed as faithfully as possible.

We might include here another safeguard concerning normative competences: it seems to be hard for any administration to accept a reduction in revenues because another level of government decided to modify regulations and reduce the tax burden of a tax whose revenue largely corresponded to it or was exclusive to it. Even if the competence belonged to the state, any modification concerning a ceded tax should necessarily be consulted beforehand with the affected administrations. They should have a right of veto where no satisfactory agreement can be reached.

Putting a fence around the topic addressed in this work, we must not go into one of the key debates of any reform of the system, which is how to arbitrate solutions that ensure all ACs can guarantee their citizens the same level of services for the same tax effort. Starting from this guarantee, autonomy would permit all ACs to change some services and to alter the tax burden. However, the model must be based on an equal starting point. Without the principle of equity and the constitutional obligations, the ACs with lower revenue ability will not accept progress in financial autonomy and co-responsibility to such an extent. Such progress would be viewed as a threat. But that analysis is for others to make.

In short, the latest reforms affecting the financing models for the territorial Spanish treasury offices have gone some way toward advancing autonomy, transparency and co-responsibility in fiscal federalism. In addition to these advances, some of the measures taken must be considered setbacks, while others have brought progress that is more fictitious than real.

Any alternative that is put forward must start from the fact that there is no ideal solution or irrefutable alternative. But thought must be given to creating a system in which the territorial treasury offices gain autonomy and co-responsibility, thereby bringing about less complexity, more transparency and a guarantee of the principle of solidarity.

NOTE

1. A more detailed version of the analysis can be found in Gimeno (1997).

BIBLIOGRAPHY

Álvarez. S., A. Aparicio and A.I. González (2004), 'La autonomía tributaria de las Comunidades Autónomas de régimen común', Working Document No. 20/04; Madrid: IEF.

Barberán, R. (2003), 'La medición del grado de discrecionalidad de las decisiones presupuestarias de las Comunidades Autónomas', Working Document No. 13/03, Madrid: IEF.

Baretti, Ch., B. Huber and K. Lichtblau (2002), 'A tax on tax revenue: incentive effects of equalizing transfers: evidence from Germany', *International Tax and Public Finance*, **9** (6), 631–50.

Cantarero, D. (2004), 'Financiación de las Haciendas regionales españolas y experiencia comparada', Working Paper No. 11/04. Madrid: IEF.

Castells, A. (2000), 'Autonomía y solidaridad en el sistema de financiación autonómica', *Papeles de Economía Española*, No. 83, 37–59.

Cnosen, S. (1990), 'Interjurisdictional Coordination of Sales Taxes', in *Value Added Taxation in Developing Countries*, Washington, DC: The World Bank, pp. 43–57.

Domínguez, J.M., A. Molina and J. Sánchez Maldonado (1989), 'El Impuesto sobre el Valor Añadido y la teoría del Federalismo Fiscal', *Cuadernos de Ciencias Económicas y Empresariales*, No. 20, 61–72.

Edo Hernández, V. (2002), 'Importancia recaudatoria y flexibilidad del sistema impositivo español según las principales fuentes estadísticas', *IX Jornadas de Economía Pública*, Vigo.

Giménez Montero, A. (2000), 'Responsabilidad y corresponsabilidad fiscal en los países federales', *Papeles de Economía Española*, No. 83, 2–24.

Giménez Montero, A. (2003), *Federalismo fiscal. Teoría y práctica*, Valencia: Tirant lo Blanch.

Gimeno, J.A. (1997), 'La utilización de la imposición sobre el consumo como instrumento de financiación de las comunidades autónomas de régimen común', *Hacienda Pública Española*, No. 141/142, 221–36.

Gimeno, J.A. and J. Ruiz-Huerta (1991), 'Financiación Autonómica: un modelo alternativo de corresponsabilidad fiscal', *Palau 14. Revista Valenciana de Hacienda Pública*, No. 15, 149–79.

Gómez, D. and A. Iglesias (2003), 'La imposición propia como ingreso de la hacienda autonómica en España', Working Document No. 11/03, Madrid: IEF.

Köthenbürger, M. (2002), 'Tax competence and fiscal equalization', *International Tax and Public Finance*, **9** (4), 391–408.

Lasarte Álvarez, J. et al. (2001), *Informe para la reforma del sistema de financiación autonómica* (White Paper), Madrid: Instituto de Estudios Fiscales.

Mitxelena Camiruaga, C. (2006), 'Descentralización fiscal y cohesión territorial en España'; *Estudios de Economía Política*, No. 4, 73–92.

Monasterio, C. (2002), 'El laberinto de la financiación autonómica', *Hacienda Pública Española*, No. 163, 157–87.

Monasterio, C. (2004), 'La corresponsabilidad fiscal en el Estado de las autonomías', *Papeles de Economía Española*, No. 100, 64–76.

Monasterio, C., F. Pérez García, J.V. Sevilla and J. Solé Vilanova (1995), *Informe sobre el actual sistema de financiación autonómica y sus problemas* (White Paper), Madrid: Consejo de Política Fiscal y Financiera, Ministerio de Economía y Hacienda.

Moreno Valero, P.A. (2001), *La armonización del IVA comunitario: un proceso inacabado*, Madrid: CES, Colección estudios 104.

Peris García, P. (1999), 'El poder financiero y sus límites: la incidencia del derecho comunitario', *Revista de derecho financiero y hacienda pública*, **49** (253), 657–92.

Ruiz Almendral, V. (2004), *Impuestos cedidos y corresponsabilidad fiscal*, Valencia: Tirant lo Blanch.

Ruiz-Huerta, J. (2000), 'Corresponsabilidad fiscal: responsabilidad y límites', *Papeles de Economía Española*, No. 83, 87–99.

Ruiz-Huerta, J. and J.A. Gimeno (1993), 'Descentralización fiscal y corresponsabilidad a través de las grandes figuras tributarias', *Cuadernos aragoneses de economía*, No. 1, 29–40.

Ruiz-Huerta, J. and O. Granado (2002), 'La Reforma de la Financiación Autonómica en el 2001. Cierre del modelo de reparto competencial y corresponsabilidad fiscal', Working Papers, Madrid: Instituto Universitario Ortega y Gasset.

Sevilla, J.V. (2001), *Las Claves de la Financiación Autonómica*, Barcelona: Crítica.

PART II

Fiscal equalization

5. Fiscal equalization: the Canadian experience[1]

Robin Boadway

1 INTRODUCTION

The Canadian federation has many of the features of a textbook system of fiscal federalism. There is a high degree of fiscal decentralization of both expenditure and revenue-raising responsibilities, with provincial budgets comparable in size to that of the federal government. The provinces, which are very diverse in size, have a significant degree of autonomy in designing and delivering their spending programs, and a responsibility for providing some of the most important public services, including those in health, education and welfare. They share with the federal government access to the major tax bases, such as income, sales and payroll taxes. Some tax harmonization exists between the federal government and the provinces, mainly in the areas of personal and corporate income taxes and sales taxes (value-added taxes). Despite the high degree of fiscal decentralization, there is some vertical fiscal gap. Over 20 percent of provincial spending is financed by transfers to the provinces. These transfers are mainly very general rather than being targeted to specific provincial expenditures. There is some asymmetry in the fiscal arrangements, mainly with respect to Quebec, which has more revenue-raising autonomy and assumes some spending and regulatory responsibilities that the other provinces do not.

More specifically, the federal–provincial transfer system is relatively simple. It has two main components. The first component is the equalization system, which consists of unconditional transfers to those provinces whose fiscal capacity is below a national norm. Fiscal capacity is determined by a so-called representative tax system (RTS) approach whereby a province's equalization entitlement is determined by its ability to raise revenue from a set of representative tax bases using national average provincial tax rates. Equalization transfers are paid to provinces whose ability to raise revenues is below the average of five provinces (excluding the very richest and the four poorest).

The second component is a set of transfers meant to contribute to financing of the provinces' provision of health, welfare and post-secondary education. These are basically equal per capita transfers nominally divided into two components: the Canada Health Transfer (CHT) to support health expenditures and the Canada Social Transfer (CST) to support welfare and post-secondary education. These transfers have some broad conditions attached to them that provincial programs must satisfy to be eligible for the full amount of the transfer. Thus, provinces must maintain public health insurance programs that are comprehensive and accessible to all and preclude user fees or extra billing by doctors. Provincial welfare programs must be available to all residents including those who migrate from other provinces. Failure to meet these conditions results in a reduction in the size of the transfer, with the federal government determining both when a violation occurs and how much the penalty should be. Given that the conditions are very general, this requires some discretion.

Both the equalization program and the CHT/CST transfers are financed out of federal general revenues. In evaluating the Canadian experience with fiscal equalization, it is important to recognize that the CHT/CST transfers are equalizing as well as the formal equalization system. Indeed, while the equalization system equalizes the low-capacity provinces up, the CHT/CST system also implicitly equalizes the high-capacity provinces down. This has implications for evaluating the vertical fiscal gap. A reduction in the vertical fiscal gap can be achieved by a reduction in the federal tax rate accompanied by a reduction in the CHT/CST transfers, with the provinces stepping in to occupy the tax room that the federal government has vacated. Such a reform increases fiscal disparities among provinces, and puts more pressure on the equalization system.

2   KEY ISSUES WITH THE SYSTEM

The federal–provincial fiscal transfer system is perpetually on the agenda for policy reform, no more so than in recent years. The Canadian economy has just emerged from a period in which both levels of government faced problems of fiscal sustainability that had built up over the years as a result of persistent budget deficits and high interest rates. The federal government responded to this by, among other things, drastically cutting its transfers to the provinces, which the provinces viewed as the federal government passing on its deficit to them. The federal government also made a number of unannounced and ad hoc changes to the system of transfers, which led to some distrust and dissatisfaction. The nation has now entered into a period of soul-searching with respect to the fiscal system, and a number of key issues have emerged that need to be dealt with. Some of the more prominent ones are as follows:

- *Adequacy and affordability of equalization.* Fiscal disparities among Canadian provinces have increased fairly dramatically in recent years owing largely to the fact that significant oil and gas revenues accrue to a small number of provinces (primarily Alberta). This, combined with the fact that low-capacity provinces are equalized to a level well below the national average and high-capacity provinces are not equalized down, seems to imply a trade-off between adequacy and affordability. It would be costly for the federal government to equalize to a national average with resource revenues fully included, partly because the federal government has no direct access to natural resource revenues.
- *Vertical fiscal imbalance.* Ever since the federal government unilaterally cut transfers to the provinces in the mid-1990s, the provinces have argued that there is a vertical fiscal imbalance. The concept is somewhat vague, but the essence is that the level of federal transfers to the provinces is low relative to the expenditure responsibilities of the two levels and the extent of the tax room that the federal government occupies. The provinces argue that either the federal government should increase its transfers or they should vacate some tax room in favor of the provinces. As we have noted, which course of action is taken will have different implications for equalization.
- *RTS versus other approaches to equalization.* Some observers argue that the RTS system is too complicated and should be replaced by a simple macro indicator of provincial fiscal capacity.[2] What that indicator should be and how it can capture revenue-raising capacity accurately is not clear. Others argue that revenue equalization alone is not enough since it does not reflect the needs for expenditures and the costs of providing public services, both of which can vary across provinces. Needs-based equalization is used in other federations, especially Australia.
- *Volatility of equalization.* Under the RTS system, a province's equalization entitlements are determined by the size of its tax bases as well as the size of tax bases in the provinces used in the standard. If equalization entitlements are calculated annually, transfers to a province can be volatile, and can actually increase the overall volatility of provincial revenues rather than insuring the province against fluctuations in own-source revenues. This has proven to be the case in the Canadian system. It arises because fluctuations in the standard bases can dominate fluctuations in a province's own base.

- *Formula-based versus discretionary approaches.* Until recently, equalization entitlements were determined fully by the formula, except in some instances when the federal government overrode the formula for budgetary reasons. Moreover, the federal government has often made ad hoc changes to the CHT/CST transfers. The incidence of discretionary interference increased substantially in recent years, and culminated in the federal government imposing a fixed cap on the total amount of equalization transfers. These kind of discretionary changes reduce the predictability of transfers from the provinces' point of view.
- *Unilateralism and abuse of the spending power.* Discretionary changes in transfers are particularly troublesome when they are done unilaterally and without advanced notice. The provinces also complain about the conditions that the federal government from time to time imposes on programs that are the legislative responsibility of the provinces. The use of conditional transfers to influence provincial spending program design and priorities is an example of the exercise of the so-called spending power by the federal government. Observers who favor further decentralizing the federation by having the federal government reduce its transfers and turn over tax room to the provinces often base their arguments on constraining the use of the spending power by the federal government. The view is that the use of the federal spending power reduces the accountability of the provinces for their own spending programs.

These issues have been addressed many times over the past several years by different bodies. These have included national royal and parliamentary commissions, various provincial commissions, studies by the federal Senate and the office of the Auditor General, and most recently reports by two panels set up to study equalization and fiscal transfers.[3] One of these was an Expert Panel on Equalization and Territorial Formula Financing appointed by the federal government and the other the Advisory Panel on Fiscal Imbalance appointed by the Council of the Federation, a body representing the provinces.[4] The reports of virtually all of these groups emphasized the importance of equalization and recommended retaining the RTS approach. The proposals differed in three ways. First, while all recognized the need for the equalization of resource revenues, they differed on whether 100 percent of resource revenues should be subject to equalization. Second, they differed in their approach to maintaining vertical balance in the federation, especially whether provinces should be made less reliant on federal transfers and more responsible for raising their own revenues. Finally, they differed in the emphasis they put on the need for changes in the process by which fiscal arrangements should be conducted, such as whether there should be an independent advisory body charged with evaluating the system and making recommendations for change.

To evaluate the role and design of an equalization system, it is useful to begin with a discussion of the principles, and then turn to issues that arise in applying those principles in practice. Although much of the discussion draws on lessons learned from the Canadian case, it has implications for other federations that are decentralized or in the process of decentralizing.

3   THE PRINCIPLES

The issue of equalization has been at the forefront of policy debates in Canada for many years.[5] Concern about the ability of the provinces to provide important public services first surfaced in the 1930s when, in the wake of the Depression, one of the provinces went bankrupt. The federal government set up a royal commission, the so-called Rowell-Sirois Commission,[6] to study the system of federal–provincial fiscal relations, and came up with some imaginative suggestions, including the introduction of an equalization system designed to ensure that all provinces had the capacity to provide comparable levels of public services. The Second World War intervened and one of its consequences was the centralization of revenue-raising to consolidate war financing. In the early post-war period, three features of federal–provincial fiscal relations emerged that heavily influenced the way the system evolved. First, the federal government began to devolve tax room to the provinces in the personal and corporate income tax fields, but in a way that maintained a harmonized income tax system that has prevailed until today. Second, as tax room was devolved to the provinces, a formal equalization system was introduced, based on the RTS approach, whose basic structure has remained intact as well. Third, the federal government through its spending power introduced major conditional grant programs in the areas of health, welfare and post-secondary education that were instrumental in developing the universal social programs that characterize the welfare state. (In Canada, the provinces have exclusive legislative responsibility in these areas.)

As time has gone on, the system has evolved. More and more income tax room was turned over to the provinces, which put some strains on the tax harmonization arrangements and increased fiscal disparities. Eventually, tax harmonization became looser, but most provinces continued to abide by a common base and a single tax collection authority. The exception was Quebec, which operates a separate system of personal and corporation income taxes and has opted out of some other federal programs as well.

The equalization system expanded to include virtually all provincial (and municipal) revenue sources, but retained its RTS formula-based approach. And, federal financing for major provincial social programs was converted to conditional shared-cost (matching) transfers to equal per capita bloc transfers with very general conditions.

3.1 Constitutional Principles

The basic values underlying the federal fiscal system are widely accepted. When the Canadian Constitution underwent a major revision in 1982, the principle of equalization was enshrined in the Constitution. Drawing on the recommendations of the Rowell-Sirois Commission, the federal government was charged with the following constitutional commitment:

> Parliament and the government of Canada are committed to the principle of making equalization payments to ensure that provincial governments have sufficient revenues to provide reasonably comparable levels of public services at reasonably comparable levels of taxation. (Canadian Constitution)

In constitutional terms, this is a strong requirement, since unlike most constitutional components, it actually imposed a spending obligation on the federal government (as opposed to proscribing the way it exercised its powers). It is unclear to what extent this commitment is justiciable in the courts, but there is no doubt that from a political and moral point of view, it places a serious obligation on the federal government, and one that all observers and political actors take seriously. In fact, it is the only element of the fiscal arrangements that enjoys constitutional status. There are federal–provincial agreements governing efficiency in the federal common market (the Agreement on Internal Trade signed in 1994) and recognizing and governing the use of the federal spending power (the Social Union Framework Agreement signed in 1999).

3.2 Economic Principles

It turns out that the obligation set out in the Canadian Constitution accords well with economic principles.[7] The decentralization of fiscal responsibilities to sub-national (provincial) governments has a number of advantages: it allows provinces to tailor their programs to local needs; it improves the cost-effectiveness of service provision; it enhances accountability; it reduces administrative costs by eliminating a layer of decision-making and lowering agency costs and it induces innovation in the provision of public services. From that point of view, decentralizing responsibility for important public services delivered to citizens enhances the efficiency of their provision. At the same time, decentralization carries some disadvantages as well that affect the efficiency and equity of economic outcomes. Equalization can be seen as one instrument among others that serves to facilitate effective decentralization while protecting the solidarity of national programs and the integrity of the internal economic union.

The main source of potential inefficiency and inequity resulting from fiscal decentralization is that different provinces have different capacities to provide public services. These different capacities lead to differences in so-called *net fiscal benefits* (NFBs) that citizens obtain from government services, that is, differences in the benefit of public services less the tax costs incurred. Otherwise identical persons living in comparable circumstances in two different provinces will receive different NFBs from provincial governments. These differences can arise from two main sources: differences in the ability of provinces to raise revenues and differences in the need for public services. Thus, if one province has larger tax bases per capita than another province, it can raise more tax revenues per capita at given tax rates. Persons of any given income level will be better off residing in the higher tax base provinces on this account. Provinces may also differ in their needs for public spending. Provinces with a higher proportion of school age children will have higher education spending requirements to provide given levels of schooling, and those with more elderly citizens will have higher health care costs.

These differences in NFBs will result in fiscal inefficiency to the extent that they induce economic activity to locate in provinces with higher NFBs, as opposed to choosing their location purely on the basis of relative productivities in different provinces. Similarly, they will result in fiscal inequity in the sense that otherwise identical persons will be treated differently by the public sector, a violation of horizontal equity. Provided there is a consensus that like persons ought to be treated alike no matter where they reside, the fiscal inequity resulting from NFB differences is a drawback to decentralization. In effect, social citizenship is violated. There may also be other inefficiencies and inequities resulting from decentralization, such as fiscal externalities that interfere with the efficient functioning of internal markets or the compromising of redistributive equity that might result from fiscal competition. However, addressing these adverse consequences of decentralization requires policy instruments that complement equalization, such as conditional grants or the harmonization of tax and expenditure programs.

Equalization is a policy instrument that can be used to address the differential NFBs arising from fiscal decentralization, assuming the requisite extent of national solidarity exists to warrant it. However, the elimination of NFBs to deal with fiscal inefficiency and inequity may conflict with other principles in a federation. For one, differences in NFBs can arise not only due to the need for public spending resulting from the composition of the population, but also due to differences in the cost of providing public services because of geographical factors, population density or wage costs. Cost differentials across provinces (or even across regions within provinces) give rise to an equity–efficiency trade-off that will preclude the equal provision of public services. Even in a unitary nation, different levels of public services will typically be provided in, say, rural versus urban areas. Given that, the design of the equalization program need not require that full compensation be given for NFB differences arising from differences in costs.

Another important principle is the desire to allow provinces to make their own fiscal choices according to their own preferences and needs rather than insisting on identical national programs. That being the case, NFB differences will necessarily arise for some persons. To attempt to equalize them away fully is tantamount to undoing one of the advantages of federalism, which is the diversity of choice than comes with decentralization. A reasonable compromise that is struck in recognition of this – and one that accords with the Canadian constitutional obligation – is to design the equalization program so that all provinces have the *potential* to provide comparable levels of public services at comparable rates of taxation should they so choose. This will undo NFB differences that arise from the different fiscal capacities of provinces while at the same time allowing those that arise solely from differences in the way provinces exercise their comparable fiscal capacities.

Finally, there is one more role that equalization systems can perform and that is an insurance function. Provincial tax bases may be subject to idiosyncratic shocks that affect their tax revenues. If it is costly for them to insure (or self-insure) against these shocks, the equalization program can serve as an insurance device. Under the RTS system, for example, reductions in a province's tax base lead automatically to increases in equalization transfers.

The design of an equalization system is informed by these principles. In the following section, we discuss some properties of an ideal equalization system, focusing in particular on lessons learned from the Canadian experience.

4   THE DESIGN OF AN EQUALIZATION SYSTEM

There is no such thing as an unambiguously perfect equalization system. Given that provinces choose different fiscal policies, it is neither desirable nor feasible to design an equalization system to eliminate NFB differentials across provinces for all persons. More generally, the concept of fiscal capacity as a measure of the ability of a province to provide public services is elusive. Some compromises must be made. In this section, we draw on practices from federations around the world to outline what might be thought of as best-practice principles of equalization design. Given that some value judgments are involved, not all observers will agree with the specifics of program design. But, there is a reasonable consensus about the general principles.

4.1 Some Basic Principles

It is useful to begin with some basic design principles that might govern any equalization system. First and foremost, equalization should be formula-based and grounded on normative principles. This serves to guard against the possibility of transfers being manipulated in a discretionary manner and based on ad hoc considerations. It especially contributes to the ability of the federal government to commit to a transfer system in advance so as to preclude a soft budget constraint. The perception by provinces of a soft budget constraint simply encourages excessive spending in anticipation of being bailed out.

Second, the system should be as incentive-free as possible so that provinces are not induced to change their behavior to increase their transfers. This means basing entitlements on indicators of fiscal capacity over which the provinces have limited control.

Third, the standard used for equalization should reflect the sorts of policies that the provinces actually choose rather than some abstract measure of fiscal capacity (such as the ability to pay). It is actual provincial policies that give rise to NFB differentials that lead to fiscal inefficiency and inequity. So, to the extent that the underlying purpose of equalization is to eliminate NFB differentials across provinces on average, actual provincial policies, or some representative average of them, should be used to measure fiscal capacity differences for equalization purposes.

Finally, in keeping with the economic argument for equalization, the system should strive to equalize the potential for provinces to provide public services (without compelling them to do so). Equalizing this potential leaves provinces with leeway to adopt policies that best serve their own residents' interests, subject to any constraints imposed on provincial policy design to avoid fiscal externalities and other deviations from national objectives. Whatever constraints are imposed on provincial policies are outside the equalization system.

4.2   The Full Equalization Benchmark

If one accepts the view that equalization should ensure that all provinces have the potential to provide the same levels of NFBs to their residents, then all provinces should have the fiscal capacity to be able to provide comparable levels of public services at comparable tax rates if they so choose. The question then becomes: what level of public services should be the standard? The accepted answer to that is the level of public services that provinces roughly do provide, as opposed to a level of services specified independently, perhaps by the federal government. More specifically, a system of full equalization would be one where intergovernmental transfers would leave all provinces with the resources to be able to provide the set of public services that the average, 'representative' province provides. Such a system is called a representative equalization system.

Since in the absence of equalization, some provinces would have above-average fiscal capacity to provide public services and others would have below-average fiscal capacity, full equalization would have to effectively equalize the former down and the latter up. In principle, this could be done in two ways. A full 'net' equalization system would be one that made positive transfers to the below-average provinces and financed them by negative transfers from the above-average provinces, so no net funding would be required from the federal government. However, negative transfers may not be politically feasible (although they are found in some countries, such as Sweden and Germany). In that case, full equalization can still be achieved by a 'gross' system of equalization. In this case, the federal government makes transfers to the provinces to bring them up to a common level of fiscal capacity. This requires a so-called top-province standard, whereby all provinces except the one with the highest fiscal capacity receive transfers such that all end up with the fiscal capacity of the latter. Unlike the net scheme, gross equalization requires federal financing, implying that there must be some minimal size of vertical fiscal gap. Note that if the amount of funding available for equalization is insufficient to bring all provinces to a top-province standard, some lower standard must be accepted. For example, a gross equalization system using a national average standard brings all low-capacity provinces up to the national average ability to provide public services, but does not bring above-average provinces down.

The implementation of a system of representative equalization involves taking account both of the ability of provinces to raise revenues and of the expenditures they require to be able to provide a common level of public services. In practice, overall equalization can be disaggregated into revenue-raising and expenditure components. Consider each in turn.

4.3 Revenue Equalization

Revenue-raising capacity is equalized when provinces are able to raise comparable amounts of revenue per capita, given their tax bases. The amount of revenue per capita that is used to determine the standard is obtained by applying a representative tax system (RTS) approach. Under a net approach to revenue equalization, the RTS approach would be such that all provinces can obtain the per capita revenues of the average province when they apply average provincial tax rates to their own tax bases. All tax bases actually used by the provinces would be included in the calculation.

The formula used in the RTS system is as follows. Consider, for example, tax base i. The per capita equalization entitlement for province j from tax base i, denoted e_i^j, is as follows:

$$e_i^j = \bar{t}_i(\bar{b}_i - b_i^j) \tag{5.1}$$

Where $\bar{t}_i$ is the average tax rate applied to tax base i by all provinces, b_i^j is the per capita size of tax base i in province j, and $\bar{b}_i$ is the average per capita size of tax base i over all provinces. Then, the total equalization entitlement for province j is given by:

$$E^j = \Sigma_i n^j e_i^j \tag{5.2}$$

where n^j is the population of province j. Given the way in which $\bar{t}_i$ and $\bar{b}_i$ are constructed, aggregate equalization entitlements over all provinces sum to zero ($\Sigma_j E^j = 0$). Thus, the system is a true net system.

If negative transfers are not feasible, the same effect can be achieved by a gross system. The simplest way to construct a gross system would be to combine the above equalization entitlements with an equal per capita transfer t to all provinces, such that the following condition is satisfied:

$$E^j + n^j t \geq 0 \text{ for all } j$$

As long as t were sufficiently large such that no province were entitled to receive a negative transfer, full revenue equalization would apply. If t were such that the highest-capacity province just received a zero transfer, the system would be a top-province standard equalization system. The larger is t, the larger is the vertical fiscal gap in the federation. That is, the larger is the amount of tax room occupied by the federal government relative to the provinces. Of course, a larger vertical fiscal gap might well serve other purposes, such as affording the federal government a lever for influencing provincial behavior, but consideration of that is beyond the scope of this chapter.

4.4   Expenditure Equalization

If the allocation of federal equalization transfers were based solely on the RTS, all provinces would have the capacity to raise equal per capita revenues if they chose to do so. But, they may still not be able to provide comparable levels of public services from those revenues since their expenditure requirements might differ.

Expenditure equalization is inherently more complicated than revenue equalization. It requires defining comparing the amount of revenues that would be required to provide comparable levels of public services. To begin with, it is difficult to define comparable levels of public services given the diversity of public services, the many dimensions in which they can differ, and the fact that public services can be of different quality. Even if indices of public service levels can be defined, taking account of the differences in expenditures required to deliver given public service levels would be complicated. The population is very heterogeneous, and measuring its needs for public services is complicated. Furthermore, even within provinces, different levels of public services are provided to different persons depending on the nature of the communities in which they reside. Thus, remote rural areas typically have less services than urban ones because the costs of provision differ. Provinces trade off the equity associated with equal provision of services with the efficiency costs of providing them.

In principle, both the needs for public services arising from the demographic make-up of the population and the costs of provision arising from geographic factors, population density and input costs (wages, property values) would have to be taken into consideration. This is a formidable task. One approach is to adopt what is called a stratified approach. Communities are stratified by some common characteristics, such as size or geographical feature, and expenditure equalization provides provinces with the resources to provide comparable public services across comparable communities. While this mitigates the problem, it does not do so entirely. Some decision must still be made about the appropriate comparable levels of services across communities. In addition, there are still all the problems of heterogeneity of services, differences in quality levels and differences in input costs to sort out. It is not at all clear that one can have confidence in the accuracy of measures of expenditure requirements that are estimated. For this reason, expenditure equalization is not used in Canada, although it is used in some other federations (for example, Australia).

One option might be to restrict expenditure equalization to a subset of expenditure categories. In many federations, a large share of provincial expenditures consists of spending on education, health and welfare programs. It might be feasible to introduce expenditure equalization on a piecemeal basis on these programs alone, especially if the programs that the provinces deliver are similar.

5   THE CANADIAN EQUALIZATION SYSTEM

In Canada, equalization applies on the revenue side only: there is no attempt to equalize expenditure needs. The RTS system is applied using the gross method. Specifically, formula (5.1) that determines each province's equalization entitlements for each tax base i is revised as follows:

$$e_i^j = \bar{t}_i(\bar{b}_i^S - b_i^j) \tag{5.3}$$

where $\bar{b}_i^S$ is the average tax base in five 'standard' provinces, which includes the oil-rich province of Alberta plus the four poorest provinces, all those on the Atlantic coast. Given that Alberta's wealth more than offsets the shortfalls in the four poorer provinces, $\bar{b}_i^S < b_i$ for most tax bases, so equalization entitlements are smaller than they would be if a national average standard is used. Indeed, the five-province standard was chosen partly to avoid the costs that would be associated with including Alberta's oil wealth in the equalization formula. The formula includes 33 separate revenue sources, of which a significant number are different types of natural resources since different natural resources are taxed differently by the provinces. Apart from natural resources, the major revenue categories are personal income tax, sales tax, corporate income tax and property tax. The latter is notable since it is a revenue source that is mainly used to finance municipal services. Thus, provincial entitlements are intended to be sufficient to enable the provinces and their municipalities to provide comparable levels of public services. (In Canada, municipalities are the responsibility of the provinces. The federal government typically does not deal with them directly.)

Actual equalization payments for province j are then determined as follows:

$$E^j = \text{Max} \; \{\Sigma_i n^j e_i^j, 0\} \tag{5.4}$$

where per capita entitlements e_i^j are determined from (5.3). Thus, provinces with a positive aggregate entitlement under the five-province standard – the so-called 'have-not' provinces – obtain equalization transfers, while the others receive nothing. Entitlements are calculated on an annual basis. However, given the volatility to which this gives rise, some measures have been undertaken to stabilize payments. For one thing, a floor provision exists whereby provinces are protected from significant decreases in their entitlements in a given year. Also, the federal government has recently moved to a system of determining equalization transfers based on a three-year moving average of most recent entitlements. This is an effective means of eliminating temporary variability.

There are some exceptions to the strict application of the five-province standard RTS system to all revenue sources. Special provisions apply when a province has more than 70 percent of the base of a given revenue source. This applies only to particular types of natural resources that are concentrated in a given province (e.g., potash in Saskatchewan). To avoid provinces having an incentive to vary the rate at which they tax resources to influence their equalization entitlements, only 70 percent of these resource bases are equalized. Special provisions have also been made for oil and gas revenues accruing to two of the Atlantic provinces (Nova Scotia and Newfoundland & Labrador) from offshore sources. These are subject to special bilateral arrangements that protect the revenues from full equalization, similar to the 70 percent rule. The treatment of personal income taxes is complicated by the fact that progressive rate structures apply. To address this, a stratified approach is adopted whereby the personal tax base is disaggregated by income groups corresponding to different tax brackets, and equalization is applied separately to each bracket. Property taxes have also received separate treatment because of differences in the way in which provinces and their municipalities have calculated property tax bases. Recently, provinces have harmonized their approach to property taxation by using consistent methods of measuring market values, and the equalization system is beginning to incorporate these into the formula.

From time to time, the federal government has introduced discretionary changes into the equalization system, and this has been a source of some controversy. A ceiling was imposed that limited the rate of growth of total equalization entitlements to the GDP growth rate, and this was binding in some years. Special provisions were made in the property tax equalization entitlements in one province (British Columbia) out of concerns for its relatively high property values, and special payments were made to Saskatchewan in recognition of some perceived difficulties in the way its oil revenues were treated. Bilateral deals protecting full offshore revenues of Nova Scotia and Newfoundland & Labrador from equalization were also initiated. Finally, growing concern with the equalization system in light of all these changes led the federal government to set a discretionary sum on total equalization entitlement and to set up its Expert Panel to make recommendations for reform of the system.

Finally, it should also be recalled that the equalization system is complemented by the system of equal per capita CHT/CST transfers. Although these are intended to support provincial social program spending and have some mild conditions attached, the funds are effectively equalizing and fully fungible. They should therefore be considered a component of the equalization system in the broad sense. There has been considerable debate about the role of these transfers. Many provinces have argued that they are inadequate and should be enriched; others argue that they represent an unnecessary intrusion by the federal government into areas of provincial jurisdiction and should be replaced by tax point transfers. Whatever is done to change the vertical fiscal gap will have implications for equalization.

6   ISSUES IN REFORMING EQUALIZATION

There is a lively debate in Canada over the reform of the equalization system. In this section, we recount the major issues in that debate. We take as given that the focus is on revenue equalization, and that the RTS system is the appropriate approach.

6.1   The Standard

Recall from (5.3) that the deviations from the standard tax base $\bar{b}_i^S$ determine entitlements for each province and revenue source: the larger is the standard base, the larger are equalization entitlements. In a net system, a national average standard makes some sense since it results in a self-financing system that fully equalizes revenue capacity. For a gross system, that is no longer the case. The standard determines the capacity to which recipient provinces are equalized, but leave wealthier provinces above the average.

An important property of the standard is found by obtaining from (5.3) the difference in entitlements between two province j and k:

$$\Delta^{jk} e_i = e_i^j - e_i^k = b_i^k - b_i^j \tag{5.5}$$

Note that this difference is independent of the base $\bar{b}_i$ used. Since this is the case for all revenue sources, changing the base changes entitlements for all provinces in equal per capita amounts. That is, horizontal balance is not affected by changes in the base. Instead, when the base increases, per capita equalization payments for all recipient provinces rise in equal amounts, and possibly more provinces become recipients. Thus, the gap between recipient and other provinces closes, while recipient provinces all have the same revenue-raising capacities. An implication of this is that if affordability of equalization is an issue, a reasonable way to let it influence entitlements is via the standard. The alternative way of responding to affordability might be to reduce the proportion of the bases that are equalized under a given standard. While this would reduce overall equalization entitlements, it would do so in a way that resulted in recipient provinces having different fiscal capacities.

While a national average standard makes sense in a net system, it is only one of many alternatives under a gross system that results in under-equalization. In that sense, a national average standard is somewhat arbitrary. Indeed, the total size of the equalization fund that is available to pay to recipient provinces could, in principle be chosen with discretion by the federal government. Under such a system, the allocation among recipient provinces could still be chosen to satisfy (5.5), thus retaining fiscal equity. However, one might want to avoid introducing discretion into the system since it leaves open the opportunity that the federal government will use the discretion for budgetary purposes on a year by year basis, thereby reducing the predictability and stability of the program to the provinces. On the other hand, if the standard that is chosen with discretion could include an escalator provision that takes it out of the hands of the federal government in the short run, its stability would be protected.

An ideal system might be a system that equalizes all provinces to the same level, presumably the national average. If a self-financing net system is not feasible, this could only be achieved by a system with a sufficiently large vertical gap, and that might be viewed as infeasible in a decentralized federation since it would limit the revenue-raising ability of the provinces.

6.2   The Number of Revenue Sources

The current RTS system has 33 separate revenue categories, including several categories of natural resources as well as a number of smaller categories. The large number of categories results from the fact that almost all provincial revenues sources are included, and these are disaggregated so that the RTS approach can be faithfully followed. More disaggregation reduces measurement problems by allowing the representative tax bases to mimic actual ones more closely, but it also increases the complexity of the system.

There are two major issues in choosing the number of revenue sources to include in the RTS system. The first concerns the scope of coverage. There are a number of provincial revenue sources whose inclusion is debatable:

- *User fees.* Some user fees serve as earmarked sources of revenue and are not pooled with general revenues available for financing public services. Examples include university tuition and cost recovery for health and safety inspection. This is recognized in the Canadian system by omitting user fees that do not go into general revenues, but the distinction is sometimes difficult.

- *Gambling revenues*. Gambling is under the direct control of the provinces, who decide which forms of gambling and how many outlets to allow. Because the revenue base is subject to discretion, incentive issues can arise.
- *Subsidies*. In principle, subsidies are equivalent to negative taxes and could be equalized as such. In fact, this is not the practice. One problem that makes it difficult is that practices differ so widely among provinces that it would be difficult to define representative tax bases. Also, since subsidies appear in provincial budgets as expenditures, equalizing them would appear to be equalizing expenditure needs.
- *Hydroelectric utilities*. A particular problem that arises is that some provinces operate hydroelectric utilities as public corporations. While some of their income or rents appear as profits of the companies, some are passed on to users in the form of lower prices. Some have argued that these forgone rents should be equalized just like other 'income'. The problem is that this would violate the principle of the RTS approach.
- *Small revenue sources*. Some revenue sources are relatively small and give rise to limited differences in entitlements. Examples include excise taxes on alcohol and tobacco products. Removing these would change equalization payments very little. On the other hand, they are not difficult to include and do not make the system more complicated.
- *Municipal revenue sources*. The main sources of finance for municipal services are included, especially property taxes and, indirectly, transfers financed out of provincial revenues. Others, however, are more like direct charges or user fees, such as water and sewage charges, and recreational fees. As with user fees discussed above, these may not enter general revenues but serve more like benefit prices.

The second issue affecting the number of revenue sources involves the level of disaggregation of tax bases. This is particularly the case for natural resource revenues. In order for natural resource bases to be treated comparably across provinces, disaggregation is required to capture the fact that different types and qualities of resources are subject to differing tax rates. Even so, questions of the accuracy of measurement of revenue-raising capacity arise, and the system appears to be quite complex. Moreover, higher levels of disaggregation imply that revenue sources are more concentrated within given provinces, leading to possible incentive problems. Aggregation could only be done by coming up with alternative measures of tax capacity. One possibility is to attempt to measure the potential rents from different revenue sources. Apart from being difficult, this would depart from the RTS principle of basing equalization on actual provincial tax practices. The other option would be to use actual revenues rather than a representative tax base. This would avoid difficulties in comparing revenue-raising capacity across resources and provinces, but it too would be a departure from the RTS. Moreover, it could increase incentive problems, to which we next turn.

6.3   Incentive Effects of Equalization

Province j's per capita equalization entitlements in (5.1) depend upon three parameters: $\bar{t}_i$, $\bar{b}_i$ and b_i^j. To the extent that it can influence any of these, adverse incentive effects can arise. It is unlikely to be able to affect national average parameters unless its tax base represents a significant proportion of the national base for a given revenue source. If it does, a so-called *rate tax-back effect* can occur. That is, it will be discouraged from increasing its own tax rate because this will cause the national average tax rate to rise, and therefore its own equalization entitlement – which is negative in this case – to fall. As mentioned above, this possibility is addressed by the 70 percent solution in the Canadian system.

The problem of rate tax-back will arise only in exceptional cases. A more likely problem is that a province may be able to influence the size of its own tax bases. If a province increases it own base, its equalization entitlements automatically fall, a phenomenon called the *base tax-back effect*. There are two avenues by which this can occur. First, to the extent that tax bases are elastic with respect to the tax rate, an increase in the tax rate will cause the base to fall. In addition to the normal fall in tax revenues that will occur, there will be a fall in equalization transfers. Technically speaking, the perceived marginal cost of public funds will be increased and provinces will have an incentive to choose tax rates that are higher than they otherwise would be. (Whether they are too high from a social point of view is not clear since there may be tax competition pressures that operate in the other direction and tend to cause them to set their tax rates too low.)

The second sort of tax-back effect that can occur is that in some instances provinces may have direct control over the size of the tax base. In the case of natural resources, they may be able to influence the rate at which natural resources are exploited if they have some property rights over natural resources (as in the Canadian case). An equalization system that offsets increases in revenue accruing to higher revenue bases will provide provinces with a disincentive to exploit natural resources.

To the extent that these base tax-back effects influence provincial behavior, one might argue that only a proportion of tax bases should enter the equalization formula, even though this would seriously compromise the ability of the system to achieve fiscal equity and fiscal efficiency in the federation. However, the relevance of these incentive effects is unclear. There is no evidence that the tax policies and economic development of provinces in Canada have been influenced by the equalization system despite the fact that relative tax capacities of the recipient provinces are fully equalized. We turn to the case of natural resources next.

6.4   The Treatment of Natural Resources

The case of natural resources is particularly germane to Canada because provinces explicitly own natural resources within their jurisdictions, and have the right to tax them as they please. Differences in natural resource revenues are the biggest sources of fiscal disparity among Canadian provinces, and have been the biggest source of debate about the design of the equalization system. A number of arguments have been proposed as to why natural resources should not be fully equalized. The most important ones, and the counter-arguments in favor of equalization, include the following:

- *Provincial property rights.* Full equalization of natural resources is said to violate the ownership rights of provinces since resources revenues are effectively 'taxed away'.[8] On the other hand, the constitutional commitment to equalization does not distinguish the ability to raise revenues from resources from other revenue sources. Proponents of resource equalization also argue that equalizing them is not equivalent to taxing them since only transfers to provinces are affected by equalization. As well, it is argued that all revenues raised by the provinces are 'owned' by them, and no one is suggesting that other revenue sources not be fully equalized. Moreover, the ownership of natural resources by the provinces is also violated by federal income and sales taxes imposed on resource firms.
- *Affordability.* The federal government faces a particular affordability problem with equalizing natural resources because, unlike with other revenue sources, it has no direct access to natural resource revenues. The counter-argument is that affordability can be better achieved by varying the standard rather than by tampering with the proportion of natural resources equalized.

- *Measurability*. The RTS system is difficult to apply to natural resources because of the heterogeneity of quality of resources and their cost of recovery, which makes their tax capacity difficult to measure. The rate of taxation applied to resources, which often takes the form of a production tax (royalty or severance tax), is limited by the quality of the resource. If provinces find it infeasible to apply a common rate of tax to their resources, the RTS system will under-equalize provinces who own low-quality resources. The response to this is that the RTS system can deal with different qualities of resources by disaggregating them into multiple bases with a stratified tax rate applied to comparable bases.
- *Incentive effects*. Natural resources are said to be especially suscepti-ble to incentive effects since provinces can exert some control over their rate of development. This is a seemingly strong argument, but its strength is belied by the fact that there is no indication that the full equalization of resources in the past has had any real influence over their rate of development. One possible explanation of that is that once resources are discovered, what is at stake is really only the timing of their exploitation. If tax-back applies, that will have no effect on the timing of exploitation. The analog is with the trapped equity argument in corporate tax theory.
- *Cost of development*. A final argument is that, since provinces incur some costs of providing infrastructure and other business inputs to generate the resource revenues, the latter do not add to revenue capacity on a one-for-one basis. However, this argument applies equally well to other revenue sources. For example, income is affected by provincial spending on education and health. More generally, once one takes account of costs of infrastructure as an element determining the equalization formula, consistency would dictate that other costs be included as well; in other words, that equalization be extended to the expenditure side.

The upshot is that some judgment is involved in deciding on the treatment of natural resources. Principles of fiscal equity and efficiency would suggest full equalization and that has been the recent practice of the Canadian system, but some may find one or other of the above arguments persuasive.

6.5 Heterogeneous Inter-provincial Tax Policies

It may be difficult to apply the RTS because provinces use different tax bases or choose complicated rate structures. Thus, provinces choose quite different sales tax bases, some opting for a value-added tax with a very broad base, others using a retail sales tax that taxes goods but few services. Also, income taxes use a progressive rate structure, implying that there is more than one tax rate applied.

There are alternative approaches that can be taken to deal with this issue. An RTS approach could be used with some sort of representative tax base adopted and a single national average tax rate used. However, the base would be arbitrarily defined, and the use of single tax rate would deviate from provincial practices. There are two other approaches. To deal with the fact that different tax rates are used, a representative tax base could be used but it could be stratified so that different national average tax rates could be applied to the relevant strata. As mentioned, this is the approach taken for the personal income tax. Another approach is to treat each province's tax system as a separate source of revenues for the purposes of equalization. Under this systems approach, entitlements for all provinces are calculated using each province's tax system. This approach avoids having to define an arbitrary representative tax base, but it does involve estimating the size of each provincially defined base in all other provinces.

6.6 Equalization of Property Taxes

The case of property taxes is a special case of the problem of heterogeneous tax rates within provinces. Different municipalities systematically levy different tax rates, with rates varying inversely with property values. Moreover, property tax rates within a given municipality differ for residential and commercial property.

In all provinces, property taxes are levied on the market value of real property (buildings plus land), and the assessment practices for estimating property values are common to all provinces. The main issue that arises is whether property values represent tax capacities. To the extent that different property values reflect qualities of the house such as its size and quality or amenity values such as its location, climate or view, one could argue that property value differentials represent differences in the benefit of the housing to the occupants and therefore different revenue-raising capacities. However, to the extent that property values are solely the result of scarcity in a given location, one could argue that higher-value properties do not necessarily have higher revenue-raising capacities.

There is no empirical evidence to support one view or the other about the main reason for different property values across jurisdictions. Despite that, one must still decide how to apply the RTS method to property taxes given the observed tendency for property tax rates to be higher in communities with lower property values. There are two approaches. One is simply to reduce the extent to which property taxes are equalized by including only a fraction of them in the RTS base. The other is to take advantage of the observed relation between average property values and property tax rates to stratify communities by average property values and equalize each separately. (This presumes, of course, that property taxes should be equalized in the first place, which is equivalent to assuming that NFBs arising from both provincial and municipal services should be equalized.)

6.7 Population as an Indicator of Need

A revenue equalization system is based on the amount of revenues that can be raised per capita. Although need is not being explicitly taken into account, one could argue that the implicit assumption is that population is a rough indicator of the need for public services. It might be argued that the equal per capita benchmark is not a reasonable one. For example, there may be economies of scale in the provision of all public services in which case less populated provinces should receive proportionately more. In the case of some provinces, which population to include may be an issue. For example, different provinces have differing proportions of aboriginal persons or military persons. Since the federal government assumes some responsibility for providing services to these persons, maybe provinces should not receive full equalization for them as well. Finally, changes in population may entail some adjustment costs. Growing provinces will have greater infrastructure requirements than others.

As legitimate as these arguments may be, they represent a piecemeal approach to taking account of differences in expenditure requirements. It would be difficult to do so without taking account of other expenditure needs as well.

6.8 Debt, Assets and Infrastructure

The ability of a province to provide public services depends not only on its ability to raise revenues and its needs for services. It also depends on its net debt situation and on the state of its infrastructure. If a province has a high level of debt per capita, it will have high debt service costs and will therefore require more revenue to provide a given level of public services. Similarly, if it has low levels of infrastructure, it will need funds to invest in upgrading infrastructure if it is to provide comparable public service levels. A revenue equalization system based on standard RTS methods does not take account of either of these two things.

There are a couple of issues that arise in dealing with debt service costs. The first is that making special provision for debt servicing would imply that the consequences of provincial decisions are being taken into account.

As a matter of principle, the equalization system should be independent of provincial behavior because of the potential consequences that this could have for incentives. In the case of debt, this could invite provinces to behave as if they had a soft budget constraint with respect to their debt financing decisions. The second issue is that taking account of debt would be equivalent to taking expenditure requirements into account, and we have argued that doing this on a piecemeal basis is inappropriate.

The case of infrastructure raises similar issues. Infrastructure requirements are matters involving provincial expenditures. If other expenditures are not being taken into account, it would be arbitrary to single out infrastructure. Nonetheless, there may be reasons for paying special attention to infrastructure requirements since these are important elements in fostering an efficient, dynamic and competitive national economy. Rather than dealing with infrastructure through the equalization program, the federal government has tended to use specific conditional grants as required.

6.9   Volatility of Entitlements

An ideal equalization system might be one that not only achieves horizontal balance among provinces but also insures them against changes in their fiscal capacity. (The insurance function might be thought of as secondary to the extent that provinces can insure themselves.) The current system does not fulfill the insurance function well for a couple of reasons. First, as equations (5.1) and (5.2) indicate, variability in entitlements can come about not just because of changes in a province's own tax base, but also because of changes in the standard tax bases. Given that the standard base is dominated by the largest province, Ontario (which is not a recipient of equalization), it is possible that equalization entitlements create volatility in a province's fiscal capacity rather than reducing it. Indeed, this has been the case in Canada over the past few decades: changes in provincial entitlements due to changes in the standard have created much more volatility than changes in the recipient provinces' bases.[9] Second, equalization entitlements are initially made on the basis of estimated data for tax bases and population, and these estimates are eventually revised in the next couple of years as estimates are updated. This can cause unexpected changes in equalization entitlements after provincial spending commitments have already been made, which leads to costly revisions of financing plans.

These sources of volatility could be addressed by changes that make equalization entitlements more predictable and smoother year by year, albeit at the expense of forsaking some accuracy on entitlements on a yearly basis. To deal with the volatility problem, a moving average procedure can be adopted whereby current year payments are based on an n-year moving average of past entitlements. This procedure was recently adopted in Canada as the calculation of equalization payments moved to a three-year moving average. A more direct way of avoiding volatility in the standard is simply to arbitrarily fix the aggregate equalization budget, and determine its allocation using the RTS procedure discussed above. The disadvantage of this is that it compromises the formula-based nature of the program and may entail more discretionary changes in the future by the federal government.

The issue of the unpredictability of revisions can only be dealt with by lagging the actual entitlement calculation by at least two years so that revisions can be avoided. Of course, this means that there is a two-year lag in adjusting to changes in entitlements that may occur, although the gain in predictability may compensate for that.

6.10   Governance Issues

A final issue concerns the procedure by which changes in the equalization system and other transfers are decided. Ultimately, changes in the transfer system must be enacted as part of the federal budget since they represent federal spending programs. The issue is how much consultation, advice and public information is involved in changes to the system of federal–provincial transfers. The federal government has been criticized in the past for making changes in the system without advance consultation and notice to the provinces. This has made the system less predictable from their point of view, and has also, from time to time, resulted in a situation where spending plans were made on the basis of expected federal transfers only to find that the latter have been cut back. Moreover, changes to the federal–provincial transfer system have often been done with short-term budgetary considerations in mind rather than the long-run health of the federation.

Some federations have arm's-length bodies that consult, study, inform and make recommendations about the evolution of fiscal transfers. Australia, India and South Africa are examples of this. The question is whether such a body could make the process of federal–provincial transfer determination more transparent and subject to public debate.

7   RECENT POLICY RECOMMENDATIONS

The issue of federal–provincial transfers, especially equalization, has been a matter of public debate in recent years. Partly this is a result of dramatic changes that are occurring in the Canadian federation, especially the growing fiscal disparities between provinces that have natural resources and those that do not. Partly it is a result of the dramatic changes that occurred in the mid-1990s when the federal government unilaterally cut transfers to the provinces with little prior notice. The issue of fiscal balance in the federation has been studied by many bodies, most recently the Expert Panel on Equalization and Territorial Formula Financing and the Advisory Panel on Fiscal Imbalance mentioned earlier. It is useful to recount their recommendations with respect to the equalization system since they are likely to form the basis for changes in the near future.

The Advisory Panel recommendations are straightforward. They recommended retaining the RTS system more or less as it is with all 33 revenue sources included and natural resources fully equalized. They would move the standard from the current five-province standard to a national average (ten-province) standard. They would address the volatility issue by lagging the calculation of entitlements by two years so no updating would be required, and by using a three-year moving average of entitlements to determine actual equalization transfers. With respect to governance, they would not create an arm's-length body to make recommendations. Instead, they would open up the current process by creating a First Ministers Fiscal Council consisting of the Prime Minster and all provincial Premiers, and also a Fiscal Information Institute that would undertake studies and provide information to the public.

The Expert Panel would also retain the RTS system but with some major changes. They would equalize natural resources by using the actual resource revenues that the provinces collect, and would aggregate them into a single revenue base. Moreover, only 50 percent of resource revenues would be included. They would reduce the number of revenue sources to the five major ones used by the provinces: personal income tax, corporate income tax, sales tax, property tax and resource revenues. In the case of property taxes, a stratified procedure as discussed above would be used. Smaller sources of revenue would be eliminated to simplify the system, and user fees would also be eliminated. A ten-province standard is recommended, although if for affordability reasons limits on equalization payments have to be made, they should be made by equal per capita adjustments thereby retaining horizontal balance among recipient provinces. Like the Advisory Panel, they would lag the calculation of entitlements by two years and adopt a three-year moving average procedure. They would make no changes to the institutional arrangements, leaving it to the federal Department of Finance to determine equalization policy. However, they recommend that the process and the information used be made more open to the public.

8   FINAL REMARKS

As we have emphasized, there is no such thing as a perfect equalization system. In a world in which provinces truly have discretion for their spending and taxing policies, heterogeneous outcomes are bound to occur. Indeed, this is a strength of the federal system. This implies that designing an equalization system, that achieves the objective of ensuring that the provinces have the fiscal capacity to provide roughly comparable levels of public services at roughly comparable levels of taxation, is a difficult task.

Despite the difficulties of implementation, the design of the equalization system should be guided by principles, and these principles should be reflected in a formula-based approach rather than one that relies on discretion. In the Canadian case, the emphasis on revenue equalization using the RTS approach accords well with the principles. The main issues that arise involve conflicts between the principle of equalization and other principles. These include the provincial ownership of resources, the incentive effects of equalization and affordability to the federal government. Different observers will have different views about the compromises this entails. Our view is that the issues of resources and affordability should be dealt with by adjusting the standard rather than by reducing the extent to which resource revenues determine equalization entitlements. Full equalization of all revenue sources for recipient provinces at least ensures that fiscal equity is achieved among recipient provinces, although not necessarily between recipient and non-recipient provinces. In a federation as decentralized as Canada, full equalization among all provinces would be very difficult to achieve. That is one reason why the country should be very cautious about further decentralizing revenue-raising responsibilities. That would make horizontal balance even more difficult to achieve.

Finally, it is worth emphasizing that achieving a successful equalization system involves non-economic considerations. Institutions can be important in ensuring that the integrity of the equalization process is respected. Equalization policy is part of the broader set of federal–provincial fiscal arrangements and is not set in a vacuum. The process requires that decisions be made from a long-term perspective and that the federal government behave in a cooperative manner with respect to the provinces. Moreover, the ability of the federal government to commit to a formula-based approach to equalization that is not compromised by discretionary changes is important to ensure that problems of soft budget constraints do not emerge. Whether that level of commitment and cooperation requires some arm's-length institution such as a grants commission found in some federations is an open question. At least, the importance of institutional considerations and process should not be overlooked in any discussion of reforming federal–provincial fiscal relations.

NOTES

1. Based on a presentation prepared for the 4th Symposium on Fiscal Federalism, Institut d'Economia de Barcelona, 30–31 May 2006.
2. See Boothe, Paul (1998), 'Finding a Balance: Renewing Canadian Fiscal Federalism', Benefactors Lecture, Toronto: C.D. Howe Institute.
3. Examples of past studies include the Breau Committee (1981), *Fiscal Federalism in Canada: Report of the Parliamentary Task Force on Federal–Provincial Fiscal Arrangements*, Ottawa: Queen's Printer; Economic Council of Canada (1982), *Financing Confederation: Today and Tomorrow*, Ottawa: Supply and Services Canada; Royal Commission on the Economic Union and Development Prospects for Canada (the Macdonald Commission) (1985), *Report*, Ottawa: Supply and Services Canada; Office of the Auditor General of Canada, *1997 Report of the Auditor General*, Chapter 8, 'Department of Finance – Equalization Program', Ottawa: Auditor General Office; Senate of Canada, Standing Committee on National Finance (2002), *The Effectiveness of and Possible Improvements to the Present Equalization Policy*; Commission on Fiscal Imbalance (the Séguin Commission) (2003), *A New Division of Canada's Financial Resources: Final Report*, Government of Quebec; Royal Commission on Renewing and Strengthening our Place in Canada (2003), *Our Place in Canada: Main Report*, St. John's: Office of the Queen's Printer; and House of Commons Standing Committee on Finance (2005), *The Existence, Extent and Elimination of Canada's Fiscal Imbalance: Report of the Subcommittee on Fiscal Imbalance*, Ottawa: Canadian Government Publishing.
4. Their reports may be found at Expert Panel on Equalization and Territorial Formula Financing (2006), *Achieving a National Purpose: Putting Equalization Back on Track*, Ottawa: Department of Finance; and Advisory Panel on Fiscal Imbalance (2006), *Reconciling the Irreconcilable: Addressing Canada's Fiscal Imbalance*, Ottawa: The Council of the Federation.
5. For summaries of the literature, see Boadway, Robin W. and Paul A.R. Hobson (eds) (1998), *Equalization: Its Contribution to Canada's Economic and Fiscal Progress*, Kingston: John Deutsch Institute for the Study of Economic Policy; Boadway, Robin W. and Paul A.R. Hobson (1993), *Intergovernmental Fiscal Relations in Canada*, Toronto: Canadian Tax Foundation; and Boadway, Robin W. (2003), 'Options for Fiscal Federalism', in *Collected Research Papers of the Royal Commission on Renewing and Strengthening our Place in Canada*, Vol. 2, St. John's, Newfoundland and Labrador: Office of the Queen's Printer, pp. 265–310.
6. Royal Commission on Dominion–Provincial Relations (1940), *Report*, Ottawa: King's Printer.
7. For a summary of the economic principles of equalization, see Boadway, Robin (2001), 'Intergovernmental Fiscal Relations: The Facilitator of Fiscal Decentralization', *Constitutional Political Economy* **12** (2), 93–121; and Boadway, Robin (2004), 'The Theory and Practice of Equalization', *CESifo Economic Studies* **50** (1), 211–54.
8. This argument is made in Courchene, Thomas J. (2004), 'Confiscatory equalization: the intriguing case of Saskatchewan's vanishing energy revenues', *IRPP Choices* **10** (2), 1–39; and Feehan, James P. (2005), 'Equalization and the Provinces' Natural Resource Revenues:

Partial Equalization Can Work Better', in Harvey Lazar (ed.), *Canadian Fiscal Arrangements: What Works, What Might Work, What Might Work Better*, Montreal: McGill-Queen's University Press.

9. This is documented in Boadway, Robin and Masayoshi Hayashi (2004), 'An evaluation of the stabilization properties of equalization in Canada', *Canadian Public Policy* **30** (1), 91–109; and Smarts, Michael (2004), 'Equalization and stabilization', *Canadian Public Policy* **30** (2), 195–208.

6. Fiscal equalization in Germany[1]

Thiess Buettner

1 INTRODUCTION

While revenue-sharing and fiscal equalization are a common characteristic of sub-national government finances in many countries of the world there is a particular emphasis on this element in Germany. To some extent this is related to German history: Germany for a long time displayed a large, loosely connected group of small countries. While the German empire established in 1871 still displayed a large degree of autonomy, the two World Wars resulted in severe fiscal pressures that led to a substantial degree of formal cooperation on the revenue side of the budget, which bears elements of centralization. While the Federal Republic still displays a non-trivial vertical structure of the public sector, the close cooperation on the revenue side results in extensive use of revenue-sharing and fiscal equalization among governments.

In order to provide some background, the following section starts with a brief overview of sub-national government finances in Germany. Afterwards, the chapter devotes attention to the local level and discusses revenue-sharing and fiscal equalization between local municipalities. This will allows us to reach a basic understanding of the basic motivation of fiscal equalization. Section 4 will then discuss fiscal equalization at state level. Section 5 concludes with some remarks on the German system of fiscal equalization.

2 FISCAL DECENTRALIZATION IN GERMANY

The three-tier structure of the public sector in Germany involves a system of vertical and horizontal fiscal equalization. Figure 6.1 provides a graphical representation where the dashed arrows depict horizontal equalization. The straight lines represent elements of revenue-sharing and vertical grants.

The vertical dimension of revenue-sharing delivers a large amount of public funds to the lower-level governments. Table 6.1 gives some comparative figures for OECD countries.

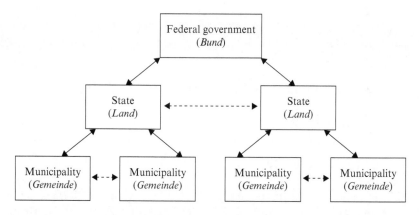

Figure 6.1   Fiscal equalization in Germany

*Table 6.1   Tax revenue decentralization in OECD countries
(1996–2001) (%)*

Country	Total Tax Revenue of Sub-national Government[a]	Autonomous Own Tax Revenue of Sub-national Government[a]	Country	Total Tax Revenue of Sub-national Government[a]	Autonomous Own Tax Revenue of Sub-national Government[a]
	(1)	(2)		(1)	(2)
Switzerland	56.9	53.0	Norway	21.8	21.4
Canada	51.8	51.8	Australia	19.1	19.1
Germany	49.3	7.2	France	18.6	18.4
Belgium	44.7	24.6	Italy	14.8	11.2
Sweden	42.8	42.8	Portugal	8.9	3.3
Japan	41.3	37.5	Luxembourg	8.0	7.9
United States	35.6	35.6	New Zealand	6.0	5.9
Denmark	34.1	32.2	Netherlands	5.1	5.1
Finland	29.7	24.2	United Kingdom	5.0	5.0
Austria	28.2	3.2			
Spain	25.9	22.3	Ireland	4.0	2.2
Iceland	25.3	25.3	Greece	1.9	0.3

Note: [a] As a percentage of total tax revenue of general government.

Source: Stegarescu (2005).

The conventional figures are provided in column (1) of Table 6.1. Only Switzerland and Canada depict a larger degree of revenue decentralization. Column (2) provides alternative figures, however, where only those revenues are assigned to the sub-national level where a lower-level government is exercising some tax autonomy. While the corresponding figures for Canada and Switzerland are not much different, the German figure is much lower.

Table 6.1 clearly shows that the large amount of funds available to the sub-national governments is not resulting from substantial tax autonomy but reflects the importance of revenue-sharing. In particular, the states receive large shares of personal and corporate income taxes as well as of the value-added tax. While the municipalities also receive a share of personal income and value-added taxes they enjoy at least some tax autonomy with regard to local business taxation. We will turn to municipal finances in the next section.

3 MUNICIPAL FISCAL EQUALIZATION

A somewhat surprising feature of municipal finances in Germany is the strong reliance on a local business tax. This tax is enforced and collected at the state level but the municipal governments set the local tax rate. Given the rather small size of the more than 10 000 municipalities, business taxation is frequently used as an instrument in the competition between municipalities (e.g., Buettner, 2001). Besides tax competition the local business tax has several other deficiencies including a severely fluctuating tax base and the necessity of intermunicipal formula apportionment. However, while the tax revenue even at the aggregate level displays severe fluctuations (see Figure 6.2) the weighted average tax rate has actually risen over the last decades.

This raises the question of why the municipalities rely on the rather inefficient business tax instead of the other local tax instrument, the land tax, which plays a negligible role. A potential explanation lies in the municipal fiscal equalization systems. While these systems differ across states, they show some strong similarities. These systems basically use some indicator of the *fiscal capacity* of jurisdictions, a measure of tax revenue at standardized tax rates, and compare it with the *fiscal need*, which is, basically, the conceded budget per resident. If a jurisdiction displays a fiscal capacity above its fiscal need it does not receive funds or is a net contributor to the revenue-sharing system. If the fiscal capacity of a municipality falls short of the fiscal need, which is typically the case, the jurisdiction is a net recipient such that grants partly compensate for the gap between fiscal need and fiscal capacity. Note that the systems are 'gross schemes' in the

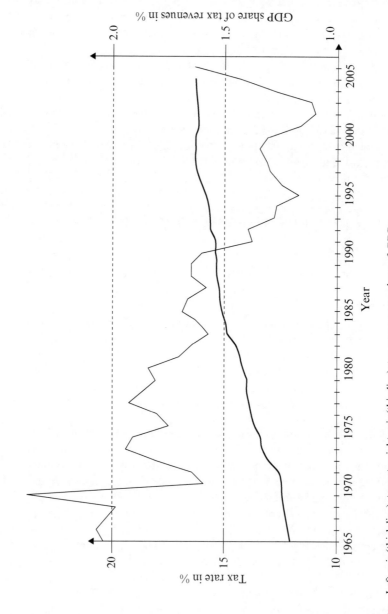

Note: Left axis (thick line): tax rate; right axis (thin line): tax revenue as a share of GDP.

Figure 6.2   Weighted business tax rate

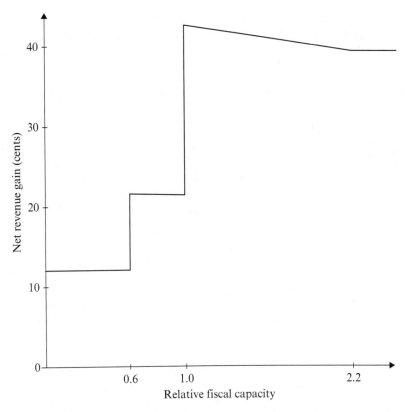

Note: Net revenue gain: increase in total revenue in cents out of one additional euro of tax revenue for a typical municipality in Baden-Wuerttemberg in 2000.

Source: Buettner (2006a).

Figure 6.3   Municipal fiscal equalization and the degree of redistribution

terminology of Boadway (2004) since the states contribute to the municipal equalization systems with substantial amounts of funds. As the grants are inversely tied to fiscal capacity, the local revenue effects of fluctuations in the business tax as well as adverse responses of the tax base to tax-rate differentials with regard to other municipalities are strongly cushioned.

The upshot of the system is displayed in Figure 6.3. It depicts the degree of redistribution for a municipality in a major German state. More specifically, it reports the revenue gain after fiscal equalization out of one additional euro of tax revenue. The system is regressive, since municipalities with a larger tax capacity tend to keep a larger share of the tax revenue, whereas jurisdictions with a low capacity tend to keep only a minor share.

The average municipality would show a relative fiscal capacity between unity and 0.6 and hence keeps about 20 cents out of one additional euro of tax revenue.

4 STATE-LEVEL FISCAL EQUALIZATION

While fiscal equalization at the municipal level has some virtues in curbing aggressive business-tax competition between municipalities and providing some sort of insurance against revenue fluctuations, the horizontal equalization system at the level of the states operates against a rather different background (for a concise description of state finances see Buettner, 2006b).

The German states do not execute any major tax autonomy but mainly finance their budgets with shares of the major federal taxes such as personal and corporate income taxes as well as value-added taxes. In what can be considered the primary revenue distribution the state share of 50 per cent of the corporate income tax is allocated to the states according to the location of the establishment either directly or through some formula allocation for multistate companies. The states' share of personal income tax revenue is currently 42.5 per cent. This revenue is distributed among states according to the place of residence of the taxpayer. Revenue-sharing with regard to the VAT is more complex. The current rule is, approximately, that a share of 46 per cent is assigned to the states distributed partly according to population and partly according to an indicator of revenue capacity. Though already the first part is obviously redistributive, the second part is usually considered as the first stage of the fiscal equalization system.

Imposed on this primary allocation of tax revenue is a second stage of redistribution by means of an explicit horizontal equalization system. As in the case of municipal fiscal equalization, equalization grants are triggered by differences between a measure of the capacity of a state and its municipalities and an indicator of the fiscal need. The fiscal need indicator is simply based on the population size and the per-capita average of all states' tax revenues. Different from the municipal equalization system, the state-level equalization can be characterized as a net system (Boadway, 2004) where equalization grants are financed with equalization contributions. Similar to tax equalization in Canada and Australia, based on so-called *representative national average standards*, the system involves huge transfers from states with high revenue capacity to low-capacity states.

The horizontal equalization system is further complemented with federal transfers to those states that after two stages of equalization are still below fiscal need. Taken together, the system of fiscal equalization between the

Table 6.2   State fiscal equalization transfers 2005 (euros per resident)

State (*Land*)	Fiscal Equalization				Other
	VAT distribution	Horizontal fiscal equal.	Fed. grants	Total	Federal Grants
Baden-Wuerttemberg		−206		−203	
Bavaria		−178		−150	
Berlin	140	720	225	966	604
Brandenburg	588	226	86	882	682
Bremen		552	183	640	90
Hamburg		−217		−377	
Hesse		−261		−308	
Mecklenburg-West Pom.	662	248	93	992	753
Lower Saxony	198	45	24	136	0
North Rhine-Westphalia		−27		−3	0
Rhineland-Palatinate	28	72	37	159	11
Saar	176	106	49	198	59
Saxony	647	234	88	953	717
Saxony-Anhalt	711	231	88	992	756
Schleswig-Holstein	71	51	28	42	19
Thuringia	638	242	91	965	736

states results in an almost complete equalization of revenue capacity across the states.

Table 6.2 provides the resulting transfers in terms of euros per capita. Given the differences among states, four states currently contribute to the system of fiscal equalization including Baden-Wuerttemberg, Bavaria, Hesse and Hamburg. The other states, in particular the states in former East Germany, get large transfers of up to about 1000 euros per capita.

Table 6.3 depicts the marginal degree of redistribution. As with the case of municipalities, it reports the revenue gain after fiscal equalization out of one additional euro of tax revenue in percentage points. Generally, small states as well as states with below-average per-capita revenue experience a larger degree of redistribution. In some cases only a few cents of an additional euro of tax revenues are kept. As the degree of redistribution is rather large a reform was enacted in recent years aimed at a reduction of the degree of redistribution. However, as can be seen from Table 6.3 the degree of redistribution is still high.

An economic assessment of the fiscal equalization system at the state level would first of all have to acknowledge that there is no substantial tax autonomy at the state level. Hence, the argument that equalization might help to reduce inefficiencies from tax competition is not applicable. In fact,

*Table 6.3   State-level fiscal equalization: degree of redistribution
               (percentage points)*

	Pre–2005 Rule	Current Rule
Saarland	1.29	1.68
Mecklenburg-West Pom.	1.91	2.44
Thuringia	2.87	3.37
Saxony-Anhalt	2.97	3.42
Brandenburg	3.44	3.57
Lower Saxony	9.82	10.80
Rhineland-Palatinate	10.60	15.67
Saxony	4.74	16.65
Schleswig-Holstein	9.34	21.70
Baden-Wuerttemberg	34.83	38.27
Hesse	28.44	39.86
Bavaria	35.74	45.45
North Rhine-Westphalia	83.29	58.98
Bremen	1.07	6.68
Berlin	5.30	16.24
Hamburg	5.30	36.38

one might argue that the states actually collude in using the federal purse
and form a *taxing cartel* (Blankart, 1999). Moreover, it is important to note
that the states not the federal government are actually collecting the taxes.
The strong degree of redistribution, therefore, creates disincentives for tax
collection effort (Baretti, Huber and Lichtblau, 2002).

An assessment of fiscal equalization at the state level would also have to
take account of the fact that there is much less need for fiscal assistance.
Since states are not restricted in incurring debt there is no general justification for risk-sharing by means of fiscal transfers.

From a general perspective, a positive aspect of fiscal equalization at the
state level might be its contribution to the rather quick process of economic
integration after Unification. However, due to the still large differences in
per-capita income the large volume of redistributive funds places a burden
on further reforms of the fiscal equalization system. As an example, consider the situation of the East German states that struggle for development
but are restricted to imposing the rather high German corporation-tax rate
on investors while the competing transition countries in the former Soviet
bloc provide many aggressive tax incentives. Though the East German
states would probably benefit from an increase in sub-national tax autonomy, they do not promote such policy changes, probably because corresponding policy proposals would put the redistributive transfers at risk.

5 CONCLUSIONS

The German system of fiscal federalism puts a strong emphasis on fiscal redistribution by means of revenue-sharing and fiscal equalization among all levels of governments. At the municipal level, the existence of a substantial degree of horizontal fiscal redistribution may be quite helpful in curbing local tax competition and providing fiscal assistance. Nevertheless, this positive role is partly offset with disincentive effects, as, for instance, the reluctance of municipalites to use the land tax to generate revenue.

At the state level, the role of fiscal equalization is much more problematic. The system provides the states with a substantial amount of public funds while it does not require the states to take responsibility for their policies against the taxpayer by deciding about the tax burden. Rather, the states live mainly on grants. At the same time, however, the extensive use of fiscal redistribution cannot be justified on efficiency grounds as is the case with municipalities. In fact, given tax collection at state level, the fiscal redistribution provides actual additional disincentives, which are not present at the municipal level.

The German example offers some interesting conclusions for the evolving fiscal federalism in Europe. The example of the German municipalities shows that under the protection of revenue-sharing, tax competition does not necessarily result in inefficiently low tax rates. At the same time, however, the example of the German states shows that fiscal redistribution should be used with caution in particular in a situation with decentralized tax collection.

NOTE

1. Notes of a lecture given at the 4th Symposium on Fiscal Federalism, Barcelona, 30–31 May 2006, 'The Experience of Federal Countries: Lessons for Spain'.

REFERENCES

Baretti, C., B. Huber and K. Lichtblau (2002), 'A tax on tax revenue: the incentive effects of equalizing transfers: evidence from Germany', *International Tax and Public Finance*, **9** (6), 631–49.

Blankart, C.B. (1999), 'Die schleichende Zentralisierung der Staatstaetigkeit: eine Fallstudie', *Zeitschrift fuer Wirtschafts- und Sozialwissenschaften*, **119** (3), 331–50.

Boadway, R. (2004), 'The theory and practice of equalization', *CESifo Economic Studies*, **50** (1), 211–54.

Buettner, T. (2001), 'Local business taxation and competition for capital: the choice of the tax rate', *Regional Science and Urban Economics*, **31** (2–3), 215–45.

Buettner, T. (2006a), 'The incentive effect of fiscal equalization on tax policy', *Journal of Public Economics*, **90** (3), 477–97.

Buettner, T. (2006b), 'The finances of the German states', *Catalan Journal of Public Law*, **32**, 211–32.

Stegarescu, D. (2005), 'Public sector decentralisation: measurement concepts and recent international trends', *Fiscal Studies*, **26** (3), 301–33.

7. Fiscal equalization in Spain

Jesús Ruiz-Huerta Carbonell and Ana Herrero Alcalde

1 INTRODUCTION

Spain has undergone an intense devolution process during the last three decades. A new level of government – regional government, namely the Autonomous Community (AC) – was created after the 1978 Constitution was passed, and although the constitutional structure of the country is not a federal one, the current degree of decentralization in both taxes and public expenditure is similar to that existing in most federations. As a consequence, the main problems that had to be resolved during that devolution process are very similar to the ones existing in federal countries.[1]

The financing system of the ACs has gone through a deep process of change since its first implementation in the early 1980s, with a progressive enlargement of regional tax resources and a proportional reduction of central government transfers.[2] However, there still is an important level of dependence on those transfers, basically on the Sufficiency Fund (Fondo de Suficiencia), which represents around one-third of ACs' total resources – approximately 24 000 million euros in 2004. This fund, which is aimed at resolving both vertical and horizontal imbalances, is the main equalization instrument of the Spanish regional financing system.

Both the regional tax resources and central government transfers were subject to a strong revision in 2001, which was accepted by all its participants. The main characteristics of that reform were the increase of regional shares in personal income tax (PIT) (33 percent); the implementation of a tax-sharing system in consumption taxes (35 percent of VAT, 40 percent of excise taxes on tobacco, alcohol and fuel, and 100 percent of taxes on electricity and car licensing) and the introduction of a new tax on fuel retail sales.[3] As a result of this increase in tax resources, central government transfers were substantially reduced, although there was also an important enlargement of regional expenditures, as a consequence of the devolution of education and health care to all the ACs.

In spite of the fact that the 2001 reform was accepted by all the ACs, and that the new system was not meant to be revised at any specific time as opposed to the previous reforms, which were passed every five years, some regional governments have been pushing for a revision ever since the first year's (2002) results were published. The dramatic demographic growth that has taken place in Spain in the last few years, linked to the absence of periodical adjustments in the transfer system in order to incorporate the new population, has caused an important change in the financial situation of some ACs. Now, the most affected areas – basically the eastern coast, the islands and Madrid – are asking the central government to compensate for the higher costs of providing services to a bigger share of national population. Moreover, all the regional governments have demanded more resources to deal with the expansion of health care costs and the high health expenditure income-elasticity.

Meanwhile, most of the ACs are in the process of reforming their own Statutes of Autonomy – the equivalent to a regional constitution – which will strongly affect their financing system. Two of the statutes already passed – the ones affecting Catalonia and Andalucía – include an increase in the share of PIT and consumption taxes.[4] At the same time, a reform of the equalization transfer is expected in order to meet new interpretations of the principles of solidarity and sufficiency.

The purpose of this chapter is to analyze the Spanish equalization system, its characteristics and problems and the main proposals for its reform in the near future. First, we will use the main guidelines of fiscal federalism to evaluate the design of the Spanish equalization transfer. Second, an explanation about the basic shortcomings and financial results of the system will be made. And finally, we will review the main topics that will have to be taken into consideration in its next reform.

2   EQUALIZATION TRANSFERS IN SPAIN: MAIN CHARACTERISTICS

The theory of fiscal federalism defines an equalization transfer as one that allows all sub-central governments to provide similar levels of public services if they have a similar level of fiscal effort. This implies that these transfers should allocate more resources to those regions with the lowest potential revenue, that is to say, the lowest fiscal capacity,[5] and/or in those areas with the highest costs of providing public services (with higher expenditure needs). According to Boadway (2004), equalization transfers are considered to enable a federal country to duplicate the results of a centralized system in terms of equity, without giving up the advantages of decentralization.[6] The political autonomy of regions can be guaranteed by a well-designed system of unconditional transfers, which allows the provision of different levels of public services responding to differences in preferences, while keeping horizontal equity among citizens, guaranteeing that the least developed areas obtain enough resources to provide a level of public services similar to the richest ones.[7]

Therefore, equalization transfers are an instrument of inter-regional redistribution. The stability of this instrument depends on how it reflects the intensity of the inter-regional solidarity desired by the country as a whole.[8] If the redistribution generated by these transfers is too intense, rich regions can argue that disincentives for economic growth can emerge for both recipients (more growth leads to bigger tax bases and larger fiscal capacity, and thus to smaller equalization transfers) and contributors (the more their economies grow, the bigger the transfers they have to pay).[9] On the other hand, if inter-regional redistribution through the equalization system is too slight, the internal cohesion of the country can be damaged, and therefore its political stability. In any case, the process of transition from an intensely redistributive system to a softer one needs time and enough consensus, if political difficulties are to be avoided.

An important issue to be resolved in this context is to establish who decides (and through which process) the intensity of the inter-regional redistribution desired by the country as a whole. It seems pretty obvious that the central government has something to say about the design and objectives of the equalization system, especially in the cases where it is implemented through vertical grants. But it is difficult to justify a decision process that completely ignores the regional governments' vision about it, if stability of the system is desired.

The participation of sub-central governments in the design of equalization transfers is important, particularly in federal countries, to make sure that the interests of all regions are taken into account. There are several ways to introduce the views of the regions in the process. Members of the German Senate are directly appointed by regional executives, while governments of the states closely cooperate with the Australian Commonwealth Grants Commission in the design of fiscal capacity and expenditure need indexes used in the equalization system. The Spanish Fiscal and Financial Policy Council (Consejo de Política Fiscal y Financiera) is a multilateral institution, where both the central government and all the ACs are represented, which agrees – among other topics – on the regional financial system reforms. Those agreements have then to be ratified in bilateral Committees (Comisiones Mixtas de Transferencias) between the national government and each region.

As stated before, the purpose of equalization transfers is to reduce (or even to eliminate) differences in the ability to provide public services, when there are differences in the fiscal capacity of regions. Thus, it is important not to confuse them with capital transfers for development purposes, which have distinct objectives and therefore require a different design and different results.[10] While in the latter there is a case for positive discrimination in favor of the least developed territories, in order to reduce the gap between them and the relatively more developed regions, such a justification does not exist in the equalization system. The idea is to guarantee that all the governments can – and not necessarily do – provide the same level of services, and that does not imply giving proportionally more resources to the poorest areas (if necessities and fiscal capacity are properly measured). In conclusion, there is no reason for an equalization transfer to modify the regional ranking in terms of fiscal capacity, allowing the lower fiscal capacity jurisdictions to provide more and better public services than those with a high fiscal capacity.[11] The result of the equalization system should be a guaranteed horizontal equity, meaning that all citizens – independently of their region of residency – can have a similar access to public services with the same level of fiscal effort. Therefore, it is important to note that these transfers should not be used to encourage the economy of the least developed regions, which is the main aim of development transfers.[12]

As we will see, the Spanish equalization system does not fulfill all the characteristics and results predicted by theory, although its basic structure was designed to guarantee the provision of similar levels of public services in all territories. In Spain, there are two main instruments with equalization purposes within the regional financing system: the Sufficiency Fund (Fondo de Suficiencia) and the Equalization Grants (Asignaciones de Nivelación).

Although the term 'Equalization Grants' would seem to reflect a structural equalization instrument, these transfers were conceived in the last reform in order to compensate for extraordinary increases in expenditure needs. They are supposed to guarantee a minimum level of basic public services – health and education – for all regions, provided that there is an increase of regional population (health) or the number of enrolled students (education) three points above the national average. These restricted circumstances, linked to the absence of clear criteria to distribute these grants, have left them unused in practice since the approval of the Spanish Constitution.

As for the Sufficiency Fund, it is a vertical, unconditional and periodical transfer, which is aimed at resolving both vertical and horizontal imbalances. It deals with the vertical imbalance by trying to allocate proportionally more resources in regions with larger expenditure needs (basically, more population), but it also tries to solve horizontal imbalances by redistributing the total amount of resources in inverse proportion to the regional fiscal capacity. Although the purpose of the transfer is to allow all regions to provide similar levels of those services devolved by the central government, its design and results have always been partially controversial.

In the following, we will try to offer a simplified explanation of the method used to calculate the Sufficiency Fund in 2002, in order to analyze its main problems in the next section of the chapter.[13]

First of all, each of the reforms of the regional financing system has assumed the cost of the previous one, preventing any change from resulting in a lower amount of resources for any territory.[14] Therefore, the first step to calculate the transfer is to obtain the quantity of resources provided to ACs in 1999, used as the base year, in three expenditure blocks – general services and education, health, and social services – the so-called 'initial restriction' (see the first column of Table 7.1).

As far as the general services and education block is concerned, the initial restriction is obtained by adding up the revenue collected through the devolved taxes (mainly on the property and transfer of wealth, and gambling taxes), the regional share of PIT, the resources obtained from the regional participation in central government taxes (the former Sufficiency Fund), and the Guarantee Fund in force between 1997 and 2001, plus the effective cost[15] of the services devolved between 1999 and 2001.

With regard to the health services block, it is important to note that the 2001 agreement represented the first time in which the decentralized health system was incorporated into the general financing system, as it had always been regulated and managed separately, and financed through conditional transfers.[16] Since 2001, its financing has been unconditional. Because some of the ACs did not receive competences on health care until 2001, the initial restriction of this block was obtained from the data of aggregated health expenditure implemented by both the ACs and the central government. The same reason led to an identical solution for the social services block, the initial restriction for each region being the total expenditure in that area.

Next, expenditure needs of each community were calculated, based on the regional participation in the variables shown in the second column of Table 7.1. In the general services and education area, three different funds can be distinguished:

- The General Fund tries to reflect the ordinary costs of providing those services in each community through its own weight in national population, area, population dispersion and non-mainland location. Obviously, this last variable applies exclusively to the case of Balearic and Canary Islands.
- The Low Population Density Fund distributes a part of this general block in response to the extraordinary costs of providing services in the least populated areas.

Table 7.1   Determining the Sufficiency Fund

Status Quo (Initial Restriction)	Expenditure Needs	Financial Resources
General services and education: + Normative collection in devolved taxes (1999) + Regional share in PIT revenue (1999) + Guarantee Fund (1999) + Effective cost of services devolved after 1999	General Fund: population (94%), area (4.2%), dispersion (1.2%), non-mainland location (0.6%) Low Population Density Fund: ACs with a density < 27 people/km² and an area < 50.000 km² Relative Income Fund: ACs with per capita income below national average Minimum guaranteed Modulation rules	+ Normative collection in devolved taxes + Regional share in PIT collection (33%) + Shared taxes (VAT and excise taxes) + Sufficiency Fund
Health: + Health expenditure in 1999	General Fund: population covered by national health system (75%), population > 65 (24.5%) and non-mainland location (0.5%) Minimum guaranteed	
Social services: + Social services expenditure in 1999	General Fund: population > 65 Minimum guaranteed	

Source: Elaborated by the authors from Ruiz-Huerta et al. (2002).

- The Relative Income Fund attributes proportionally more needs to those ACs with a per capita income below the national average.

After expenditure needs in general and education services were obtained, they were compared with the regional initial restriction, and if they were below this restriction, the status quo clause (minimum guaranteed) was applied. Furthermore, if the increase of resources attributed to the region, as compared with the ones resulting from the previous system, was too large or too small, a number of modulation rules applied.

Regional expenditure needs in health care were calculated based on the figures of the regional share in population covered by the National Health System,[17] population over 65 and non-mainland location. As for the social services expenditure needs, the index was obtained from the number of residents over 65. The status quo rule also applied in health and social services, so no AC could be worse off after the reform.

Finally, once the regional needs in all services were known, the Sufficiency Fund was obtained by subtracting the regional tax collection from those expenditure needs (third column in Table 7.1). If the result was below zero, as was the case of Madrid and Balearic Islands, a negative transfer would be implemented, reducing the regional share in VAT and excise taxes.

Although the current legislation does not contain an explicit equity target to be achieved by the equalization system, its design seems to be trying to close 100 percent of the fiscal gap between regional fiscal capacity and expenditure needs. However, a number of ad hoc adjustments in the calculation of the expenditure needs index – namely the status quo and modulation rules – have made it impossible to meet that objective with the same intensity in all territories. Some of them have had a large cut in their own calculated needs, because the introduction of new variables and their particular weights would have generated a large increase in the resources allocated to them, which would have resulted in an excessively high cost for the central government. On the other hand, the mentioned adjustments allowed some ACs to maintain their share in expenditure needs, in spite of the fact that the new variables within the needs index would lead them to a lower share of regional resources.

The fiscal capacity index used to calculate the Sufficiency Fund is also pretty remarkable. An estimation of the normative collection that each AC should have obtained through devolved taxes – over which they have regulatory and administrative powers – is obtained by updating the real collection in the year of devolution with the central government's taxes growth rate. This peculiar system was introduced in the mid-1980s, to avoid the disincentives generated by the previous system, which calculated central transfers by subtracting the actual collection from the regional expenditure needs assessment. Because the ACs do not have regulation powers over the shared consumption taxes, actual collection of these taxes is used in order to clarify the fiscal capacity assessment. As for the PIT, the federal tax administration provides information on the regional potential yield, given that regional governments have powers over deduction and tax rates. This is calculated as the normative collection that would result if no changes regarding the original central deductions and rates system were implemented.

From the dynamic point of view, each territory's Sufficiency Fund evolves annually with the growth rate showed by central government taxes.[18] Therefore, it does not address the particular evolution of regional fiscal capacity and expenditure needs.[19]

3 MAIN RESULTS AND SHORTCOMINGS OF THE IMPLEMENTATION OF EQUALIZATION TRANSFERS IN SPAIN

The first thing that should be noted about the design of equalization transfers in Spain is the unclear terminology used. One could expect the Equalization Grants – as they were included in Article 158 of the Constitution – to be the main equalizing instrument within the regional financing system. However, as it was remarked before, those transfers have not been used, and the main equalization transfer is the Sufficiency Fund. This denomination does not set out a clear objective in terms of desired inter-territorial redistribution. Although its design does correspond with the usual structure of Equalization Grants, the philosophy behind the transfer maintains the crucial role of the central government to guarantee a certain level of public services. By using the 'sufficiency' term, oriented to the achievement of the sufficiency principle – stated in the financial legislation applied to ACs[20] – the national government seems to be responsible ad infinitum for any increase of regional expenditure needs in the area of devolved services. From our point of view, this idea has contributed to the existence of a soft budget constraint, and therefore to a loss of accountability of the whole financial system, as it has always been believed that any shifts in regional expenditure would finally be assumed by the central government through the enlargement of regional shared taxes and/or transfers.

Another important problem of the Spanish equalization system concerns the fiscal capacity index, which systematically underestimates the regional collection of devolved taxes. As noted before, the normative collection used to calculate the Sufficiency Fund is obtained with the pre-devolution yield of each tax, updated with the federal tax resources growth rate. Because of the strong increase of tax bases – especially in those on property transfers – and the generalized improvement of tax administration, actual collections are far from the normative ones. In some territories, like Andalucía, Balearic Islands and Murcia, the actual collection is more than double the normative yield. As is shown in Table 7.2, the difference between both figures amounts to almost 7000 million euros.

From our point of view, if the fiscal capacity assessment is correct, some ACs would have potential revenue over, and some under, the real yield of these taxes, because of their different levels of fiscal effort.[21] A correct fiscal capacity index would attribute to each territory the revenue that it would receive with the standard tax rate, breaking away from the historical criterion and from the evolution of fiscal resources of the central government's budget.

Table 7.2   Actual and normative collection in devolved taxes

	Actual Collections (thousands €)	Normative Collections (thousands €)	Actual/Normative Collections (ratios)
Andalucía	2 734 732	1 275 395	2.14
Aragón	481 734	334 240	1.44
Asturias	284 625	239 672	1.19
Balearic	456 824	204 759	2.23
Canarias	486 073	384 831	1.26
Cantabria	215 373	110 996	1.94
Castile-León	726 800	502 348	1.45
Castilla-La Mancha	479 490	256 290	1.87
Catalonia	3 447 198	1 985 877	1.74
Com. Valenciana	2 093 283	1 118 371	1.87
Extremadura	187 570	132 395	1.42
Galicia	590 748	476 465	1.24
Madrid	3 364 702	2 047 264	1.64
Murcia	453 882	173 069	2.62
La Rioja	121 866	64 000	1.90
TOTAL	16 124 900	9 305 972	1.73

Source: Elaborated by the authors from Ministerio de Economía y Hacienda (2006).

With respect to expenditure needs, we have already explained the complex system of assessment, which introduces a number of ad hoc adjustments, distorting the result of the measurement obtained using the agreed variables. The most important of those adjustments, the status quo rule, maintains the link between the system and the historical criterion of the effective cost, thus perpetuating pre-devolution existing differences in public services provision.

Another important issue that has always been controversial relates to the variables – and their weights – used in the expenditure needs measurement. It is true enough that all of them try to reflect differences in the cost of providing services due to special geographical or demographical conditions. However, there is no empirical background to support the variables that were chosen, and particularly their respective weights. In this context, it is not inaccurate to say that the expenditure needs assessment has always been a political negotiation, in which the desired results oriented the process.

There is one important matter related to the expenditure needs assessment that should be noted. As it was pointed out before, there is an adjustment that distributes part of the Sufficiency Fund within low per capita income ACs. Because there is no empirical background showing the greater costs of providing public services in less developed territories, this leads to an over-weighting of the fiscal capacity index in the equalization system.[22]

As a result of all the aforementioned, the expenditure needs index does not adequately reflect differences in the demand and supply conditions regarding public services. A technical approach to the issue is necessary if stability of the whole system is desired. With no empirical background, there is an important incentive to re-negotiate continuously the design of the equalization transfer, in order to alter the variables used, and their respective weights.

There is another problem that should be solved if equalization transfer stability is to be achieved. We already pointed out the inexistence of an explicit equity target within the current equalization system legislation. Therefore, it is difficult to evaluate its results in terms of redistributive effects. However, the implicit equity target of the system is, as it was explained above, aimed at closing 100 percent of the fiscal gap between regional fiscal capacity and expenditure needs. Thus, all the ACs should have the same resources per adjusted population[23] after the distribution of the Sufficiency Fund. This net equalization result is by no means achieved in the current system, due to the important adjustments suffered by the assessed expenditure needs. The information in Figure 7.1 shows that there is an important difference between those communities that benefited the most from the effective cost method and the status quo rule, like La Rioja and Extremadura, with resources per adjusted inhabitant that exceed in more than 15 points the national average, and those regions that were more affected by the effective cost and some modulation rules, like the Balearic Islands, whose resources are almost 20 points below average.

Apparently, the results display no clear distributive pattern, and that encourages some regions to renegotiate the whole system with the argument that they are being penalized by the equalization system, through an incorrect expenditure needs assessment. And because those renegotiations have always guaranteed the status quo, the central government has to provide a bigger share of its own resources. In this context, we think that the government of the nation should be highly interested in finding an equalization system that has an explicit equity target, accepted by both its recipients and contributors.

In spite of the problems just mentioned, it does not mean that no equalization is achieved. In fact, an important redistribution is implemented, with a substantial reduction of inter-regional differences, as is showed in columns (2) and (5) of Table 7.3. The ratio of the largest and the lowest

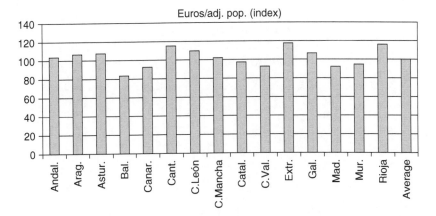

Euros/adj. pop. (index)

Note: * The information in the figure corresponds with the financial situation of each AC related to a homogeneous level of expenditure competences. Therefore, resources devoted to finance public services that have been singularly devolved to some regions are not included. The adjusted population was obtained with the share of the regions in the variables used in 2001 to assess expenditure needs (with 2004 values).

Source: Elaborated by the authors from Ministerio de Economía y Hacienda (2006) and Instituto Nacional de Estadística (Padrón 2004)

Figure 7.1   Total guaranteed resources (normative tax collection plus Sufficiency Fund) per adjusted population*

fiscal capacity is 3.18, while the ratio of the regions with the highest and the lowest total resources descends to 1.40.

Another important shortcoming of the current equalization system is that re-ranking is performed with no clear criteria: if we assume that fiscal capacity and expenditure needs are properly measured, some of the high fiscal capacity ACs – namely Balearic Islands, Madrid and Catalonia – end up having less per capita resources than some of the low fiscal capacity regions. This is one of the most controversial results of the Sufficiency Fund at the moment, because it shows that a positive discrimination with developing purposes is implemented through equalization grants. We already pointed out that equalization and development transfers have different targets, and thus require distinct designs. For that reason, mixing them up in the same instrument can lead to a lack of transparency and horizontal equity, and it makes it difficult to evaluate its results.

Finally, there is an important problem in the Spanish equalization design from the dynamic point of view. In contrast with most of the equalization systems studied, the Sufficiency Fund is not periodically adjusted with the regional evolution of fiscal capacity and needs. The transfer allocated to

Table 7.3   *Regional resources per adjusted population before and after the distribution of the Sufficiency Fund*

	Fiscal Resources			Total Resources (Taxes and Transfers)		
	(1) Euros/adj. pop.	(2) Index	(3) Position	(4) Euros/adj. pop.	(5) Index	(6) Position
Balearic*	1804	139.4	1	1548	83.5	15
Madrid*	1770	136.7	2	1709	92.2	2
Catalonia	1584	122.4	3	1801	97.2	10
Aragón	1447	111.8	4	1977	106.7	6
La Rioja	1336	103.2	5	2151	116.1	2
Cantabria	1320	102.0	6	2133	115.1	3
Asturias	1316	101.7	7	1991	107.5	5
Valencia	1268	98.0	8	1716	92.6	12
Castilla-León	1242	96.0	9	2030	109.6	4
Galicia	1111	85.8	10	1975	106.6	7
Murcia	1032	79.7	11	1754	94.7	11
Castilla-La Mancha	1031	79.7	12	1890	102.0	9
Andalucía	1027	79.3	13	1923	103.8	8
Extremadura	896	69.2	14	2176	117.4	1
Canary	566	43.8	15	1716	92.6	13
Average	1294.79	100		1853	100	

Note: * Because of their respective negative Sufficiency Funds, these ACs have final resources that are lower than their respective fiscal ones.

Source: Elaborated by the authors.

each community was calculated for the first year of the current system, and updated each of the following years with the central government's collection growth rate. As a result, and taking into consideration the strong increase in the population of certain regions, the whole system shows a slight diverging trend, in the sense that the differences shown in Figure 7.1 and Table 7.3 are slowly increasing.

4   THE REFORM OF THE SPANISH EQUALIZATION TRANSFER SYSTEM

The whole regional financial system will very likely be reformed in the near future, at least to incorporate some of the changes included in the Statutes of Autonomy just passed. Thus, it is a good time to try to gather all the important issues that should be changed, as well as the different alternatives that can be used to solve the problems mentioned above.

In the current context, the search for a new Equalization Grant should deal with some restrictions. First of all, it should try to achieve more equitable results, responding to an explicit equity target. For that purpose, the system should tend to produce relatively more benefits for the worst positioned regions. However, it is difficult to think about a reform that translates into direct losses for regional governments. From a realistic point of view, it has to be assumed that no community would accept a new equalization system that would result in a worse-off financial situation.[24] Thus, it is likely that the convergence of the results will be more easily implemented from the dynamic point of view and that the gradualism of the reforms seems to be a clear solution for the main financial restrictions. And last, but not least, the reform of the system should generate the lowest possible cost to the central government.[25]

The first task of the reform should be to determine explicitly the equity standard of the equalization system. In this matter, we have to insist on the idea that the central government plays the main role in deciding on how much equalization will be achieved. However, if the inter-regional redistribution generated by the equalization transfer is not accepted by both its recipients and contributors, instability of the system is guaranteed. Thus, the participation of regional governments in the decision process is crucial, trying to find a formula that fits everyone (or at least most of its participants).[26] How much redistribution is socially desired is a political decision anyway. From the technical perspective, we can just show the alternatives, and its advantages and shortcomings.

There are basically two alternatives in choosing the intensity of equalization. On the one hand, a *net equalization* can be achieved, meaning that all regional differences will be assessed and eliminated. As a result, all sub-central governments will be able to supply the same level of public services. On the other hand, *gross equalization* tries to reduce, but not to eliminate, inter-regional differences; that reduction of differences can be done from both sides (over and under the average or standard value), or just from the lower perspective of the standard. In the former case, positive transfers to low capacity regions are (at least partially) financed by negative grants (payments) of the richest territories. In the latter, although the poorest areas receive positive transfers with equalization purposes, high fiscal capacity regions remain in a better-off financial position, being able to provide more public services.

There seems to have been a bigger support for a net equalization scheme in the Spanish system, although the current statutory debate argues that equalization grants should be devoted to finance just essential, and not all devolved, public services. So, it is possible that, from now on, the equalization system will not try to assess all inter-regional differences in fiscal capacity, but only those that could generate distinct conditions in the access to essential services.

What seems to be obvious from a technical point of view is that the distribution of equalization transfers should not generate large changes in the ranking of the regional abilities of providing services. It is difficult to justify the purpose of equalization if re-rankings are allowed. However, it would be important to define what we mean by that, as there has been some confusion in the political debate about it. We have to insist on the idea that the purpose of an equalization transfer is to allow all territories to provide similar levels of public services with similar levels of fiscal effort. Therefore, not allowed ranking changes refer to the financial situation of sub-central governments before and after the distribution of the grant. The evaluation of the system design should compare regional fiscal normative collection with total (fiscal and transfers) resources. As far as it improves equity, there is a case for a reduction (or even elimination) of regional differences. On the contrary, such a justification does not exist from an equity point of view if re-rankings are achieved.[27]

As far as the special foral regime regions (Comunidades Forales) are concerned, it has to be remarked that the Basque Country and Navarra participate neither in the equalization system, nor in the ordinary regional financial system. This absence is the origin of an important horizontal imbalance, resulting in much larger public resources for these territories. Any reform of the equalization system aimed at guaranteeing similar levels of public services in all the regions should take into account this circumstance.

Once the equalization target and the desired redistribution intensity are decided upon, there are different ways of implementing the transfer. Even in the context of bigger tax shares in PIT and consumption taxes, a vertical grant will still be necessary, because some vertical imbalance will remain – amounting to approximately 8000 million euros if 2004 figures are used.

Provided that the historical criterion (through the effective cost method) is still the main distribution pattern behind the results of the system, and taking into account that the economical and demographical characteristics of ACs have changed substantially since the beginning of the devolution process, we would suggest making a shift in the whole philosophy of the system, trying to steer it towards a scheme that takes into account the overall regional budget, and not only devolved services and taxes. This could be possible using a standardized budget methodology, which would determine both the regional standard of expenditures and taxes.

As far as the fiscal capacity index is concerned, it should be assessed in a more realistic way, although real collections may not be used if incentives for an efficient administration of devolved taxes are to be maintained. While no official figures on regional tax bases are available, a proxy variable (GDP, for instance) could be used to calculate the normative tax rate. Regional fiscal capacity on those taxes where ACs have regulation and administrative powers would therefore be obtained by applying the normative rate to the regional tax base. In the case of taxes regulated and administered by the central government, there should not be any problem when using actual collections for the measurement of fiscal capacity.

It seems that a new method for assessing expenditure needs is required, as it was remarked previously, to avoid the instability of the current system. First of all, we would suggest avoiding the use of variables that have no empirical background regarding higher provision costs. Any inclusion – and the corresponding weight – of the variables should be empirically justified. Meanwhile, the simplest and most transparent expenditure needs index is probably the weighted number of potential users.

There are some services, like the police, that are used by all citizens, while others, like education, are just devoted to a certain group of them. In the former case, regional population would be a good approach to expenditure needs, while in the latter, enrolled students would do better. Furthermore, it is important to note that if we use the number of real users as a measure of needs, we would discriminate against those territories that, having fewer resources and public inputs, cannot supply enough services, thus reducing the number of users. In that case, the number of people under a certain age would fit better than the number of enrolled students (except for compulsory education, where both numbers should coincide). Finally, it is known that there are certain groups of population (the elderly and children) that use certain public services (health) more intensively than others (young people). If the potential demand was to be estimated, and considering that the demographical characteristics of each region are diverse, it would be necessary to weight those groups to assess those kinds of differences in the expenditure needs index.

A more specific question that should be taken into account is the necessity to separate education from general services in the expenditure needs assessment. As it was previously remarked, educational services are used by a certain group of population, the weight of which in each territory does not have to be the same as the total population weight. For that reason, it seems that using a special expenditure needs index for education services would enhance equity and transparency, without making the system too complex.

Whatever the methodology of the expenditure needs measurement, it is absolutely essential to avoid ad hoc adjustments. These kinds of special rules have always helped to reach political agreements in the short run, but at the same time they have reduced transparency and simplicity, encouraging log-rolling and constant re-negotiations of the system.[28]

From a dynamic point of view, a good equalization system requires periodical adjustments, which can address the evolution of regional fiscal capacity and expenditure needs. From our point of view, it is correct to have the total amount of the equalization transfer evolve with central tax collection, therefore guaranteeing its sustainability within the central budget. However, it is by no means justified to have each region's share unchanged with regard to the evolution of its own resources and population, because divergences on that evolution would lead to differences (or to their enlargement) in the resources allocated to each region.

A different matter is how often the whole regional financial system should be evaluated. To that purpose, we think that the usual five-year periodical revision is good enough to capture the long-term trends that cannot be addressed by the proposed annual adjustments. In these revisions, changes in the central–regional share of public resources could be adjusted if the income-elasticity of their respective expenditures shows important differences.

We are aware that most of the proposals above are difficult to implement without generating some costs to the central government and/or certain regions. However, we think that they would help in building up a more stable regional financial system, while they would achieve better results from the equity perspective. Besides, those costs could be dissolved in the long term, by a gradual application of the reform.

Finally, we would like to remark that intergovernmental cooperation and exchange of statistical and fiscal information should be fostered in order to improve the transparency and accuracy of the equalization system.

NOTES

1. Nevertheless, there is still an intense debate about the state model underlying the Constitution. An important part of the Spanish population and some ACs have interpreted the constitutional text in a way that leads to a highly uniform provision of public services, with a narrow margin for diversity, while some argue about the necessity of reinterpreting it in federal terms, allowing for more inter-regional diversity.
2. See Herrero (2005) for an explanation of this process.
3. The recently passed Statute of Autonomy of Catalonia stipulates an enlargement of regional shares in PIT (50 percent), VAT (50 percent) and excise taxes (58 percent), which will presumably be extended to the rest of the ACs.
4. The first Autonomous Community that passed a new statute, Valencia, did not introduce such a change explicitly but, in an attempt to avoid certain future problems, a special clause was included to guarantee that the Community of Valencia will never be worse off in financial terms than any other community. Nevertheless, in the current state of

affairs, the main opposition party, which did not accept the Catalonian Statute, has filed – just as the Spanish Ombudsman has – a claim of unconstitutionality before the Constitutional Court against this statute, which is still being discussed. The other statutes, from Valencia and Andalucía were accepted by the main parliamentary parties, in spite of the fact that the Andalucian statute contains several norms that are identical to the Catalonian ones.

5. It is important not to identify the concept of fiscal capacity with revenue collection, because the latter is a result of both the level of economic activity and regional fiscal policy. An assessment of fiscal capacity based on actual collections would introduce an undesirable disincentive for an efficient administration of taxes; as the collected amount grows larger, the equalization transfer grows smaller. Therefore, a good fiscal capacity index should be a reflection of the evolution of tax bases, but not of tax rates in the region. For a further explanation of fiscal capacity indexes, see Boex and Martínez-Vázquez (2004). Although this is a controversial issue, we think that fiscal capacity and fiscal effort should be distinguished in the design of Equalization Grants. If a region has a high fiscal capacity, it should lead to a lower regional share of equalization transfers. On the contrary, a higher regional fiscal effort (higher tax rates, lower fiscal benefits or more efficient tax administration) as compared with the national standard should be irrelevant in the calculation of equalization transfers.

6. The intensity of equalization varies among countries, from very centralized perspectives (Australia) to others that do not accept any general equalization transfer (USA), or where the target is to reduce differences to 'tolerable' levels (like in the case of Switzerland).

7. See Boadway (2006) for an explanation of the main arguments that justify the use of equalization transfers in a decentralized context.

8. Ahmad and Brosio (2006, p. 20): 'While the grounds for establishing equalization transfers are clear, the degree of equalization to be introduced into the system is subject to controversy. First, in general, people have different views about equity. Second, satisfying horizontal equity may conflict with welfare maximization applied at the level of the whole country.'

9. This payment can be explicit or implicit, depending on the design of the equalization system. In Germany, the richest *Länder* have negative transfers (payments) that are used to finance the positive ones allocated to the low fiscal capacity regions. In Canada, on the other hand, it is the federal government that distributes a vertical transfer within those provinces with scarce fiscal resources. Although it is the central government that holds the burden of the transfer, it is obvious that the resources it allocates through equalization transfers come from taxes that are collected mainly in the richest territories.

10. In this case, the country as a whole tries to improve the situation of the poorest regions, trying to apply effectively the constitutional principle of inter-territorial solidarity.

11. Here we accept the concept of fiscal capacity as a general expression of the amount of resources that can be obtained as a consequence of some kind of control over the tax bases. We do not take into account the more general problem of territorial assignment of taxes, like the efforts put into trying to attain a fiscal balance between central and sub-central governments.

12. See Herrero and Martínez-Vázquez (2007).

13. A further explanation can be found in Ruiz-Huerta, Herrero and Vizán (2002).

14. It could be said that, because of political restrictions, the objective of the different negotiations was to obtain the maximum consensus, and the only way to do so was to assure a strong Pareto improvement for all the regions. This line of negotiation has created a biased incentive to get more money from the central government and to elude a clear assumption of fiscal responsibility.

15. From the beginning of the fiscal decentralization process, the devolution of resources was linked to the so-called effective cost, which was supposed to be the cost of maintaining the pre-devolution level of public services. It was the sum of direct and indirect current costs of supplying the services, plus the replacement investment. The central government was committed to guaranteeing an amount of resources to the ACs that would, at least, cover that cost.

16. In the 2001 agreement negotiation process, the central government obliged the communities that did not have competences on health care to accept them as a condition to enjoy the advantages of the new financing system.
17. This includes basically all population, except for those citizens who have statutory health coverage.
18. In the case of negative transfers (Madrid and Balearic Islands), this rule applies only if the national growth rate is larger than the regional one. If it is smaller, then the regional growth rate is applied.
19. The only guarantee rule introduced into the system was the one applied to cover the increase of health care expenditure. It has had a very restrictive interpretation and so the quantities assigned have been very small (for a wider interpretation, see López-Laborda, 2006). Nevertheless, the intense growth of health care expenditure led to a new agreement in 2005 between central government and the ACs, as a result of which, new resources for the sub-central health system were allocated by the central government.
20. Ley Orgánica de Financiación de las Comunidades Autónomas LOFCA (Financial Act of the Autonomous Communities), passed in 1981, and reformed in 1997 and 2001.
21. The differences in terms of fiscal effort could come from the regulatory changes of tax elements and/or the improvements in administration and collection of the taxes that are managed by the ACs. There is no change in fiscal effort if tax bases increase or decrease because of economical or non-economical reasons independent of regional policies.
22. For a further explanation on this matter, see Castells, Sorribas and Vilalta (2005).
23. We are now referring to the regional population adjusted by the need variables included in the system and summarized in Table 7.1.
24. There is something that should be noted about the impossibility of generating losses on some or all of the regional governments. If an absolute perspective is used, the total amount of money received by each community should not decrease, but it could be possible that some territories would make some progress in financial terms. But if losses are measured in relative terms, meaning that no community could accrue a smaller share of the total pool of regional resources, then it would be impossible to implement any reform.
25. The end of the devolution process, from the expenditure side, calls for a more stable financial system, based on a hard budget constraint that pushes the ACs towards a more responsible behavior in fiscal terms.
26. What we are trying to point out is that it is not a good strategy to ignore the interests of regional governments in the decision-making process. The best way to assure some stability to the sub-central financial system would be the unanimity rule. However, as clearly set out with the German model, and particularly with the decision-making process within the Bundesrat, unanimity can lead to a consensus trap, preventing any reforms from being passed.
27. However, we have to insist on the idea that this lack of justification of re-rankings only applies, as we said before, if fiscal capacity and expenditure needs are properly measured.
28. At least it would be necessary to avoid the consolidation in the AC budgets of those resources that are used at specific times to assure the participation and acceptance of a new agreement by some of them.

BIBLIOGRAPHY

Ahmad, E. and G. Brosio (2006), 'Introduction: Fiscal Federalism – A Review of Developments in the Literature and Policy', in E. Ahmad and G. Brosio (eds), *Handbook of Fiscal Federalism*, Cheltenham, UK and Northampton, MA, USA: Edward Elgar, pp. 1–29.

Boadway, R. (2004), *How Well is the Equalization System Reducing Fiscal Disparities?* http://www.econ.queensu.ca/faculty/boadway/PEI-equalization.pdf. Accessed 22 November 2007.

Boadway, R. (2006), 'Intergovernmental Redistributive Transfers: Efficiency and Equity', in E. Ahmad and G. Brosio (eds), *Handbook of Fiscal Federalism*, Cheltenham, UK and Northampton, MA, USA: Edward Elgar, pp. 355–80.

Boex, J. and J. Martínez-Vázquez (2004), 'Designing Intergovernmental Equalization Transfers with Imperfect Data: Concepts, Practices and Lessons', Conference on Challenges in the Design of Fiscal Equalization and Intergovernmental Transfers, Atlanta, 3–5 October 2004.

Castells, A., P. Sorribas and M. Vilalta (2005), *Las Subvenciones de Nivelación en la Financiación de las Comunidades Autónomas: Análisis de la Situación Actual y Propuestas de Reforma*, Barcelona: Universidad de Barcelona.

Herrero, A. (2005), 'Aplicación de un fondo de nivelación en el marco de un sistema de financiación autonómica estable', *Investigaciones*, Instituto de Estudios Fiscales, No. 1/05.

Herrero, A. and J. Martínez-Vázquez (2007), 'La Nivelación en el Marco de la Financiación de las Comunidades Autónomas', *Papeles de Trabajo*, Instituto de Estudios Fiscales.

Instituto Nacional de Estadística (2004), *Padrón 2004*, http://www.ine.es/jaxi/menu.do?type=pcaxis&path=%Ft20%2Fe260&file=inebase&L=0. Accessed 20 November 2007.

López-Laborda, J. (2006), 'Las Haciendas Autonómicas en 2005: La Financiación del Gasto Sanitario y la Propuesta de Reforma Del Estatut', in various authors, *Informe de Comunidades Autónomas 2005*, Barcelona: Instituto de Derecho Público, pp. 599–616.

Ministerio de Economía y Hacienda (2006), *Financiación de las Comunidades Autónomas por los Impuestos Cedidos (IRPF, IVA e Impuestos Especiales), Fondo de Suficiencia y Garantías de Financiación de los Servicios de Asistencia Sanitaria, en el Año 2004 y Liquidación Definitiva de Dicho Ejercicio*, Madrid, http://www.meh.es/Portal/Estadistica+e+Informes/Estadisticas+territoriales/. Accessed 20 November 2007.

Ruiz-Huerta, J. and A. Herrero (2005), 'La financiación de las comunidades autónomas españolas: evolución, situación actual y perspectivas de futuro', *El Debate Político*, **3**, pp. 118–56.

Ruiz-Huerta, J., A. Herrero and C. Vizán (2002), 'La Reforma del Sistema de Financiación Autonómica', in various authors, *Informe de Comunidades Autónomas 2001*, Barcelona: Instituto de Derecho Público, pp. 485–511.

PART III

Tax administration

8. Tax coordination under the Canadian tax system[1]

Paul Berg-Dick, Michel Carreau, Deanne Field and Mireille Éthier

1 INTRODUCTION

Canada is comprised of ten provinces and three territories. The responsibilities of the federal and provincial governments are set out in the Canadian Constitution. Provinces delegate some powers and responsibilities to municipalities within their jurisdiction, and the federal government delegates some of its powers and responsibilities to territorial governments.

Under the Constitution, the federal government and provincial governments have access to most of the major tax bases. Provinces are limited, however, to direct taxation within their jurisdiction:

> A direct tax is one which is demanded from the very person who it is intended or desired should pay it. Indirect taxes are those which are demanded from one person in the expectation and intention that he shall indemnify himself at the expense of another. The direct/indirect test is a legal, not economic, one. (John Stuart Mill, [1848] 1909, Book V, Chapter 3, p. 1)

Within Canada's relatively decentralized structure, provinces have considerable flexibility with respect to taxation. Federal and provincial governments use a variety of tax fields to raise revenue to ensure that no one item or activity bears an excessive tax burden. This means that, in practice, both the federal and provincial governments jointly occupy most tax fields.

The three main tax fields jointly occupied by the federal and provincial governments in Canada are: income taxes on individuals (personal income tax), income taxes on businesses (corporation income tax) and sales taxes. The federal and provincial governments occupy all of these taxation fields to varying degrees.

The Figures 8.1 and 8.2 demonstrate the amount, and breakdown by source, of federal and provincial revenue raised by governments in Canada for the 2004–05 fiscal year. In 2004–05, the Government of Canada raised $212 billion in tax revenue. Provinces raised an amount comparable to that

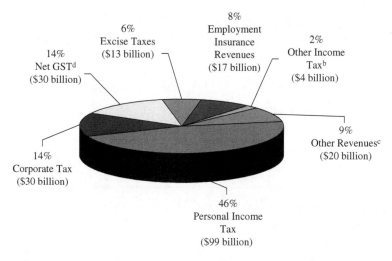

Notes:
ᵃ Does not include Canada Pension Plan/Quebec Pension Plan (CPP/QPP) contributions.
ᵇ Includes non-resident income tax and other withholding tax.
ᶜ Includes revenues from Crown corporations and program revenue.
ᵈ Goods and services tax (GST) revenues net of GST credit.
   Public Accounts Basis.

Source: 2006 Budget, Finance Canada.

Figure 8.1   Federal revenue[a]

of the federal government ($204 billion in 2004–05). In addition, provinces receive, on average 39 percent of total revenues as federal cash transfers. The three main tax fields – personal income tax, corporation income tax and sales tax – generated 74 percent of federal revenues and 54 percent of provincial revenues.

The personal income tax system is the largest source of revenue for Canadian governments. Personal income tax is levied on the income of individuals and the tax base is individual taxable income earned in a calendar year. The income base is broad and includes income from employment, investment, non-incorporated business and pensions. While the personal income tax system is based on self-assessment, a large portion of personal income tax revenues are deducted at source by employers and remitted to governments.

The corporation income tax system imposes a tax on the profits and capital gains of incorporated businesses prior to their distribution to individuals. The income base on which the corporation income tax is applied is broad with most sources of income being subject to tax, net of the

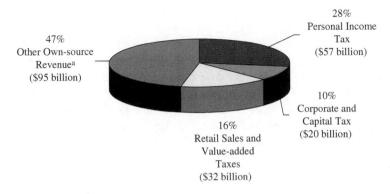

Note: ᵃ Includes Crown royalties, lotteries, gaming and liquor revenues.
Financial Management System Basis.

Source: Statistics Canada.

Figure 8.2 *Provincial own-source revenue*

deductions for expenses incurred to earn that income. Corporations may choose any 12-month period as their taxation year.

In contrast to taxes that are linked to income, sales taxes are linked to the amount of consumption by taxpayers. At the federal level, a value-added tax – the goods and services tax (GST) – is very broadly based[2] and is levied at a single rate of 6 percent throughout the production chain. However, to ensure that the tax applies only to the value added by the business enterprise, input tax credits are provided. Generally, these are equal to the value of GST paid on business inputs.

As a result of the joint occupancy of these three main tax fields, the federal government and many provincial governments have entered into administration agreements covering each of the tax fields. These administration agreements represent one of the main components of tax coordination between the federal and provincial governments.

This chapter will focus on efforts to coordinate taxation by the two main orders of government in Canada – the federal and provincial/territorial[3] governments. For income tax, Tax Collection Agreements cover the administration and collection of both personal and corporation income tax. For sales tax, Comprehensive Integrated Tax Coordination Agreements cover the harmonized sales tax, which exists in three provinces in Atlantic Canada. An administrative agreement has also been put in place in Quebec under which the Government of Quebec collects the federal GST within the province, along with the province's own value-added tax. The chapter will analyze the coordination elements inherent in each of these agreements.

2   INCOME TAX COORDINATION

The Tax Collection Agreements (TCAs) are the mechanism that was developed in Canada to deal with the fact that both the federal and provincial governments have the constitutional right to impose income taxes. These agreements are the major instrument for coordinating the federal and provincial income tax systems in Canada. They facilitate the joint occupancy of the income tax field in a coordinated manner.

When income taxes were first introduced, there was no coordination among the federal and provincial governments. There were many stages in the development of today's TCAs. Following Confederation in 1867, economic expansion and development were prominent. In order for the provinces to fund their new responsibilities and obligations, they sought a new source of revenue. As a result, provinces became the first order of government to tax income, with British Columbia imposing a provincial personal income tax in 1876, followed by other provinces taxing both personal and corporate income.

The federal government entered the income tax field in 1917, initially as a means of financing the costs of the First World War. This marked the beginning of joint occupancy of the income tax field. Subsequently, in the 1930s, as a result of falling government revenues and little or no cooperation between governments, joint occupancy of the income tax field led to a situation in Canada commonly described as a 'tax jungle'. During this time, combined federal and provincial marginal tax rates were very high and conflicting income tax rules were dominant.

The Great Depression (1929–39) marked an era in which Canada's economy began to falter, with governments running short of revenues. There was much tax competition among various jurisdictions across Canada. As a result, the federal government began to enter into tax collection arrangements with provinces. This led to the beginning of some coordination in the tax system. However, as discussed in the following sections, these arrangements were neither comprehensive nor universal.

2.1   Beginning of Income Tax Coordination

The Canadian tax structure changed profoundly during the Second World War. The major tax sources were gathered under a central fiscal authority to distribute the enormous financial burden of the war equitably, to raise funds efficiently and to minimize the impact of inflation.

In 1941, the provinces agreed to surrender both the personal and corporate income tax fields to the federal government for the duration of the war and for one year thereafter. In exchange, they received fixed annual payments.[4] Under the 1941 Wartime Tax Agreements, the federal government became the sole taxing authority. There was a single tax system across the country.

After the war ended in 1945, Tax Rental Agreements replaced the Wartime Tax Agreements. Under these new agreements, the federal government continued to be the sole taxing authority, with provinces receiving rental payments, that is, the federal government paid tax revenue to the provinces determined by agreed-upon per capita amounts. The Tax Rental Agreements were quite similar to the Wartime Tax Agreements, continuing the notion of a single tax system across the country. In 1947, Quebec decided to end its agreement with the federal government and created its own tax collection system for both personal and corporate income taxes. Quebec continues to design and administer its own personal and corporate tax to this day. The Tax Rental Agreements with the other provinces remained in place, with little modification, for several years.

In 1954, various factors, including an economic recession, changed the balance of federal–provincial spending and revenue-raising. As a result, the Tax Rental Agreements came under review once again. The era of Tax Sharing Agreements between federal and provincial governments began.

Under the Tax Sharing Agreements, the system of per capita tax rental payments changed to one of payments based on tax capacity, or a jurisdiction's ability to raise revenues. These payments were coupled with separate Equalization[5] payments for provinces based on tax 'incapacity'.

While Tax Sharing Agreements put provinces on a more equal footing with the federal government in the area of income taxation, and continued to ensure a certain degree of efficiency in the tax system, provinces could not set their own income tax rates nor could they use the income tax system for policy purposes. Even though tax revenues were shared with the provinces, the fact that the federal government set policy and collected taxes meant that there was a strong tendency for taxpayers to continue to see the federal government as the only entity taxing them. The inherent provincial component was not apparent.

2.2 Tax Collection Agreements

As a result of provincial demands, new Tax Collection Agreements (TCAs) were negotiated and put in place in 1962. While these agreements have been modified somewhat over the years, the basic principles underlying their creation have remained unchanged and they have become an important component of the current federal–provincial tax structure. The purpose of these agreements is to facilitate the imposition of income taxes by provinces, while maintaining the federal interest of a harmonized national income tax system.

Under the TCAs, provinces are responsible for their own income tax systems with provincial tax legislation and provincial tax policies operating alongside federal legislation and federal policy. This is not simply a federal system with payments to provinces.

TCAs exist with nine provinces (except Quebec) and three territories for personal income tax. For corporate income tax, these agreements are in place with seven provinces (except Quebec, Ontario[6] and Alberta) and three territories.

TCAs are the major instrument for coordinating the income tax systems in Canada, and they facilitate the joint occupancy of the income tax field. The TCAs provide a degree of consistency and harmony in the national tax system and simplify compliance for taxpayers. These agreements affect both policy and administration. Under the terms and conditions of the TCAs, the provincial tax structure is required to be harmonized to a certain degree with federal tax structure.

One of the major characteristics of the TCAs is agreement by provinces to adhere to a common tax base. A single, common, tax base prevents

---

BOX 8.1

The terms and conditions of the TCAs are relatively straightforward. The federal government agrees to:

1. Take responsibility for the actual collection of both federal and provincial taxes;
2. pay provinces the value of income tax assessed; and
3. administer (including issuing notices of assessment, auditing, and so on) provincial personal and corporate income taxes virtually free of charge.

In return, provinces agree to:

1. apply their tax rate to a common tax base;
2. maintain legislation similar to that of the federal government; and
3. provide the Minister of Finance and the Canada Revenue Agency (CRA) with the legal powers necessary to collect and administer their income taxes.

economic distortions across jurisdictions by ensuring that the treatment of income is uniform across provinces even though provincial tax systems may differ. Harmonization of the tax base also prevents double taxation, ensuring that all income is taxed, and is taxed only once. The adherence to a common tax base keeps the tax system simple for both taxpayers and administrators. It is such policy harmonization that makes the TCAs unique instruments of tax coordination – they are fundamentally different than a fee-for-service administrative agreement. The adherence to a common tax base is the primary reason for the federal government to absorb virtually all of the administrative costs associated with the collection of provincial taxes.

Policy harmonization among the federal and provincial governments is further assisted through the operation of the Federal–Provincial Committee on Taxation. This committee, chaired by the Assistant Deputy Minister, Tax Policy Branch, Department of Finance Canada, provides a forum in which the federal and provincial governments may discuss tax policy issues and examine their consequences for both the national and provincial economies. These discussions can be extremely useful in providing an exchange of information, with the potential of guiding policy developments in a common direction for the benefit of both national and regional economies. The committee meets at regular intervals to examine proposed tax policy changes, and ensure that these changes are regionally and nationally effective and appropriate. These discussions then form the basis for federal–provincial meetings in which Ministers of Finance shape national tax policies.

Single administration of federal and provincial income taxes benefits both taxpayers and governments. Taxpayers benefit from a reduction in overall compliance costs and increased simplicity in the operation of the tax system. These benefits arise as a result of:

1. more integration of federal and provincial tax policy, administration and rules of operation;
2. a single tax return;
3. a single audit;
4. a single appeal process; and
5. a single judicial process.

This results in an income tax system in Canada that is streamlined and efficient, also reducing administrative costs for governments.

Governments also enjoy cost savings because of economies of scale, benefiting all Canadians. The waste and duplication of dual administrations are avoided. To achieve these efficiencies, as noted earlier, the federal government has agreed to incur the costs of administration associated with the provincial tax systems.

All governments in Canada recognize the value of some harmonization in the national tax system. This is evidenced by the fact that there is a certain degree of consistency even among the provinces that have chosen not to enter into a TCA. For example, all provinces use the calendar year as the tax year for the personal income tax system, with individuals paying tax based on their province of residence as of 31 December. Within the corporation income tax system, non-agreeing provinces all start with the federal definition of income, and then make adjustments to that definition depending on provincial priorities. As a result, the default case is that the provincial definition would change as the definition of income changes at the federal level. In other words, provinces without a TCA must take specific legislative action if they do not wish to follow a change in the definition of income at the federal level. All provinces use the same 'permanent establishment' concept and an allocation formula under which taxable income is allocated based on a common formula, usually as the average of total gross revenue and total salaries and wages attributed to each jurisdiction.[7]

There is no specific coordinating organization that oversees the TCAs. There are three federal government entities involved in the administration of the agreements:

1. The Department of Finance is responsible for the policy matters relating to the TCAs and for making payments to provinces in respect of their share of assessed income taxes, as well as for informing provincial auditors about these payments.
2. The Canada Revenue Agency (CRA) collects, assesses, audits and enforces provincial legislation.
3. The Auditor General of Canada conducts an audit annually of the tax collection account.

2.2.1 TCAs from 1962 to 2001

Under the original TCAs, for personal income tax, the provincial governments agreed to base their tax as a percentage of federal tax (a tax-on-tax system). In other words, the federal government determined both the tax base and tax progressivity. Provinces could use surtaxes, low-income tax reductions and province-specific tax credits to alter the degree of progressivity in their province. Under these TCAs, provinces exercised the bulk of their policy flexibility through the use of tax credits. For corporate income tax, provincial governments agreed to the federal definition of taxable income. In this system, provinces set both tax rates and provide tax credits.

BOX 8.2   MacEACHEN GUIDELINES (1981)

Effective administration   The tax measure must be capable of being administered in an effective manner in order to preserve the efficiency and credibility of the system. This includes being within the legal jurisdiction of provinces.

Common tax base   The tax measure must respect the common tax base by not changing the federally defined personal and corporate income tax bases.

Free movement of capital, labor, goods and services   The tax measure must not impede the free flow of capital, goods, service and or labor within Canada.

Thus, provincial policy flexibility under these arrangements was largely provided through the use of tax credits under both personal and corporate TCAs. The federal government would, for a nominal fee, administer special measures on behalf of provinces so long as these measures satisfied certain criteria – often referred to as the 'MacEachen guidelines'. These guidelines were communicated in the 1981 federal Budget (see Department of Finance, 1981) tabled by the Honourable Alan MacEachen, and again discussed and summarized as in Box 8.1 in the federal government's publication *Federal Administration of Provincial Taxes: New Directions* (Department of Finance, 2000).

The tax arrangements provided a certain degree of flexibility in provincial tax policy but some provinces believed that their options for credits were limited and that the procedures to ensure that the guidelines were followed were cumbersome and insufficient. The federal government also faced challenges in the application of the MacEachen guidelines, sharing provincial concerns that they were not transparent.

The federal government found itself in the position of having to impose an imprecise set of criteria that affected provincial flexibility and created, at times, serious irritants. The criterion concerning the economic union caused the most difficulty. Provinces did not always accept the federal assessment of provincial measures as being harmful for the economic union. Provinces, while acknowledging the potential role for the federal government in protecting the economic union, believed that, on balance, those concerns did not warrant the loss of their tax policy flexibility, particularly if they viewed any potential negative impact of a provincial action to be relatively small.

If the federal government refused to administer a particular provincial tax credit because it did not meet the tests of the MacEachen guidelines, provinces did maintain the ability to self-administer these measures. In certain cases, provinces opted to do so, if they believed that the credit warranted the additional administrative burden.

While making important strides toward an appropriate balance between national harmonization and provincial flexibility from the previous tax rental arrangements, the original 1962 TCAs were seen, over time, as not meeting the evolving needs of both provinces and the federal government. However, change was slow to come and these agreements remained virtually unchanged until 1999, when another period of negotiations was initiated, with the major changes put in place in 2001 and the final agreements being signed in 2004.

2.2.2   2001 to present

The primary concern of the provincial governments was to be allowed more flexibility in determining the progressivity of their personal income tax, and not have to automatically match federal changes to the personal income tax rate structure, which could often have a serious impact on provincial revenues. In 2001, the TCAs for personal income tax were revised such that provincial governments could base their taxes as a function of federally determined taxable income. This made the personal income tax system more consistent with that of corporate income tax.

Both the federal government and provinces now have the flexibility to impose their own tax rates and brackets on a single definition of taxable income. Provinces apply separate multi-rate tax structures on federally determined taxable income. The ability to decide on their own tax rates gives the provinces more control over a major revenue source. Choosing separate tax brackets allows provinces to control the degree of progressivity in the provincial tax system in a more straightforward manner. Provincial governments, who often took criticism for federal policy decisions, have embraced this additional degree of 'insulation' from federal tax changes.

At the same time as the TCAs were modified to use taxable income as the common tax base for both personal and corporation income tax, new guidelines were developed for evaluating whether the federal government would administer provincial tax programs. The guidelines included in the current TCAs encompass the following principles:

- *The tax measure should not materially alter the common tax base, except by granting relief by way of a credit in respect of an outlay or an expense.* In other words, provinces may put in place tax credits in respect of certain expenses. In this way, they can encourage certain activities such as research and development or film production to be carried on in their jurisdiction. They are restricted to the use of credits since providing accelerated or additional deductions would result in a different tax base for federal and provincial purposes – that being viewed as the major benefit of a TCA. Provinces are also precluded from putting tax credits in place that would target particular components of income, and therefore encourage the reporting of that income in their jurisdiction.

- *The tax measure should not impede the free flow of capital, labor, goods and services.* In evaluating the tax measure, consideration will be given to whether the measure would have a material impact on the economic and fiscal base of other provinces. In particular, a tax measure should not provide preferential treatment only to income, capital or labor located outside the borders of the province with the requirement that these factors relocate to the province offering the measure.
- *The tax measure should be consistent with Canada's international obligations.* The federal government will not, for example, assist a province in the administration of a tax measure that would contravene a tax treaty.

These new guidelines are viewed as more transparent and precise by both the federal and provincial governments. While still relatively new, it is envisioned that these guidelines will be easier to apply and give rise to fewer irritants in the future.

Under the new TCAs, provinces can now use tax rates and brackets to achieve certain policy goals, in addition to the surtaxes, low-income tax reductions and province-specific tax credits, available previously. Provinces are using this additional freedom in different ways. In the current personal income tax system, the federal government utilizes four tax brackets and rates. One province has only one rate, while another province uses five brackets and rates. Each provincial government controls the progressivity of its own personal income tax. Tables 8.1 and 8.2 depict the provincial personal income tax rates that were in effect in 1999 under the original 'tax-on-tax' TCAs, as well as the rates and brackets for 2006 (under 'tax-on-income').

3   SALES TAX COORDINATION

There are currently two arrangements in place between the federal government and some provinces that provide for coordination of sales tax. The first

Table 8.1   Provincial tax rates – tax-on-tax – 1999

	Basic Rate	Surtax[c]
Newfoundland and Labrador	69.0	10.0
Prince Edward Island	58.5	10.0
Nova Scotia	57.5	10.0
New Brunswick	60.0	8.0
Quebec[a]		0.3
Ontario	39.5	20.0, 56.0
Manitoba	48.5[b]	2.0
Saskatchewan	48.0[b]	15.0[d]
Alberta	44.0[b]	8.0
British Columbia	49.5	30.0, 49.0
Nunavut	45.0	–
Northwest Territories	45.0	–
Yukon	50.0	5.0

Notes:
[a]   Not readily comparable because Quebec maintains its own PIT system and applies
      provincial rates directly on taxable income. Rates range from 20% to 26%.
[b]   Flat tax: Manitoba and Saskatchewan – 2% of net income; Alberta 0.5% of taxable
      income.
[c]   Provincial surtaxes apply on provincial PIT payable in excess of: NF – $7900; PEI –
      $5200; NS – $10 000; NB – $13 500; SASK – $4000; ALTA – $3500; YUK – $6000. ONT
      surtax – 20% on provincial PIT payable between $3750 & $4681; 56% on provincial PIT
      payable in excess of $4681. BC surtax – 30% on provincial PIT payable between $5300 &
      $8660; 49% on provincial PIT payable in excess of $8660. QUE surtax on basic
      provincial tax net of non-refundable tax credits. MAN surtax on those with net income
      in excess of $30 000 through application of a formula.
[d]   Additional debt reduction surtax, on the aggregate of basic Saskatchewan tax and flat
      tax, of 10% less a general reduction of $150.

arrangement is the Comprehensive Integrated Tax Coordination Agreements
(CITCAs), under which the federal government is the administrator of the
tax for Newfoundland and Labrador, Nova Scotia and New Brunswick.
Similar to the TCAs, the CITCAs are policy and administration agreements.
The second arrangement is between Canada and Quebec, under which the
province is the administrator of federal and provincial value-added taxes
within Quebec. Unlike the CITCAs, the arrangement with Quebec is more of
an administration instrument than a policy instrument.

3.1   Prior to Sales Tax Coordination

The federal government first introduced a federal sales tax in 1924, which
was levied on the price of goods sold by the manufacturer. The tax also

Table 8.2   Provincial tax rates – tax-on-income – 2006

	Basic Tax		Surtax
	Rates (%)	Brackets ($)	
Federal[a]	15.25	0	No surtax
	22.00	36 378	
	26.00	72 756	
	29.00	118 285	
Provincial or Territorial			
Newfoundland and Labrador	10.57	0	9% of tax above $7032
	16.16	29 590	
	18.02	59 180	
Prince Edward Island	9.80	0	10% of tax above $5200
	13.80	30 754	
	16.70	61 509	
Nova Scotia	8.79	0	10% of tax above $10 000
	14.95	29 590	
	16.67	59 180	
	17.50	93 000	
New Brunswick	9.68	0	No surtax
	14.82	33 450	
	16.52	66 902	
	17.84	108 768	
Quebec	16.00	0	No surtax
	20.00	28 710	
	24.00	57 430	
Ontario[b]	6.05	0	20% of tax above $4016
	9.15	34 758	+ 36% of tax above $5065
	11.16	69 517	
Manitoba	10.90	0	No surtax
	13.50	30 544	
	17.40	65 000	
Saskatchewan	11.00	0	No surtax
	13.00	37 579	
	15.00	107 367	
Alberta	10.00	0	No surtax
British Columbia	6.05	0	No surtax
	9.15	33 755	
	11.70	67 511	
	13.70	77 511	
	14.70	94 121	

Table 8.2   (continued)

| | Basic Tax | | Surtax |
	Rates (%)	Brackets ($)	
Nunavut	4.00	0	No surtax
	7.00	36 378	
	9.00	72 756	
	11.50	118 285	
Northwest Territories	5.90	0	No surtax
	8.60	34 555	
	12.20	69 110	
	14.05	112 358	
Yukon	7.04	0	5% of tax above $6000
	9.68	36 378	
	11.44	72 756	
	12.76	118 285	

Notes:
a   In Quebec, the federal component of tax is reduced by 16.5% abatement of basic federal tax.
b   Provincial health premium also applies on taxable income in excess of $20 000.

applied to imports, based on their value at the border. Alberta was the first province to impose a sales tax, doing so in 1936, and ending it the following year. To this day, Alberta has not reintroduced a general sales tax. However, other provinces have put in retail sales taxes over the years – Saskatchewan in 1937, Quebec in 1940, British Columbia in 1948, New Brunswick and Newfoundland in 1950, Nova Scotia in 1959, Prince Edward Island in 1960, Ontario in 1961 and Manitoba in 1968.

3.2   Beginning of Sales Tax Coordination

In 1991, the federal government replaced its outdated federal sales tax on manufactured products with a value-added tax – the goods and services tax (GST). At the onset, the tax was charged at a rate of 7 percent but was reduced to 6 percent as of 1 July 2006. The GST applies to the majority of goods and services sold in Canada. However, there are a number of areas where the GST does not apply, such as basic groceries, most health and dental services, most financial, legal, educational services and child care services, exported goods and services and residential rents.

At the time of the GST introduction, all of the provinces except Alberta levied some form of retail sales tax. This meant that in most parts of the country, businesses and consumers continued to contend with two different sales tax systems. The federal government recognized the inefficiencies inherent in such a system and began to take steps toward improving coordination and harmonization between the federal and provincial sales tax systems.

The benefits of these arrangements are numerous. For vendors and suppliers, it means one set of rules for the collection and remittance of sales taxes, and usually one set of forms. Also, there is some consistency with respect to the application and interpretation, by governments, of sales tax legislation. For consumers, because the tax bases are similar, there is uniform application of sales taxes in any one transaction. This makes it easier for consumers to know when tax will or will not apply. For governments, the benefits of joint administration are clear. The virtual elimination of overlap of services by governments provides savings. Such savings, ultimately, benefit all taxpayers. In addition, the arrangements provide for some harmonization of sales taxes. Such consistency between governments is desirable.

3.3　Comprehensive Integrated Tax Coordination Agreements

In 1994, the Government of Canada, through its House of Commons Standing Committee on Finance conducted an extensive review of sales tax reform options. In a 1994 Report entitled *Towards Replacing the Goods and Services Tax* (Department of Finance, 1994), the Finance Committee concluded that a harmonized value-added tax was the best option. After the release of the Finance Committee's report, the federal government actively sought agreements with provinces interested in harmonization. In April 1996, the federal government announced that Memoranda of Understanding between the federal government and the governments of Nova Scotia, New Brunswick and Newfoundland and Labrador outlining the process to harmonize the federal and provincial sales taxes had been agreed to. In a 23 October 1996 News Release it was announced that harmonization of the sales tax systems would take place on 1 April 1997. As described in the same News Release, broad elements of the final agreements included the replacement of the current federal and provincial sales tax systems with a single combined value-added tax – the harmonized sales tax (HST) – and single administration of both federal and provincial sales taxes. The detailed agreements are known as the CITCAs.

As noted earlier in respect of the TCAs, the CITCAs have both policy and administration elements. The federal government and the three participating provinces have established a Tax Policy Review Committee. The committee, chaired by the Government of Canada, is responsible for reviewing issues regarding the legislation and administration governing the HST. This includes the tax base, tax rates, tax structure and management of the shared revenue pool. On an ongoing basis, the committee reviews the harmonized tax system and its operation to ensure that it is working at its most efficient and optimal level.

The tax base on which the provincial portion of the HST rate is applied is common with the tax base on which the federal portion of the HST tax rate is applied. Changes to the provincial portion of the tax base are possible. Proposals for changes of this nature must be brought to the attention of the Tax Policy Review Committee.

Federal changes to the tax base are relatively straightforward, partly because the GST/HST is a federal tax, imposed under the Excise Tax Act, which is shared with the participating provinces. Where the Government of Canada proposes a tax base expansion that would result in an increase in revenues of more than 1 percent, a province may object in writing. The objection gives the province a right to request that the federal government administer a relieving measure in the form of a credit or point-of-sale rebate within the province, subject to certain conditions.

The parties also agreed that a common provincial tax rate will be maintained. For an increase in the provincial portion of the rate, a simple majority of participating provinces is required, while a reduction calls for unanimous approval of all participating provinces. In addition, mechanisms are in place to ensure that all participating provinces will implement any change to the provincial portion of the HST rate simultaneously. Changes to the federal portion of the HST would not affect the provincial common tax rate since such changes would be implemented in all participating provinces simultaneously. For example, when the federal government reduced the GST rate from 7 percent to 6 percent, the HST rate was reduced to 14 percent in the three CITCA-participating provinces. If the federal portion of the rate has been raised from the base rate by two increments of 0.5 percent, the federal portion of the rate cannot be further increased until the rate of the provincial portion has been increased from the base rate.

Another notable aspect of the CITCA relates to inter-provincial sales. Generally, where a good is purchased in a province for delivery to another province, purchasers are required to self-assess and remit the sales tax to the province where the good is delivered if they do not have a presence in that province. Under the HST system, the HST applies to all inter-provincial taxable supplies. Vendors in non-participating provinces are required to collect the HST in respect of taxable supplies made to a recipient in New Brunswick, Newfoundland and Labrador, or Nova Scotia because HST is administered under federal law. Goods imported into participating provinces must be remitted by vendors outside the HST zone. For the CITCA provinces, this essentially protects provincial sales tax revenues generated from inter-provincial sales. This makes the system fair for business, and gives the participating provinces a more effective tax collection system by minimizing tax-revenue leakage on inter-provincial sales of goods and services.

Responsibility for the administration of the HST lies with the Canada Revenue Agency (CRA), an agency of the federal government. Administration includes everything from the registration of suppliers and vendors for collection and remittance of the HST, to the conduct of litigation under the HST.

The sharing of HST revenues between governments is achieved through a formula and is based on assessment data gathered by the CRA. In short, the formula attempts to approximate the share of the HST raised in each of the participating provinces, and the amount that applies to each province is then transferred to the province.

3.4 Administration of GST by Quebec

Similar to other provinces, prior to 1991, Quebec levied a retail sales tax. The province then engaged in a sales tax reform of its own, which included discussions with the Government of Canada about harmonization of the new Quebec Sales Tax (QST) base with the federal tax base, and about the possibility of single administration.

On 30 August 1990, the federal government and Quebec signed an agreement regarding principles that would govern the administration of the federal GST within the province by the Quebec government. Under the arrangement, both parties would remain solely responsible for matters relating to their respective sales tax policies.

Canada and Quebec both recognized the importance of maintaining consistency in their tax bases on a going forward basis. At the time of the agreement, the federal government had already recommended to Parliament legislation to establish the GST. Quebec agreed to recommend to the Parliament of Quebec to amend the Quebec consumption tax base in order to make it substantially comparable with the GST base.

Under the arrangement, both parties agreed that they 'would avoid duplication, reduce administration costs, simplify compliance for vendors and be economically efficient for the GST to be administered within the province of Quebec by Quebec along with the provincial tax.' (Memorandum of Understanding between the Government of Canada and the Government of Quebec, August 30 1990, p. 1). To ensure a smooth implementation of the GST on 1 January 1991, and transfer to Quebec of the administration of the GST within the province, the governments agreed to a transitional period from 30 August 1990 to 31 December 1991. The transfer of the administration of the GST to Quebec was to take place on 1 January 1992 (this date was later changed to 1 July 1992). At the beginning of the post-transitional period, the Government of Canada would turn over to Quebec the administration of the GST in the province.

Under the August 1990 agreement, the parties agreed that they would conclude another agreement with more concrete details about the principles that would govern the administration of the GST by Quebec after the transition period. The new agreement came into effect in July 1992.

BOX 8.3

The objectives set out in the July 1992 agreement included:

1. minimizing costs by eliminating overlap in the administration of the two taxes;
2. reducing costs of administration;
3. guaranteeing the integrity of revenues for both levels of government;
4. facilitating the application of the GST and the QST by vendors and suppliers; and
5. providing a high level of service to the public.

Under the July 1992 agreement, Quebec agrees to administer the GST within the province along national parameters used by the Government of Canada in administering the GST in other provinces. Quebec is responsible for all administration aspects of the GST within the province, from registration of suppliers and vendors for collection and remittance of the GST, to collection of taxes and audits. However, the Government of Canada remains responsible for matters related to GST policy, as well as legislative changes to, and interpretation of, the GST legislation.

It can sometimes be difficult and inefficient for a sub-national government to collect and administer its sales tax because taxes can in some cases be avoided by purchasing goods outside of the province. The Quebec government gains efficiencies from being the administrator of the federal GST within its jurisdiction. As noted earlier, the federal and Quebec governments' value-added taxes are similar in design and have very similar tax bases. Since the GST/HST applies in all of the provinces, the information Quebec gathers as a result of tracking federal credits paid to registrants on business inputs provides a very useful input to protect its own tax base. In terms of purchases in neighboring jurisdictions, provinces bordering on Quebec to the east are party to the CITCA with a similar overall tax rate. In the case of Ontario to the west, the tax on goods to final consumers is equivalent. Also, Quebec and Ontario exchange information about vendor sales for delivery in the neighboring province, in order to protect their respective bases. As a result, Quebec has a unique opportunity to ensure that its sales tax is not avoided.

Unlike CITCA where HST revenues are shared between governments based on a formula, under the arrangement with Quebec actual GST collected is transferred to the Government of Canada. Costs of the joint administration of the GST and QST within Quebec are shared basically equally between the Government of Canada and Quebec. The joint administration costs are calculated on the basis of an agreed-upon formula.

4   NEXT STEPS – TAX COORDINATION

In its 2006 Budget, and an accompanying paper entitled *Restoring Fiscal Balance in Canada* (Department of Finance, 2006a p. 50) the Government of Canada set out a number of priorities including furthering provincial sales tax harmonization. The government stated that 'A key to maintaining an efficient tax system that provides governments with the flexibility to raise the revenues they need is to harmonize taxes to the greatest degree possible.' It is also stated:

> The existence of provincial retail sales taxes substantially increases the effective tax rate on investment by taxing business capital goods and intermediate materials, thereby impairing the competitiveness of our tax system. Having to comply with different sales tax systems also greatly increases the complexity and the cost of doing business. The Government invites all provinces that have not yet done so to engage in discussions on the harmonization of their provincial retail sales taxes with the federal GST.[8]

In a document released in November 2006 entitled *Advantage Canada – Building a Stronger Economy for Canadians* (Department of Finance, 2006c), the government reiterated its commitment to encouraging harmonization of the remaining provincial retail sales taxes with the GST as a key element to improving Canada's competitiveness.

5   ROLE OF THE CANADA REVENUE AGENCY IN TAX COORDINATION

The Canada Revenue Agency (CRA) plays a key role in administering provincial taxes that have been subject to a TCA or a CITCA. Effective administration and good communication with provinces is key to demonstrating to provinces that their taxes are being collected in an appropriate fashion. Because of the importance of the role of the CRA in tax coordination in Canada, as the principal revenue collector for both the federal and provincial governments, this section will provide some additional information about the agency and its mandate.

The CRA is responsible for administering taxes and benefits on behalf of governments and government institutions in Canada. Annually, it collects over $300 billion in taxes and other revenues, and distributes benefit payments to millions of families and individuals on behalf of the federal, provincial and territorial governments, as well as First Nations (the aboriginal peoples of Canada).

Recently, it increased cooperation with other federal departments and agencies. New services were also provided to provinces, territories and First Nations governments. It participated in recent discussions with the Government of Ontario that led to an agreement on the collection of provincial corporate tax.

The CRA is a relatively new organization that was formed on 1 November 1999 at the instigation of the federal government to achieve three objectives:

- provide better service to Canadians;
- become a more efficient and effective organization; and
- establish a closer partnership with the provinces and territories.

The legislation contains five major elements: mandate and governance of the agency; accountabilities; partnership responsibilities; human resource authorities and administrative authorities.

The legislation established a governance regime for the agency that is unique in Canada. The federal Minister of National Revenue retains full responsibility and accountability for the administration by the agency of federal tax and benefit legislation, notably the Income Tax Act and the GST legislation.

The Act created a Board of Management from the private sector (except for the Commissioner's position) to oversee the human resources, financial and administrative authorities, which were formerly the responsibility of central agencies of the federal government. It created a Commissioner who is effectively accountable to the federal Minister for the day-to-day administration of the program legislation and to the Board for the day-to-day administration of the human resource and administrative authorities.

The partnership provisions of the legislation give the agency the authority to implement agreements (under certain conditions) with other federal departments and agencies, with provincial and territorial governments, and with aboriginal governments. The important relationship with provinces and territories is strengthened by the requirement that 11 of the 15 members of the Board of Management be nominated by them.

The accountability provisions round out the legislation by putting in place a strong and transparent regime that ensures agency actions are reported upon and given proper scrutiny by appropriate authorities. Indeed, the agency is arguably subject to stronger accountability requirements than virtually any other federal organization. Accountability to Parliament is guaranteed by the longstanding concept of ministerial responsibility, coupled with the fact that the Auditor General is named as the agency's auditor.

In the human resource area, it replaced a more process-oriented and rules-based staffing system with one where employees are recruited, selected and promoted based on a common set of competencies matched to the organization's business needs. Staffing recourse was similarly overhauled and replaced with a system that promotes openness and dispute resolution.

The agency assumed the responsibility of a separate employer for labor relations, compensation and collective bargaining. In order to recognize and strengthen the importance of the management function in the agency, a new Management Group encompassing most managers below the Executive level was created along with a new Senior Management level within the Executive level.

In the financial and administrative areas, the Board of Management oversaw similarly profound changes. Costs were reduced and internal services vastly improved through a broad range of technology-based re-engineering. Overall savings of $37.4 million were realized between 2002 and 2004, with the potential for further savings over the following two years. Savings were also realized in real property as a result of a number of innovations introduced in partnership with Public Works and Government Services Canada. The Board of Management's strong emphasis on the comptrollership function resulted in more comprehensive and clear disclosures on financial matters and performance, both internally within the agency and to outside stakeholders.

The changes in human resource administration, in the management structure, and in the internal administrative area have had a beneficial impact on management–employee relations in the agency. This is evident in the results of two employee surveys: one completed in 1999, the year the CRA was created, and the other in 2002. They demonstrate that over this three-year period, employees' satisfaction with their jobs and work environment improved considerably.

Overall, the changes clearly demonstrate both the willingness and desire of the CRA to work collaboratively in designing services that meet the needs of various client governments.[9]

6   CONCLUSION

Within the income tax field, Canada has achieved a substantial degree of tax harmonization between the two orders of government, without severely compromising either's policy flexibility. The recently revised and signed TCAs, which promote a common tax base and a single administrator for both corporation and personal income taxation, illustrate how efficiency and flexibility can be combined. These agreements help to reduce compliance costs for taxpayers and administration costs for governments. Even in the case of provinces that have not entered into such agreements, a significant degree of harmonization in the definition of the tax base has been maintained. This reflects an acknowledgment by all governments in Canada of the importance of some degree of commonality, or harmonization, in the shared tax fields.

However, there remain areas where additional harmonization would provide substantial benefits, and governments continue to work toward this goal to improve competitiveness and efficiency in Canada. On 6 October 2006 the Government of Canada signed a Memorandum of Agreement with Ontario under which the federal government will collect and administer the provincial corporate income tax, beginning in 2009. In the 2006 federal *Budget Plan*, it was stated 'the Government is committed to working with remaining provinces that want to enhance their economic competitiveness and productivity by harmonizing their retail sales taxes with the GST' (Department of Finance, 2006b, p. 68). This commitment was reiterated in the document released in November 2006 entitled *Advantage Canada – Building a Stronger Economy for Canadians* (Department of Finance, 2006c).

Within the sales tax field, harmonized value-added taxes are now in place in Newfoundland and Labrador, Nova Scotia and New Brunswick, and Quebec administers a provincial value-added tax as well as collecting the GST on behalf of the federal government. The absence of a provincial sales tax in Alberta eliminates the need for a sales tax coordination arrangement with that province.

Separate provincial retail sales taxes continue to be collected and administered in five provinces. There is an opportunity for governments to transition to a more competitive and efficient provincial tax system by lowering the cost of capital, broadening the tax base, removing economic distortions, reducing the cost of intermediate goods, and reducing compliance costs for businesses and government. The 2006 federal *Budget Plan* and the *Advantage Canada* document invited all provinces that have not yet done so to engage in discussions on the harmonization of their retail sales taxes with the GST. Given that a number of provincial tax reviews have explored the possibility of sales tax harmonization, it is to be hoped that in the future both levels of government will be able to have a productive discourse that will lay the groundwork for further sales tax harmonization.

NOTES

1. This chapter was prepared by Paul Berg-Dick, Michel Carreau, Deanne Field and Mireille Éthier, with technical assistance from Jasmine Alam. It expands upon the presentation by Paul Berg-Dick entitled 'Tax Collection Agreements and Canadian Tax Administration' prepared for the 4th Symposium on Fiscal Federalism sponsored by the Institut d'Economia de Barcelona, 31 May 2006. The chapter reflects the views of the authors and no responsibility for them should be attributed to the Department of Finance. Comments on the chapter are invited and may be sent to the authors.
2. The main elements of consumption that are not taxed are basic groceries, most health and dental services, most educational, financial, legal and child care services, exported goods and services and residential rents.
3. Throughout this chapter, references to provinces will include territories, unless otherwise stated.
4. Carter, George E. (2007), 'Taxation', in, *The Canadian Encyclopedia*, Historia Foundation, http://www.canadianencyclopedia.ca/index.cfm?PgNm=TCE&Params= A1ARTA0007883 (Accessed 10 January 2008).
5. Equalization is a federal transfer program that ensures that less prosperous provinces can provide reasonably comparable public services without their taxes being out of line with those of more affluent provinces. Territories are subject to a different transfer program entitled Territorial Formula Financing.
6. On 6 October 2006, the Governments of Canada and Ontario signed a Memorandum of Agreement, under which the federal government will collect and administer Ontario's corporate income tax. Under the agreement, businesses will make combined payments starting in 2008 and file a single return beginning in 2009 for taxation years ending after 31 December 2008.
7. The allocation formula differs by industry with different rules in place for banks, trust companies, insurance companies and pipeline companies. Again, all provinces have adopted similar rules. An administrative mechanism exists for government officials to meet and attempt to resolve different interpretations of the rules that might otherwise lead to double taxation at the provincial level. The CRA also undertakes to review the allocation results for firms as part of its service commitment to provinces.
8. Department of Finance (2006b, p. 68).
9. More information about the CRA can be found at: http://www.cra-arc.gc.ca/agency/ review/2005/fv_yr_rvw_web-e.pdf. Accessed 26 November 2007.

REFERENCES

Canada Revenue Agency (2005), *CCRA Annual Report to Parliament 2004–2005*, Ottawa: CRA.

Department of Finance, Budget (1981), *Fiscal Arrangements in the Eighties – Proposals of the Government of Canada*, Ottawa: Department of Finance.

Department of Finance (1994), *Towards Replacing the Goods and Services Tax*, http://fin.gc.ca/GSTOV/gstovepdf. Accessed 25 November 2007.

Department of Finance (1991), *Personal Income Tax Coordination: The Federal–Provincial Tax Collection Agreements*, Ottawa: Department of Finance.

Department of Finance (2000), *Federal Administration of Provincial Taxes: New Directions*, Ottawa: Department of Finance.

Department of Finance, (2006a), *Restoring Fiscal Balance in Canada*, Ottawa: Department of Finance.

Department of Finance (2006b), *The Budget Plan 2006: Focusing on Priorities*, http://www.fin.gc.ca/budget06/pdf/bp 2006c.pdf. Accessed 25 November 2007.

Department of Finance (2006c), *Advantage Canada – Building a Strong Economy for Canadians*, Ottawa: Department of Finance.

Due, John F., (1951a), *The General Manufacturers Sales Tax in Canada*, Toronto: Canadian Tax Foundation.

Due, John F. (1951b), *Provincial Retail Sales Taxes in Canada*, Toronto: Canadian Tax Foundation.

Eaton, Kenneth (1966), *Essays in Taxation*, Toronto: Canadian Tax Foundation.

Mill, John Stuart ([1848] 1909), *Principles of Political Economy*, London: Longmans, Green and Co., ed. William James Ashley, http://www.econlib.org/library/Mill/mlP65.html. Accessed 25 November 2007.

Perry, J. Harvey (1990), *Taxation in Canada*, Fifth Edition, Toronto: Canadian Tax Foundation.

Whalley, John and Deborah Fretz (1990), *The Economics of the Goods and Services Tax*, Toronto: Canadian Tax Foundation.

9. The decentralization of tax administration in Germany: consequences

Alexander Ulbricht

1 INTRODUCTION

Germany (and Bavaria, as one of its *Länder*) is usually taken as a model case because of its well organized and efficient decentralized tax administration. After giving a brief overview of the main features of the German tax system, this chapter will focus on the organization of the German tax administration and will give examples of the consequences of a decentralized administration in the German case.

2 MAIN FEATURES OF THE GERMAN TAX SYSTEM

Germany is a federal, federative state. This means that Germany consists of individual states – called *Länder* – which have their own rights, powers and tasks, but which are also part of a single, larger entity – the Federation. The government is divided into three basic levels (Federation – 16 *Länder* – communities). Each level has certain tasks determined by the German Constitution (*Grundgesetz*, GG) and has to finance the expenses incurred by fulfilling their constitutional responsibilities. This is called the 'connectivity of task and expense responsibility', which is one of the central principles in the German tax system. Therefore, the Constitution also regulates the assignment of tax revenue. This generally ensures that each level is able to fulfil its tasks.

Table 9.1 shows some examples of the tasks and tax revenue assigned to the specific political levels. At the federal level, for instance, social security appears as a constitutional responsibility. In order to finance this, the Federation receives a portion of the income tax.

As can be seen, some kinds of taxes, for instance income tax, appear at every level of government, while other taxes are limited to only one level. This

Table 9.1   Tasks and tax revenues assigned to the three political levels

	Task	Tax Revenue
Federation	Social security Foreign affairs Defence/armed forces Federal roads Business development	Portion of income and corporation tax, VAT Excise duties
Länder	Cultural programmes Schools, universities Police, jurisdiction Tax administration	Portion of income and corporation tax, VAT Inheritance tax Motor vehicle tax Real estate transfer tax Beer duty
Communities	Water supply Public transport Kindergarten Social welfare Building licence	Portion of income tax and VAT Trade tax Real estate tax Local taxes

is due to a crucial feature of the German tax system: the German 'separation and bonded' system. For the purpose of tax revenue assignment, the taxes are categorized into two groups (Art. 106 GG): 1) taxes that are assigned to just one level of government and 2) taxes that are assigned to more levels. These two tax categories form the basis of the separation and bonded system. Most of the taxes are primarily allocated to just one level. They accrue only to the Federation, the *Länder* or the communities. Here are some examples:

- Federation:
  - spirits duty;
  - mineral oil duty;
  - tobacco tax;
  - coffee tax;
  - sparkling wine duty;
  - insurance duty;
  - solidarity surcharge.
- *Länder*:
  - beer tax;
  - real property transfer tax; (participating *Länder*);
  - motor vehicle tax;
  - lottery tax;

- fire protection tax;
- inheritance tax.
● Communities:
- real property tax;
- entertainment tax;
- beverage tax;
- hunting tax;
- local taxes, for example, dog tax; secondary home tax.

There are, however, also taxes that are distributed between more than one level of government (Art. 106 Sec. 3 GG). These taxes, called common taxes, are generally the most important and provide the highest yield. The different levels of government receive a specific percentage of the revenue derived from the different taxes. If we consider that the common taxes usually represent approximately 70 per cent of the annual tax revenue, it is clear why distribution quotas, particularly for VAT, constitute one of the most commonly disputed issues between the different levels of government involved.

The following are examples of common taxes and their distribution quotas:

● Income tax:
- Wages tax and assessed income tax: Federation 42.5 per cent; *Länder* 42.5 per cent; communities 15 per cent.
- Capital gains tax: Federation 50 per cent; *Länder* 50 per cent.
- Interest deduction tax: Federation 44 per cent; *Länder* 44 per cent; communities 12 per cent.
● Corporation tax:
- Federation 50 per cent; *Länder* 50 per cent.
● Value-added tax:
- The Federation receives 5.63 per cent of the total revenue in advance (as a compensation for a higher contribution used to stabilize the old age insurance system).
- Of the remainder, the communities receive 2.2 per cent as a compensation for their losses due to the reformation of corporation tax.
- The remaining amount is shared between the Federation (50.25 per cent) and the *Länder* (49.75 per cent).
● Trade tax:
- Federation 7.9 per cent; *Länder* 18 per cent; communities 74.1 per cent.
- The Federation and the *Länder* receive their share by apportionment.

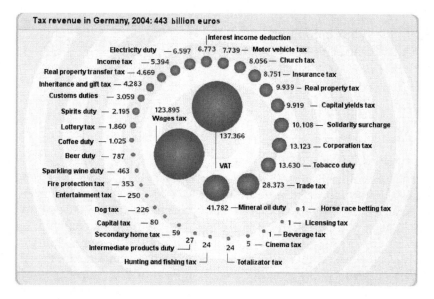

Note: In million euros.

Sources: BMF, Statisisches Bundesamt.

Figure 9.1 The tax helix.

When considering the advantages and the disadvantages of the German tax administration, it is always necessary to take into account the separation and bonded system and its effect on the system as a whole. The final part of this section gives some statistics on German and Bavarian tax revenue.

Figure 9.1 shows what is known as the tax helix. It depicts the tax revenue for 2004 and illustrates how this can be broken down between the various different taxes and duties. As can be seen, the two main contributors are common taxes: VAT, and wages tax, which is a special form of income tax. As stated above, this is the main reason that tax quotas are always heavily disputed.

The figures below in Table 9.2 show that the German tax revenue was approximately 415 billion euros in 2005. About two-thirds of this total were bonded taxes.

The statistics below show the relation between the total tax revenue and the cost of administration at the state and federal levels:

- Federation:
  - federal tax revenue, 2005: €190.8 billion;
  - expenses for the federal tax administration: €3192 million.

Table 9.2   Tax revenue 2004/05

	Fiscal Period (million €)		Rate of Change	
	2005	2004	Million €	%
Bonded taxes	307 890	302 130	5 760	1.9
Separate federal taxes	83 508	84 557	−1 046	−1.2
Separate land taxes	20 579	19 774	805	4.1
Customs duties	3 378	3 059	319	10.4
German tax revenue (without separate local taxes)	415 355	409 517	5 838	1.4

Source: Federal Ministry of Finance, February 2006.

- Bavaria:
    - Bavarian tax revenue, 2005: €25 759.6 million;
    - expenses for the state tax administration: €1625 million (43 per cent for the staff). (*Source:*   Budget reports of the Federal Ministry of Finance and the Bavarian State Ministry of Finance.)

3   THE ORGANIZATION OF THE GERMAN TAX ADMINISTRATION

3.1   General Principles

The German administration (see Figure 9.2) is split into two main parts: the federal and the *Länder* administrations. Above both government levels are the ministries, while below them are the regional and finally the local offices. It is interesting to note that the regional offices often house both the federal and the state departments and have a common president, who in this case is partly a federal and partly a state civil servant.

The tax administration – like the tax system itself – is regulated by the German Constitution (Art. 108 GG). Customs duties, tax monopolies and federally regulated excise duties are administered by federal offices. The same applies to duties levied by the European Union. All of the remaining taxes (i.e., VAT, income tax) are managed by the state offices. The administration of those separate taxes, which are communities-only taxes, can be allocated to the community itself by the respective *Länder*.

Unlike the regional authorities, the local tax offices are solely state offices and administer the federal property and traffic taxes on behalf of the

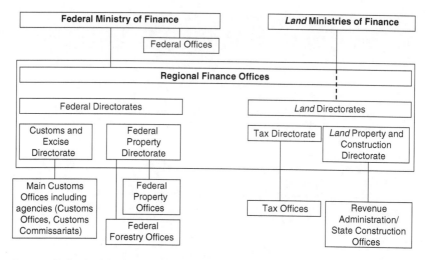

Source: Federal Ministry of Finance, *An ABC of Taxes*, 2005.

Figure 9.2   Structure of Federal and Länder *administrations*

Federation. They also control all state taxes and several community taxes. Furthermore, the local tax offices assign the assessed value of national real property (as a basis for determining real property tax or inheritance tax, for example).

The customs and excise offices are federal offices and administer the customs and excise duties and the beer duty, although the receipts for the latter accrue wholly to the *Länder*. They also administer the duties for the EU.

Most tax administration is carried out at state level, either because it is a state responsibility or because the state is acting on behalf of the Federation. The *Länder* are free to choose the organization of their administration. There is no federal rule concerning how to administer taxes and organize the administration other than the constitutional guidelines and, of course, the law. The only rule to follow when organizing the administration, besides the law, is the principle of 'uniform taxation in compliance with the law'. Regardless of how the administration is organized in each *Land*, there must be no differences in taxation for a taxpayer, irrespective of the *Land* or community of residence. The only exceptions to this are the local taxes in each community, such as second home tax. The communities have legislative powers over some of their local taxes and, therefore, the tax rate may differ at community level.

The Bavarian tax administration consists of a state ministry, one regional tax office and 108 local tax offices. There are approximately 18 000 civil servants and employees and last year the Bavarian state had an overall tax yield of 59 139 billion euros. Since August 2005, the Bavarian tax administration has maintained only one regional tax office. The two former regional offices merged and the new Bavarian state tax department is now responsible for all local tax offices in Germany. The regional office has a president, who is a state-only public servant as Bavaria decided against sharing an office with the Federation. Consequently, there is no longer a customs department or any other federal organizational structure in the Bavarian regional office. In addition to the president, there are two vice-presidents, each of whom is the head of one department, which altogether have seven divisions (one organizational division, one personnel division, two tax divisions, two programming/organizational divisions and one electronic data processing centre). Additionally, the president has four more presidential positions at his office (presidential office, two staff positions and issuing authority).

Bavaria used to have one local tax office in every administrative district but 26 of these were downgraded to outposts of larger tax offices for organizational and (particularly) financial reasons. The number of employees in one office ranges from 35 to 590 and the offices are generally organized according to the type of tax. In several special areas, however, such as enforcement or investigation, the offices are structured according to their respective tasks.

The organizational structure in Bavaria is not necessarily reproduced in every other state. Not every state has a regional tax office; in some states the responsibilities are distributed between the departments of the state ministry and sometimes even between some of the local tax offices. As the following list shows, the organizational structure varies in terms of the different levels of government (besides the ministries). The existing number of tax offices (there may in fact be no specialized office) also differs from *Land* to *Land*:

- Bavaria: one regional tax office, 108 local tax offices (two specialized enforcement offices, 1 specialized corporation tax office);
- North Rhine-Westphalia: two regional tax offices, 137 local tax offices (ten specialized investigation offices, 15 specialized offices for the examination of affiliated groups);
- Berlin: 17 local tax offices (four specialized corporation tax offices, one specialized investigation office);
- Mecklenburg-Western Pomerania: 15 local tax offices.

Another significant organizational difference is the usage of tax administration software. Each state initially had its own software, and there are still incompatibilities between a number of *Länder*, although in 1993 the project FISCUS (Federal Integrated Standardized Computer Supported Tax System) was set up to develop a uniform tax administration software. This project failed to provide the *Länder* with any usable software till 2000, so the state ministers of finance for all states except Bavaria resolved to launch a new initiative. They decided to create Fiscus GmbH, a private sector enterprise with the *Länder* and the Federation as shareholders. The Bavarian Minister of Finance withdrew from the project altogether and set up the EOSS (Evolutionary Oriented Tax Software) project. Instead of constructing a completely new system, as Fiscus GmbH planned to do, he decided that the IT division of the Bavarian tax office should enhance the software already in use.

Although the Fiscus corporation produced four software solutions, the ministers of finance decided on 19 July 2005 that the company was to be closed. This was, in part, due to the fact that all of the *Länder* in East Germany, as well as the Saarland, joined with Bavaria in 2002 to found the EOSS network. Subsequently, these states even abandoned Fiscus GmbH, and the rest of the participating *Länder* could only maintain the enterprise by asking the Federation to pay the monthly contributions for the former members. In 2005, Hamburg, Bremen and Schleswig-Holstein also joined the EOSS network, which meant that by this point ten of the 16 states took part. Therefore, the ministers decided to call an end to the FISCUS project, which is said to have cost between 250 and 700 million euros, depending on the source. The following list outlines the history of the regional differences in software development:

- 1953: punchcard;
- 1970s: first software program;
- 1993: first attempt to create a nationwide standard software application (FISCUS);
- 2000: first signs of failure – Fiscus GmBH founded; Bavaria separated and founded EOSS;
- 19 July 2005: termination of FISCUS developments; EOSS and KONSENS (Consensual New Software Development) represent future software solutions.

The new KONSENS has become responsible for creating a uniform software solution and Bavaria is again part of this new attempt. The state-internal North-Rhine Westphalian project and the EOSS project will be the basis for the new initiative and the five largest German states (Bavaria, North-Rhine Westphalia, Lower Saxony, Hesse and Baden-Württemberg) will develop the new software and provide it to the other *Länder*. The Federation no longer has an active role in this project.

Another regional difference in Germany is the financing and budgeting of the tax administration. In Bavaria the regional tax office is given its own budget to work with – excluding staff and construction costs, which are paid by the regional financial office and the construction directorate. The regional tax office also administers part of the budget for the local offices (again, except for staff and construction costs) whereas the local offices are responsible for the other part, in particular office equipment. There are other *Länder* in Germany in which the local tax offices control their own budgets, which include staff costs. As there is no nationwide board or work group, all states are free to choose their own budgeting strategies.

However, not all aspects are different. As mentioned above, the results of a tax refund have to be the same in every state because of the principle of 'uniform taxation in compliance with the law'. The *Länder* may not vary the tax rates since fiscal law and special tax laws are the only bases for taxation. No *Land* has the power to change the existing tax law. Therefore the tax refund is the same, regardless of the state.

The same applies to the training system for tax officers. The German Constitution states that the training for public servants shall be governed by federal law, in this case the StBAG (Steuerbeamten Ausbildungs Gesetz). This Act (consistently and bindingly) governs the training of revenue officers in all 16 states and is supplemented by the training and examination regulation for revenue officers (StBAPO).

In addition, the entrance requirements for the training programmes are the same in all *Länder*. There is a lower civil service grade (postal services, caretaker), a middle grade (handling of tax refunds and tax registration, enforcement, auditing), an upper grade (handling of tax refunds, legal remedies, audit and revision services, administration of sensitive matters and criminal cases) and the highest grade (head of a respective functional area, chief officer). For middle grades, a secondary school graduation level one is required, for upper grades a university entrance diploma or advanced technical college entrance qualification is required. For higher grades, prospective participants need a university degree in law, finance or economics.

The training in all grades is the same nationwide. It comprises a mixture of on-the-job training and field-specific learning at a financial academy. All higher-grade officers receive their theoretical training together at a federal academy, while middle and upper-grade trainees attend state academies. The final part of upper-grade training is a closing examination (these exams are state-specific, but the content is defined by the training and examination regulation for revenue officers (StBAPO)). The actual exam may therefore be different, but the teaching content referred to is the same. The trainees become tax officers, either by passing their examination or by successfully completing two years as a trainee and receiving a positive assessment in case of the higher-grade service.

Since the basic wages are governed by federal law – the federal public servant salary law Bundesbesoldungsgesetz (BBesG) – all officers receive the same wage, regardless of the state in which they are working. This applies only to the basic salary, whereas bonuses (for instance, the so-called Christmas allowance) can vary (for example, in Baden-Württemberg the Christmas allowance is divided into 12 parts and added to the monthly salary). The weekly working hours are also different and vary from 39 to 42 hours a week.

However, this system is not specific to the tax administration: it is based upon the fact that almost all tax officers are public servants and are there-fore subject to standard regulations concerning public servants. The forth-coming 'Major Federal Reform' is likely to change some of these aspects. One of its aims is to assign responsibility for the salary of public servants to the states. This may cause the basic salary to change – many poorer states even fear that the richer ones will raise the basic salary and start a compe-tition between states to hire the better qualified trainees.

3.2   The Tax Administration Explained Using the Example of Wages Tax

Having presented the general principles of the German tax administration, it is useful to take a closer look at how a tax (in this case wages tax as a special form of income tax) is actually administered.

Wages tax, a special income tax that has to be paid on the wages and salaries of employees and public servants, is collected through deduction at source. This deduction usually serves to conclude a taxation procedure, unless the employee is assessed for income tax after the end of the calendar year or an annual adjustment of the tax paid is to be carried out. The tax office responsible for the deduction is the office that is also responsible for the area in which the wages are processed for payment – usually the head office. The annual adjustment is made at the tax office that is responsible for the employee, that is, the office that covers the area of residence.

The employer is obliged to deduct wages tax from each salary payment. Tax is withheld on the basis of wage tax cards, which are issued by the municipal authorities at the beginning of each calendar year to those employees registered in the district, determined using the data contained in their records (for example, in the civil register). On the wage tax card the community certifies the tax class, marital status, the number of child allowances for children under 18 and the religious affiliation of each employee. This last detail is necessary because the local tax offices deduct the church tax together with the wages tax on behalf of the churches.

Therefore, the tax offices have to know if an employee is a member of a church that levies church tax.

Any lump-sum allowances for surviving dependants and for those whose earning capacity is reduced by physical disability are also entered on the card, if such allowances are to be taken into account in the taxation of the employee. If the employee is entitled to additional allowances, or if there are children over 18 years who need to be taken into account, data entered on the wage tax card may be corrected or supplemented by the tax office at the employee's request. The employer is required to transfer the wages tax for all employees in a single sum to the local tax office on certain pre-arranged dates (monthly, quarterly or annually – in Bavaria usually quarterly). The payment is accompanied by a wage tax return (which must be submitted in electronic form) that states the total amount of tax withheld. No further information is required for employees whose wages tax is included in the remittance.

Any excess of tax withheld during the calendar year is refunded to the employee at the end of the year. This takes the form of an annual adjustment of wages tax, which is carried out in certain cases by the employer, although an application for assessment may also be made (for instance, to assert a subsequent claim for tax relief). In certain cases, the income tax assessment is mandatory even for employees, in order to determine their annual tax liability. This applies in particular to cases in which the employee has other income in addition to his or her wages, or when a tax-free allowance is entered on the wage tax card. While any excess of tax withheld will be refunded when an employee is assessed for income tax, additional tax will also be demanded in the event of underpayment. Liability for wages tax is attached to the employee, but the employer is responsible for the correct deduction and remittance to the tax office. If the tax office determines on examination that insufficient tax has been withheld, it may enforce payment of the amount still due from the employer or directly from the employee.

The revenue authorities of the *Länder* monitor the withholding and payment of wages tax by employers. After the tax has been deducted, the amount is declared to the state ministries, which report these amounts to the federal ministry where the correct amount for each state is assessed and the respective shares are distributed. The Federation and the *Länder* each receive 42.5 per cent of the wage tax revenue, whilst the communities are entitled to a share of 15 per cent.

3.3 Distribution of Corporation Tax Income

One of the main questions concerning distribution of taxes is the distribution of corporation tax in the case of multi-state corporations. The distribution of corporation tax in such a case, in which several *Länder* are involved, is based on the rules for the distribution of trade tax and therefore depends on the payroll. If the corporation tax is greater than €500 000, the corporation is obliged to inform the local tax office that is responsible for the registered office of this corporation (the segmentation tax office) of where all its workers are located and how the payroll is distributed between the states. The corporation is therefore obliged to provide information on how the tax must be distributed between the states. If the tax levied is less than €500 000 the state in which the registered office of the corporation is located receives the entire amount and no segmentation takes place.

This information – as declared by the corporation – can only be verified by external audits. The only other reference is the trade registration. Whenever a corporation opens a new branch or a new place of work, it has to contact the authorities of the local community. The registration form is used to inform the community authorities whether the corporation is new or part of an already existing one. In the latter case the community sends a copy of the registration form to the local tax office and also to the segmentation tax office (even if this is in one of the other *Länder*).

All these assignment and control procedures take place only at state level. Even if the tax offices concerned disagree over the distribution quota, there is no federal intervention. The offices involved report the dispute via the regional offices to the state ministries, which try to broker an agreement. If no solution can be agreed, the state ministry to which the segmentation office belongs has the final decision and issues the segmentation notice. The other state ministries involved can then lodge standard legal appeals against this segmentation notice.

3.4   Coordination of a Decentralized Administration

It is obvious that differences between the *Länder* exist within the tax administration due to the decentralization. The main problem to arise is that the administrative tasks – which are not a state-only responsibility – have to be coordinated. As there is no superior coordination authority, the *Länder* have to rely on several boards, committees and work groups to reach informal or formal agreements. The board that is closest to a coordination authority is the board of the State Ministers of Finance. This board has the final vote on every decision concerning nationwide boards or work groups. However, this only applies to boards and work groups in which all states are represented. In 1998, Germany had more than 900 of these nationwide boards that covered all areas of its administration, including tax administration. This was reduced to 210 necessary boards by 2005. Of these 210 necessary boards, 26 belong to the tax administration. There are a number of other tax committees and boards, of which only some states are members.

A useful example is the project group called 'Leistungsvergleich der *Länder*' ('Performance Comparison Between *Länder*'). The aim of this project is to assess the performance of every local tax office by creating several key parameters (such as task completion, taxpayer and staff satisfaction and efficiency). These key parameters are then used to compare the departments within each local tax office and the offices within each state. The basic idea is that less efficient employees and offices should learn from the most efficient. The final goal is to establish a comparison of the offices within all participating states.

Only seven of the *Länder* participate in this project, while the other *Länder* all have their own control systems. The difficulty of trying to coordinate the different control systems is that the resulting key parameters will always be different, because every control system creates its parameters differently. Even if these parameters have the same name and the same background, their composition may be different. For instance, the 'Leistungsvergleich' project only takes into account positive increases for the key parameter 'higher revenue generation' used by auditors. Other *Länder* and other control systems also consider the decrease in losses due to the work of auditors when generating this key parameter.

If we now compare these two methods of calculating a 'higher revenue generation', it is easy to see which will yield a higher revenue figure and be viewed favourably in a cross-state comparison. This leads to the next and, once again, crucial point: the consequences of these various efforts to coordinate the system.

4 CONSEQUENCES OF DECENTRALIZATION IN GERMANY

First, due to the different organizational methods, the cross-state cases sometimes pose a major problem, particularly if the taxpayer happens to move from one state to another. If the two states involved use different software, it may take some time to re-establish a working administration for the individual case. The same can occur – even if the states share the same software – if the organization of the tax offices differs too greatly. It is even possible that the taxpayer's file will have to be split into several parts if the file has been sent from a tax office that is organized by tax type to an office that is organized by tasks.

Tax equalization is also a significant obstacle. Although it may seem inconceivable, it appears that some states are not willing to invest money and personnel in a more extensive auditing process. This may be because the states know that most of the money will be sent to other states or that they will receive their own share of the tax revenue as a result of the equalization, even without investing money and personnel.

Both problems arise from political influences. Each *Land* has different plans and visions for its own administration. For example, to refer again to the 'Leistungsvergleich', one *Land* prefers a short time lapse between the tax return and the notice of assessment. Another *Land* may give greater importance to an accurate auditing process. This may take longer but the tax revenue is greater and more changes are made by the auditors. Therefore, the political influence and the individual plans and goals of each *Land* make coordination difficult.

Yet this does not mean that the decentralized system as such is not working. The German decentralized system is much more democratic than a centralized administration. It provides the states with greater responsibility and means that they are no longer dependent on assignments in order to meet targets. Unlike in a centralized administration, the *Länder* do not have to ask the Federation to provide them with the money required to fulfil their tasks – they have a legal right to their share of the annual revenue.

However, in as far as it can be measured, the decentralized tax administration does seem to have an influence on tax compliance, if not on the attitude of taxpayers. To the taxpayer, every tax office and every member of the tax administration is part of a single system. Due to the fact that only the Federation is able to change the law and influence the taxation system, the states have no real possibilities of changing public opinion. They can certainly act to a minor degree, for instance by assisting the taxpayers (through the creation of adult education programmes or by installing service centres at every local tax office to answer questions regarding taxation problems), but as soon as the Federation has a new policy and raises a tax like VAT, all of the tax offices are seen as members of one overall administration.

The decentralized system has also had a significant impact on the administration and different auditing structures have caused loss of revenue. It is not in itself the greatest cause of tax evasion in Germany, but it certainly contributes to the problem. It can be likened to the problem of VAT evasion in Europe, although on a smaller scale. Due to the different approaches to fighting tax evasion and encouraging the compliance, and due to the lack of coordination in this area of tax administration, most of the measures lose their effectiveness the moment another state becomes involved.

To reduce the impact, the structure and the organization of the tax administration could be improved. First, the current German system suffers from a lack of cohesion. In some cases the states can do what they want, whereas in others they are bound by federal regulations. It is impossible to act independently if certain restrictions remain in place. On the other hand, it is impossible to work effectively – considering the scale of the German economy, its tax revenue and level of tax evasion – if all the states have complete fiscal autonomy. One of the German State-Secretaries of Finance, Barbara Hendricks, and the former Federal Minister of Finance, Hans Eichel, therefore proposed a federal tax administration, but they were not able to convince the states of its viability.

The aim was to transfer the administrative powers over common taxes (income tax, corporation tax and VAT) from the states to the Federation. This administrative model was already part of the first draft of the German Constitution but had to be abandoned due to the objections of the Allied High Commission. Therefore, the Federation and the states arranged the system in which the states administer taxes on behalf of the Federation. But, as a result, countless work groups and coordination boards had to be created. Those boards have multiplied and a serious effort is now required in order to reduce the number. This procedure is one of the obstacles that an effective and efficient tax administration has to overcome.

The former Federal Minister of Finance was of the opinion that unnecessary costs are created by the fact that the states have to administer taxes that belong entirely, or at least to a large degree, to the Federation – an opinion that I share. This system also delays the consequent modernization of the German administration because, once more, every state has its own ways of dealing with the modernization process.

The former Federal Minister of Finance shared his opinion not only with the State-Secretary, but also with the Federal Court of Auditors, and declared that 16 independent tax administrations with different organizational models for auditing and implementation, different approaches to the role of public servants and different equipment are incapable of administering tax according to the principle of 'uniform taxation in compliance with the law'. To compound the problem, the interference of state policy cannot be totally ruled out. The states often have to deny the accusation that they provide local companies with advantageous locations simply to obtain more tax revenue or secure jobs, thus contravening the principle of 'uniform taxation in compliance with the law'.

In my opinion, Germany has no real guidelines for quality control and lacks a nationwide system of control based on consistent figures. In order to work effectively, a centralized tax administration is not required, and is probably even more obstructive than a decentralized one. The only necessity is a superior coordinating authority with a greater influence on the way in which the states organize their tax administration: a federal tax office, for example, that provides all state tax offices with an annual list of topics to focus on during the auditing process. It should have the right to oblige a state or local office to re-inspect taxpayers with greater diligence. Another possibility would be a complete decentralization, which would give the states full control of every part of the tax administration. This would, however, require a more extensive modification of the German Constitution than the construction of a federal tax office – particularly where the responsibilities of the Federation are concerned.

Ultimately, the risk of failing to meet the 3 per cent maximum annual government deficit demanded by the Maastricht criteria cannot be conveyed to the taxpayers as long as Germany continues to lose more than 10 per cent of its tax revenue through tax evasion or the inefficient implementation of legislation due to a lack of state cooperation. Some adjustments are necessary in this field of administration and it is to be hoped that a superior coordinating authority with power over the respective *Länder* will eventually be created, remembering that this does not necessarily have to be a federal tax office.

This analysis of the decentralized German tax administration concludes with a quotation from Prof. Dr Kurt Faltlhauser (April 2006), the Bavarian State Minister of Finance and a strong defender of the decentralized administration, who provides the following analogy:

> In a decentralized tax administration the quality of the finance minister is not the linchpin – it's the quality of the head officials at the local tax offices. . . . Compare it to a restaurant chain. Regardless of the quality of the management at the HQ – it's the local management that's responsible for the quality of the restaurant on site.

10. Current situation and proposals for reform of Spain's tax administration[1]

Alejandro Esteller Moré

1 INTRODUCTION

Since the mid-1980s, successive reforms to the financing of Spain's Autonomous Communities (ACs) have largely focused on the ongoing correction of vertical fiscal imbalances, on the revenue side, and on increasing the degree of tax autonomy. As for the latter aspect, greater AC tax autonomy has basically been achieved by means of assuming legislative power over personal income tax and other ceded taxes (i.e., wealth tax, inheritance and gift tax, and capital transfer tax). Under the present financing model, in effect since 2002, tax autonomy has been expanded yet further (see, for example, Durán and Esteller, 2005).

Obviously, such reforms must be described as positive overall, although certain ACs may well still wish to take such reforms further, raise what they consider to be insufficient levels of financing, and/or widen the range of taxes over which they can exert tax autonomy (e.g., VAT and corporation tax). However, in recent years, these types of demands from ACs have been joined by calls for institutional reform of the tax administration. In particular, they would like to play a more active role in the setting of taxes in their respective territories. In fact, this can be seen as a demand for greater fiscal autonomy. After all, responsibility for administering taxes may be characterized as 'fiscal autonomy in the widest sense' as opposed to 'fiscal autonomy in the strictest sense', which would involve the exercise of legal powers (Ramallo and Zornoza, 1995, p. 40).

In this chapter, certain basic legal principles on tax setting in Spain are described in Section 2.1. Then, Section 2.2 summarizes the current institutional structure of tax administration in Spain. Next, reasonable grounds for reform are set out, identifying dysfunctions that the present institutional structure causes or may cause, as well as justifying a more active AC role (Section 2.3). To conclude Section 2, the chapter describes, first, the reforms that have arisen as a result of various official reports on the AC financing system (Section 2.4.1) and, second, AC reforms or statutory projects for reform (Section 2.4.2), with special emphasis given to Catalonia's recently passed Statute of Autonomy. In light of the observed dysfunctions and the proposed reforms, Section 3 evaluates the issues at stake based on the relevant economic literature. Finally, the chapter offers a number of conclusions.

2   AN OVERALL VIEW OF TAX ADMINISTRATION IN SPAIN

In this section, an overall view of tax administration in Spain looks at the basic legal principles that may be of interest when assessing proposals for institutional reform (Section 2.1); the present institutional structure (Section 2.2) and the structure's dysfunctions (Section 2.3). Then, in Section 2.4, we spell out in detail the reform proposals put forward on the basis of two official reports on the financing system (Section 2.4.1) as well as reforms associated with the AC Statutes of Autonomy (Section 2.4.2).

2.1   Legal Principles

The financing of the Autonomous Communities must be governed by three fundamental principles: financial autonomy, coordination and solidarity among territories. These principles are asserted in Art. 156.1 of the Spanish Constitution, which states: 'The autonomous communities shall enjoy financial autonomy in the development and exercise of their powers, in conformity with the principles of coordination with the State Treasury and solidarity among all Spaniards'. Therefore, on the one hand, any advance in financial autonomy must be compatible both with coordination with the central administration and with solidarity among territories. On the other hand, as experts in tax law recognize (and which will be justified from an economic standpoint in Section 3.3) the concept of financial autonomy – interpreted broadly – can include the tasks of tax administration. In particular, authors such as Ramallo and Zornoza (1995, p. 40) have characterized tax-setting power as 'fiscal autonomy in the widest sense', basically associating this wide level of autonomy with increasing taxpayer proximity to the level of government that levies a tax.

Indeed, with respect to the application of taxes, Art. 156.2 of the Spanish Constitution recognizes that 'the autonomous communities may act as delegates or agents of the State for the collection, management and assessment of the latter's tax resources, in conformity with the law and their statutes'. This is also reflected in Organic Law 7/2001 on AC financing, which states that tax administration functions (including audit) correspond to the tax administration of the state, but ACs may also act as delegates of the state, or collaborate when necessary (Art. 19.3). Law 21/2001 specifies the detail of the present financing system. In Art. 46.1 and Art. 46.2, respectively, the law identifies the ceded taxes to be administered by the ACs and those that will be managed by the central administration even though they are shared. In Section 2.2 of this chapter, AC administration powers concerning the first of these two groups of taxes are described.

Therefore, it is clear that the ACs will be delegated to assume the administration of some state taxes, and to do so using mechanisms of collaboration and coordination between administrations.[2] Indeed, adopted in the interests of guaranteeing effectiveness in the application of the tax system, the following areas of cooperation or coordination can be identified in the legislation:[3]

2.1.1   Collaboration/coordination

2.1.1.1   Information sharing
Art. 94.1 (General Tax Act): All authorities, including ACs, are required to provide to the tax administration any information with consequences on taxation and to assist in its functions.

Art. 53 (Law 21/2001): The state and ACs will work together in the administration of taxes. They will help each other with all required information, establishing precise procedures for technical intercommunication.

2.1.1.2   Tax auditing
Art. 50.1 (Law 21/2001): With regard to ceded taxes, the ACs will apply state regulation in audit activities and will follow audit plans, which will be elaborated jointly by both administrations. The ACs will account annually to the Ministry of Finance and Parliament.

Art. 50.2 (idem.): Whenever an audit body of the state or the ACs knows a relevant fact for other tax administrations, it will communicate the fact to them.

2.1.1.3   Institutions
Prior to 1997, existing regulation allowed for a 'plethora of interadministrative relations and institutions that have apparently never been set up' (Ramallo, 1994, p. 173). In that year, the AC financing system for the period 1997–2001 took effect. It involved the creation of two forums – one multilateral and the other bilateral – for interactions between the Spanish tax authority (Agencia Estatal de Administración; AEAT) and the

AC tax administrations. Although their performance was deemed 'useful and fruitful', improvement was considered appropriate (see Fiscal and Financial Policy Council, 2001, p. 78 onwards). In 2002, the Autonomous Communities gained representation on the AEAT Board, which will shortly be described.

By law, the General Inspectorate of the Ministry of Public Finance undertakes an annual inspection of the way regions develop their various powers over ceded taxes. All the information is published in an official report. The reading of the annual reports shows that collaboration and coordination between the AEAT and the corresponding AC tax administrations have improved substantially over time, especially since 2002. Even so, the reports mention certain problems in the sharing of information (delays and difficulties in interpreting transferred data, often because of systems incompatibilities or simply because of the absence of suitable channels to process the required data). Additional problems are noted in working together to carry out audit tasks (in certain cases, joint audit plans as envisaged by law do not exist). In any case, the improvements occurring since 2002 seem to lead to the conclusion that effective collaboration and coordination between administrations requires the creation of institutions to make such procedures automatic. This underpins our interest in understanding the composition and main functions of the institutions created in 1997 and strengthened in 2002.

The institutional forums of AC participation in the AEAT are as follows:

● Joint Commission on Tax Coordination reports directly to the president of the AEAT. All the ACs are represented on the commission, which has the following main functions:
  – conducting studies in order to adjust the procedures of the AC taxation system in keeping with the state's tax framework and to harmonize state and AC regulations concerning ceded taxes;
  – analyzing and reporting on drafts of new laws that may modify the regulation of ceded taxes;
  – designing the general management policy for ceded taxes managed by the AEAT and to establish guidelines for its application;
  – setting uniform performance standards, as well as standards for coordination and exchange of information among the ACs and between the ACs and the Spanish Ministry of Public Finance;
  – coordinating the standards used in tax assessment;
  – evaluating management of ceded taxes and the performance of the Autonomous Communities' tax authorities (which will be addressed next);
  – designing the basic outlines of programs to be included in the control plans, in relation to the ceded taxes managed by the AEAT;

– setting guidelines for the execution of coordinated actions specified in such programs in the control plans;

– receiving and analyzing an annual report on ceded taxes managed by the AEAT;

– proposing the implementation of telematic systems for information exchange concerning matters that may be of mutual interest to the AEAT and the ACs.

• Territorial Councils on Taxation (Consejos Territoriales de Dirección para la Gestión Tributaria) are the AEAT delegations in each AC, which carry out the following functions:

– adopting agreements on information exchange between the state and AC administrations;

– coordinating and collaborating in tax management;

– designing and planning the execution of coordinated actions set out in the control plans;

– furthermore, regarding ceded taxes managed by the AEAT, developing the functions listed below in keeping with the guidelines set by the Joint Commission: 1) the management of said taxes; 2) the analysis of results; 3) the study of any proposals and adoption of any decisions that would contribute to improved management; 4) the drafting of management improvement proposals, given available resources and 5) the development and specification of programmes included in the control plans.

• AEAT Board (Consejo Superior de Dirección) is presided over by the president of the AEAT. Six AC representatives sit on the board and their positions rotate annually.[4] The board's main functions are:

– making each year's objectives plan public before its approval;

– receiving the results of the previous year's objectives plan and being updated on performance against the current plan;

– proposing strategic lines of action and functional priorities for the Joint Commission and, through it, the ACs' Territorial Councils on Taxation;

– advising the AEAT president on issues relating to tax revenue management policy, the needs and issues caused by application of the state tax system, and coordination and cooperation between the Spanish Ministry of Public Finance and the AC tax administrations.

In a document approved by the Joint Commission in 2004 (Joint Commission, 2004), a set of specific action steps is described. Among them are included the opening of an internal debate to identify shortfalls in the use of co-official languages in the Special Delegations of the AEAT; the establishment of an annual plan that specifies the information that the AEAT must provide to the ACs and a set of steps aimed at strengthening AC management, for instance, by consolidating census information in a single database. In conclusion, while these issues are difficult to evaluate and some of them are merely projects yet to happen,[5] it seems that the ACs have, as noted previously, gained greater access to AEAT information and can, to some extent, participate – or, at least, receive information – on the decisions taken by the AEAT that may affect them (e.g., on issues related to the management of income tax or revenue forecasting).[6]

2.1.2 Administrative effectiveness *versus* equality in the application of the tax system

Art. 103.1 (Spanish Constitution): The Public Administration shall serve the general interest in a spirit of objectivity and shall act in accordance with the principles of efficiency, hierarchy, decentralization, deconcentration and coordination, and in full subordination to the law.

Art. 3.2 (General Tax Act): The application of the tax system will be based on the principles of proportionality, effectiveness and minimization of compliance costs.

Therefore, any reform of the tax administration should take into account both effectiveness and compliance costs. However, the principles of deconcentration and decentralization, which are recognized in the Spanish Constitution, could hinder equality in the application of the tax system across the entire country. For that reason, Garcia, Pérez and Zornoza (1998) and Garcia (2000) defend a strict interpretation of the equality principle, particularly regarding income tax, because of its special role within the tax system. However, the Constitutional Court provides a less strict interpretation, indicating that the equality principle cannot be taken as monolithic, which is to say, equality in the application of the law does not imply complete uniformity.

In short, any reform of the tax administration must be guided by the principle of effectiveness, but also equality in taxpayer treatment. These two principles may be complementary, but also contradictory. If contradictory, it would be necessary to resolve the dilemma of which principle was more important. Thus, some inequality could promote effectiveness gains if, for example, tax application required non-uniform audit policies across territories because of differences in the nature and/or the level of tax fraud. Another instance would be gains arising from lower compliance costs if decentralization led to more streamlined administrative procedures.[7]

However, according to Garcia et al. (1998), such divergences would be limited in the case of income tax because of its key role in the tax system. In any case, the dilemma of effectiveness versus equality – in both examples mentioned above: lower tax compliance and lower compliance costs versus uniform taxpayer treatment across the national territory – is fundamental when considering any institutional reform of the tax administration that followed decentralization criteria. This is because it would affect income tax,[8] currently a shared tax between the central administration and the ACs.

2.2 Institutional Structure

As reflected in Figure 10.1, there are 20 tax administrations in Spain leaving aside the local level.

The tax administration levels in Spain can be described as follows:

2.2.1 The state tax authority (AEAT)

The AEAT is in charge of the application of centrally administered taxes and some other taxes shared between the central government and the ACs. In particular, it administers income tax, corporation tax, VAT, excise and import taxes, and shares the administration of wealth tax with the ACs under the common regime. Created by Law 31/1990, the agency began work on 1 January 1992. It is a public body falling under the aegis of the Ministry of Economy and Finance, but usually treated as an independent organization (Ortiz-Calle, 1998).

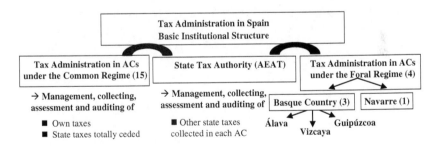

Source: Sánchez-Saché (2006).

Figure 10.1   Tax administration in Spain: the AEAT and AC tax administrations

In 2004, the agency had a staff of 27 415 people, which means that the ratio between yield and personnel was 5.14 million euros per person.

2.2.2   The Directorate General of Taxes (DGT) in each AC

Table 10.1 displays a summary of the main characteristics of the tax administration in ACs under the common regime. In fact, the institution in charge of administering taxes is not always denominated DGT. Unlike the AEAT, none of the DGTs have (yet) adopted the administrative format of an agency. Most of the ACs had taken on tax administration authority by the mid-1980s, with Catalonia being the first to do so and the Autonomous Community of Madrid being the last.

The ratio between the amount of tax yielded (in thousands of euros) and the number of people devoted to the application of the taxes shows great heterogeneity. The range varies from €7480 (Catalonia) to €1485 (Castilla-La Mancha).[9] This may be due to differences in the way ACs are organized, resulting in differences in the sums attributed to personnel.[10] It may also, however, arise from possible differences concerning personnel requirements, which may depend on the socioeconomic features of an Autonomous Community's taxpayers and/or the composition of its tax bases, that is to say, the difficulties in guaranteeing tax compliance within its territory.[11]

The last column of the table shows a selection of various areas of collaboration between the AEAT and the AC tax administrations. All of the ACs have signed a collaboration agreement covering mandatory collection (i.e., collection of taxes once the voluntary timing for voluntary tax compliance has run out), and they collaborate in the annual income tax filing campaigns (see endnote 6). In the case of Catalonia, there is a working group (referred to as 'Language' in Table 10.1), whose objective is to promote, as far as possible, the use of Catalan in all internal documentation, such as in AEAT documents and programs. Most of the ACs have created a technical committee through their Territorial Councils on Taxation to address the relationship between VAT and TCT (tax on capital transfers and stamp duty). The committees resolve operational conflicts concerning which tax is applicable, VAT or TCT. Finally, some ACs have signed an agreement concerning the use of information technology in taxation (Andalucía, SOUTH project; Asturias, project TRASGU; Balearic Islands, project SEAS; Canary Islands; Cantabria, project MOURO; Castilla-La Mancha, project GRECO; La Rioja, project ORIA; Valencia, project TIRANT). The agreement aims to improve information exchange between the ACs and the AEAT by creating integrated, modern tax management systems linking the administrations.

Finally, it is worth spelling out the administration powers of the ACs under the common regime over taxes that are totally ceded to the AC or

Table 10.1 Basic characteristics of AC tax administrations under the common regime

	Name	Year	Staff	Revenue per Staff (in thousands)	Collaboration with AEAT
Andalucía	Directorate General of Taxes (DGT)	1985	881	€1911	Income tax campaign/Mandatory collection/TCT-VAT
Aragón	DGT	1985	139	€2885	Mandatory collection VAT
Asturias	Finance and Inland Revenue Office	1986	63	€3638	Income tax campaign/Mandatory collection
Balearic Islands	Tax Department	1986	94	€4090	Idem.
Canary Islands	DGT	1985	165	€2396	Idem.
Cantabria	Inland Revenue Office	1986	39	€3713	Computing/Income tax campaign/Mandatory collection
Catalonia	DGT	1982	355	€7480	Income tax campaign/Mandatory collection/TCT-VAT/Language
Castile-Léon	DGT	1985	331	€1823	Mandatory collection/TCT-VAT
Castilla-La Mancha	DGT	1985	196	€1485	Computing/Income tax campaign/Mandatory collection
Extremadura	General Revenue Office	1984	87	€1565	Mandatory VAT collection
Galicia	DGT	1985	342	€1567	Idem.
La Rioja	DGT	1987	42	€2298	Computing/Income tax campaign/Mandatory collection
Madrid	DGT	1995	345	€6484	Mandatory collection
Murcia	DGT	1987	141	€1945	Idem.
Valencia	DGT	1984	314	€4832	Computing/Income tax campaign/Mandatory collection

Note: VAT: value-added tax; TCT: tax on capital transfers and stamp duty.

Source: Reports on the collection of ceded taxes, General State Budgets over several years.

shared with the state (Table 10.2). With respect to IGT and TCT, the powers of management and assessment, auditing and collection correspond to the ACs. Filing returns for the two taxes can be done not only through the offices of an AC's own DGT, but also through 'assessment offices of the pertinent district', which are run by the local recorder's office. Such offices invoice the corresponding DGT for their services, and do not have audit power. This 'decentralization' or 'externalization' in the application of the cited taxes in each AC generates dysfunctions in certain cases described in the reports of the cession of taxes, namely when transferring the collections made by those offices and/or when sharing the information that they have. Wealth tax administration is done jointly by the AEAT and the ACs. As a result, a tax-payer must file the tax return with the AEAT together with the income tax return. The wealth tax return forms – unlike those for other taxes – cannot be adapted by the ACs. However, ACs can perform tax control tasks at that point in the process (e.g., verifying data or monitoring the obligation to file tax returns). They have the power of collecting assessments made by their own DGT, during the voluntary period, and all the debts in the mandatory period. Finally, with respect to auditing, the AEAT can also commence audit procedures and verification of wealth tax.

In Table 10.2, tasks that are the exclusive competence of the ACs appear in darker grey, whereas shared WT administration is shown in lighter grey. Regarding income tax administration, the ACs only participate through the Joint Commission, their Territorial Councils on Taxation and the AEAT Board. As for the excise duty categories, it is envisioned that they can be administered by the ACs alone, if they should demand to do so. After all,

Table 10.2   AC responsibilities in the application of ceded taxes

	Management/Assessment	Auditing	Collection
Wealth tax (WT)			
Inheritance and gift tax (IGT)			
Tax on capital transfers and stamp duty (TCT)			
Income tax (IT)			
Excise duties on retail sales of hydrocarbons (EDH) & excise duty on certain means of transport (EDMT)			

Note: The darker the cell the greater the level of responsibility for the AC.

Source: Own elaboration, from Law 21/2001.

yielded revenues belong completely to the ACs, even they are currently administered by the AEAT.

2.2.3 Tax administration in the ACs under the foral regime

As recent institutional reforms in tax administration solely affect the ACs under the common regime, we will only briefly describe the institutional organization of tax administration under the special foral regime (pertaining to the Comunidades Forales of the Basque Country and Navarre). In the case of the Basque Country, power corresponds to the three foral provinces, Álava, Vizcaya and Guipúzcoa. Specifically, they are in charge of administering all taxes within their territories. The central administration only has the exclusive power – through the offices of the AEAT in the AC – of regulating, managing, auditing, reviewing and collecting import taxes and excises and VAT on imports. However, the AEAT is also in charge of managing corporation tax and VAT returns for those companies that are required to file returns under state law, following the geographic criteria of both tax bases, even though they are fiscally domiciled in the Basque Country.

The main mission of the Tax Coordination Agency of the Basque Country (see Figure 10.2) is to promote harmonization, coordination and collaboration among the foral provinces themselves in order to improve greater effectiveness in tax management. The Commission on Tax Coordination and Regulatory Evaluation must take charge of many tasks including facilitating uniform performance standards, plans and software as well as articulating instruments, procedures and methods for

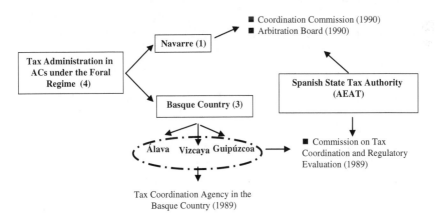

Source: Sánchez-Saché (2006).

Figure 10.2   Relationships between the AEAT and the foral provinces

collaboration and information exchange. Furthermore, it must analyze any question raised in the course of auditing that affects the state tax authority and the respective foral provinces, and it must tackle problems from evaluating tax effects.[12]

The tax administration in Navarre is an autonomous administrative body and, as in the foral provinces of the Basque Country, it takes responsibility for the management, assessment, collection and inspection of most taxes. As in the case of the Basque Country, the AEAT also has a presence in Navarre.

The Coordination Commission basically has the same functions as its counterpart in the Basque Country. An arbitration board has been created to resolve any conflict that may arise between the state administration and the Autonomous Community of Navarre or between Navarre and the administration of any other AC. Such conflict may arise in the application of taxes or the assessment of the share corresponding to each administration in the case of joint taxation such as corporate tax or VAT. Finally, it may occur when applying liability criteria in the case of traditional ceded taxes.

2.3   Main Dysfunctions

Most of the dysfunctions described below arise from the fact that common regime ACs do not take part directly in administering income tax.

2.3.1   Financial effect caused by how income tax revenues are allocated to the ACs

According to the present model of regional financing, the income tax share corresponding to each AC is administered by the AEAT. Each month, the AEAT makes payments on account based on each AC's predicted collection. Until now, the basic characteristics of this procedure have been as follows: 1) forecast revenues have turned out to be calculated systematically in a lower-bound estimate; 2) monthly payments on account are supposed to be 98 percent of forecast and (3) the final assessment (calculated as the difference between 98 percent of forecast and 100 percent of final revenues) is done with a delay of almost two years.[13]

In the case of Catalonia in the year 2003, this way of making the corresponding payments has cost the regional government 36 million euros (in 2006 prices), according to calculations done by Sánchez-Saché (2006). Taking into consideration the new regulation (Royal Decree-Law 12/2005) whereby payments on account are to be 100 percent of forecast, the financial cost diminishes slightly to 33 million euros. Therefore, the reform has reduced the initially calculated cost.

Similar situations have also been identified by Grady (2004) in the Canadian case, arising from the mistrust of certain provinces concerning the computing procedure used to calculate their share of taxes administered by the federal government. The federal government's confirmation of financial costs brought with it a commitment to compensate provinces for such costs, so they reformulated how the assessment was calculated in order to avoid such costs befalling the provinces. In any case, this type of dysfunction does not imply an institutional reform of the tax administration, but rather – given a certain institutional structure – an improvement in assessment procedures and implementation of a system of compensation for such financial costs (at least, when they surpass a certain threshold).

2.3.2 Income tax withholding mechanism

In section 2.1, it was noted that some legal experts consider tax administration to confer a degree of 'fiscal autonomy in the widest sense' (Ramallo and Zornoza, 1995, p. 40). They make the argument on the grounds that tax accountability is greater when rule-making and administrative powers are connected. In that sense, it would be interesting to see whether income tax withholding at source could differentiate which percentages correspond to the state and which correspond to the AC where the taxpayer has tax residence. It would also be interesting to see whether the withholding percentages were affected by reforms carried out at each level of government. Both cases would make income tax more accountable to the taxpayer, and the revenue yielded would be adjusted automatically to the expenditure needs of the corresponding AC.

In the new income tax law of 2007, the above differentiation is not taken into account. The dysfunction would not require any institutional reform of the tax administration, but it would instead call for administrative procedures to be adapted regarding the withholding mechanism. In such case, the (possible) greater management costs would be traded off against greater taxpayer accountability and the immediate adjustment of the income tax collection to each AC's expenditure needs.

2.3.3 Income tax information

As noted previously, AC access to AEAT information has improved substantially, especially since 2002. Nevertheless, when reading the reports on the collection of ceded taxes, certain dysfunctions are still apparent. For example, in the 2002 report, the Directorate General for Tax (DGT) of Galicia complained about its difficulties in including a forecast of income tax revenues in its revenue budget, due to the lack of information provided by the AEAT.

The lack of information also affects the legislative reform processes that certain ACs are attempting to carry out. Without sufficiently detailed, up-to-date information on its taxpayers, an AC cannot devise a suitable design for the legislative changes that it intends to make. Therefore, it is understandable that an AC does not embark on substantial tax reform. To a certain extent, this may explain the limited income tax reform undertaken by the ACs. This dysfunction, however, would not require an institutional reform of the tax administration. It could simply be solved by providing sufficiently timely and complete access to the tax information held by the AEAT (see Joint Commission, 2004, p. 11).

2.3.4   Income tax auditing

On the one hand, decentralizing audit tasks can improve tax compliance, if we assume that the closer a tax administration is, the greater its knowledge is of the level of fraud in its territory. In any case, this amounts to pure speculation. It is evident, on the other hand, that, when an AC makes use of its legal powers over income tax, the regional income tax presents peculiar features (e.g., a greater amount of regional tax credits),[14] which might make it essential to establish 'specific control filters' for tax audit purposes (Costa i Solà, 2006, p. 6).[15] In that sense, it is essential to adapt auditing plans to fit better with each AC's own specific social and economic reality. Furthermore, it is necessary for plans to be designed and executed in a decentralized manner, based on the assumption that ACs possess a knowledge of local idiosyncrasies that is (somehow) superior in the fight against tax fraud.[16,17]

Along these lines, the Joint Commission (2004) has sought to harness the AEAT Board by proposing that the General Regional Plan be redefined with a twofold objective: 1) clearly specifying the plan's content and 2) setting AEAT objectives at the AC level, that is managing the degree of compliance according to AC-specific indicators. The aim is that AC tax administrations should have real influence when the AEAT takes fundamental strategic decisions and sets performance objectives. Without any doubt, these questions could only be resolved through institutional reform involving some kind of institutional decentralization in the application of income tax.

2.3.5   Better taxpayer service

In Section 2.3.4, decentralization is shown to result in improved levels of tax compliance – subject to essential coordination between administrations. This would fit with Art. 103.1 of the Spanish Constitution (see Section 2.1.2) and could be supplemented with better service to the citizen (Art. 3.2 of the General Tax Act, see Section 2.1.2 again). In particular, better service to the citizen could be delivered through wider use of Spain's

co-official languages (i.e., Basque, Catalan, Galician) in the tax administration. After all, this is an issue that is currently being considered by the
corresponding Territorial Council on Taxation. Another improvement
would be to move tax offices (physically) nearer to the taxpayer and, therefore, clearly lower tax compliance costs. This could occur because decentralization could combine the points of contact between the taxpayer and
the AEAT and the DGT, so that the DGT could independently process
returns or deal with any other type of tax information, regardless of the
government level to which the tax legally corresponds.

In order to promote the use of the co-official languages and to guarantee greater physical proximity between the taxpayer and the administration,
it would not be essential to enact institutional reform of the tax administration. It would simply be necessary for the AEAT to increase the number
of delegations or administrations.[18] However, that would have an economic
cost, so it seems more sensible to combine the resources of the different
administrations to facilitate taxpayer compliance.

2.3.6 Direct management control over shared taxes

In Canada, the Canadian Revenue Agency (CRA) is the federal agency in
charge of applying the Canadian tax system. With the provinces of Canada
participating in its direction, it was created in 1999 in part to guarantee
fairer treatment to the provinces, because they had expressed their concerns
over the degree of effectiveness shown by Revenue Canada (a department
of the federal government) in administering their taxes. This is an example
of the distrust that can arise when a tax administration is different from the
one that corresponds to all or part of the tax revenue collected.

In the case of Spain, that situation also appears as a problem in the
reports carried out by the General Inspectorate of the Ministry of Public
Finance. For example, Extremadura reported in 2002 that the number of
wealth tax audits had been falling over time, because the audit board of the
AEAT was intensifying its audits on VAT, corporation tax and income for
businesses in the income tax. Valencia complained in its 2002 report that
the AEAT was mainly concentrating on income tax without making
enough effort in publicizing wealth tax compliance. After all, a wealth tax
return must be filed with the AEAT along with the income tax return. Thus,
the AEAT could carry out a wealth tax inspection as a result of its income
tax inspection (see Section 2.2.2). In both cases, the economic explanation
lies in the AEAT's limited incentives to audit or promote voluntary wealth
tax compliance, since it only incurs costs for the AEAT and the revenue
would correspond to the AC in question.

At the empirical level, Esteller (2005b) has found that in ACs whose
income tax share is smaller (throughout the period under analysis,

1993–2000, the percentage was not constant, since after 1994 not all the ACs accepted that shares of income tax revenue be differentiated by AC, among other factors), the efforts of the AEAT in guaranteeing income tax compliance are less strenuous. Again, the fact has a straightforward economic explanation: asymmetry occurs in certain shared taxes (e.g., income tax) between the AEAT's assumption of costs (100 percent) and its collection percentage (< 100 percent).

In this case, mistrust can only be overcome through AC management involvement in the application of shared taxes; through access to performance information against control objectives set at the beginning of the year (as suggested by the Joint Commission with respect to the AEAT Board's functions, see Section 2.3.4); and preferably, through direct AC participation in tax administration.

To sum up, this section has established the existence of certain dysfunctions in the Spanish tax administration. Thanks to forums of institutional collaboration and the passage of time, most of them have tended to be solved. However, overcoming some of them will probably require institutional reform of tax administration in Spain, such as giving direct management control over shared taxes to the ACs, or adapting tax control plans to the unique nature of each AC. It may only require minor agreements between the AEAT and the ACs to address other issues, such as improved information access, a better income tax withholding mechanism, improved calculation of payments on account with respect to AC shares of income tax payments and, to a certain extent, the better service to the taxpayer.

2.4 Reform Proposals

Section 2.4.1 describes the main aspects of the reform proposals made by two working groups set up by the Spanish Fiscal and Financial Policy Council. In Section 2.4.2, Catalonia's new Statute of Autonomy is highlighted, along with, to a lesser extent, the proposed reform of Andalucía's Statute of Autonomy and the already passed statutory reform for Valencia.

2.4.1 Reports on reform of the AC financing system

2.4.1.1 *An integrated tax administration (1995)*
In 1995, the study group set up by the Spanish Fiscal and Financial Policy Council (CPFF) published its *Report on the Present System of Autonomic Financing and Its Problems* (Grupo de Estudio, 1995). The report proposed the creation of a new entity, an integrated tax administration. This proposal could be considered forward-looking because it was prepared with

the notion in mind that the ACs and the state's central administration might share certain taxes, as currently happens.

For the authors, the touchstone of any institutional reform of the tax administration must be essential collaboration when administering taxes of a personal nature. With respect to these taxes (for example, income tax and VAT), the taxpayer may reside in one AC, yet earn income and engage in consumption in another. As result, the authors raise two potential reform options: either setting up information exchange mechanisms, or pooling management of services. Given the high costs of inter-institutional collaboration and, according to the authors, the difficulty of implementing the first option, they come down strongly in favor of the second option. The second option would involve the creation of an agency, but it would not mean a decrease in AC financial autonomy, because it is perfectly possible, according to the authors, to differentiate the political scope of tax system design and the technical scope of its application. Benefits would derive from AC coordination within a single integrated agency. It would even permit taking advantage of present economies of scale in the administration of taxes. In addition, AC representation in the agency would be equal to the state's central administration's participation. No dependency would be established between them. Both levels of government would act with functional independence.

Among the proposal's basic elements, one of some importance is the fact that the agency 'would need to be structured using decentralized criteria for the political organization of our country' (Grupo de Estudio, 1995, p. 162). The point is not much developed in the text of the proposal (on p. 165, regional representation on the agency's control body is mentioned), but it refers, in all likelihood, to the administrative structure of the agency, whereas its direction would be unitary. If so, it is worth asking how the agency could simultaneously internalize the (potentially different) objectives of each of the entities represented in the agency (i.e., each AC under the common regime and the state's central administration) when making tax reforms or, simply, deliberating decisions with respect to tax treatment that was (slightly) different from the treatment given to its own taxpayers (vis-à-vis the principle of equality, see Section 2.1.2).

2.4.1.2 *A single, shared tax agency (2002)*

Another *Report on Reform of the Autonomic Financing System* (Secretaría de Estado de Hacienda, 2002) was also prepared by a committee of experts at the request of the CPFF. The report was structured on the basis of questions formulated by the CPFF. In particular, regarding tax administration, the question (No. 11) addressed the 'possibility of adapting AEAT regulation and economic-administrative jurisdiction to a Spanish decentralized framework in the service of greater cohesion in the management and application of the Spanish tax system' (p. 85).

Identifying problems in the present institutional structure (e.g., lack of information sharing, and duplicated or overlapping tasks), the committee proposed the creation of a single, shared tax agency, in which all ACs and the state central administration would participate. The new tax agency would be made fully responsible for managing state taxes, including those totally ceded to or shared with the ACs. The experts note that the proposal does not undermine the principle of regional autonomy, since the principle would be embodied by AC participation in the agency. Thus, the exercise of fiscal autonomy would be guaranteed, according to the report, by means of the exercise of legal competences and the agency's own actions, which the citizen would perceive as partially regional in nature.

The advantages of this institutional form are: economies of scale (as with the first proposal for institutional reform); the centralization of tax information; better service to the taxpayer, who should only have to address a single administration and the formulation of common standardized criteria for all tax legislation, so that all taxpayers would be treated equally by the tax administration and any possible problems of tax responsibility would be avoided.[19]

Both the 1995 and 2002 reports try to integrate (1995) or to share (2002) the application of taxes in Spain in a new entity, bringing together taxes that are currently administered by both the AEAT and AC tax administrations. The similarity stems from the key principle on which they were both based: promoting coordination between administrations and common assessment standards for all state taxes. (In particular, the second aspect is explicitly mentioned by the 2002 report.) The 2002 report definitely tends to emphasize that such reform would not involve curtailing AC tax autonomy. However, given the steps taken in this area, it would probably be more difficult to argue that now than in 1995.

2.4.2. Statutory reforms
Catalonia's 2006 Statute of Autonomy came into effect on 9 August 2006.[20] Art. 204 of the statute makes reference to the 'Tax Agency of Catalonia' and states the following:

1. The Taxation Agency of Catalonia is responsible for management, collection, settlement and inspection of all Generalitat of Catalonia taxes and also, when delegated by the State, of State taxes which are totally ceded to the Generalitat.
2. The Taxation Administration of the State is responsible for management, collection, settlement and inspection of other State taxes collected in Catalonia, without prejudice to any delegation to the Generalitat in this

respect or to any collaboration that may be established especially when required by the nature of the tax.

For implementation of the content of the previous paragraph, a Consortium, or an equivalent entity, shall be constituted, within two years, with parity of participation by the Taxation Administration Agency of the State and the Taxation Agency of Catalonia. The Consortium may be transformed into the Taxation Administration in Catalonia.

3. The two taxation administrations shall establish the necessary mechanisms to permit presentation and reception in their respective offices of tax forms and other taxation-related documentation which may have a bearing on the other administration, with a view to facilitating taxpayer compliance with tax obligations. The Generalitat participates, in a manner yet to be established, in State taxation entities or bodies with responsibility for management, collection, settlement and inspection of partially ceded State taxes.

4. The Taxation Agency of Catalonia shall be created by means of an Act of Parliament and shall have full power and attributes for organization and exercise of the functions referred to in Section 1.

5. Management functions in relation to local taxes may be delegated to the Taxation Agency of Catalonia by the municipalities.

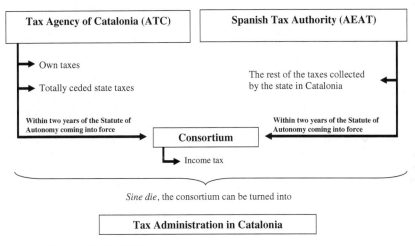

Source: Sánchez-Saché (2006).

Figure 10.3   The tax administration in Catalonia, according to the Statute of Autonomy of 2006

Figure 10.3 is intended to display the content of Art. 204 of the statute. The elements emphasized in the article are as follows:

1. It is anticipated that taxes shared between the state and the Generalitat (e.g., income tax or VAT) can be jointly administered by the two

administrations. In fact, a two-year deadline is set for the initiation of joint administration through a consortium (or equivalent entity) in which the two levels of government would take equal part.[21]

2. Both administrations will facilitate tax compliance by establishing the necessary collaborative mechanisms in order to offer so-called 'one-stop shopping', making it possible to address any tax issue there concerning any administration (which would be totally congruent with what is recommended in the 2002 report, enabling the taxpayer to have dealings with no more than one administration).

3. It provides for creation of the Taxation Agency of Catalonia, which in its new format will do the administrative tasks done by the DGT until now. In this sense, it will have the same status as an AEAT agency, which is of relevance in setting up the consortium.

4. Last, although no deadline is set, the statute also anticipates that the consortium can eventually be turned into the Tax Administration in Catalonia, that is to say, applying all taxes levied in Catalonia.

Consequently, the reform seems to combine most of the characteristics that could be demanded of tax administration in a decentralized context. On the one hand, it includes what could be expected of a centralized administration. In other words, according to the nomenclature of the reports cited in the previous section, it would be 'integrated'. Thus, it would allow coordination between the AEAT (that would take part in the consortium) and the other ACs. It would give access to a global database and have the advantage of economies of scale. In contrast to the ACs under the foral regime, for example, or the German case, in which the administration is decentralized at the level of the *Länder*, these advantages would all arise because the AEAT would work together with the Catalan agency in the application of taxes in Catalonia, under decentralized management, with a degree of non-uniformity vis-à-vis other territories that was compatible with a minimum level of equality in the application of taxes (especially, concerning income tax).[22] In addition, the reform would contribute to reducing the costs of tax compliance by raising the number of points of contact between the taxpayer and the tax administration in the territory (Art. 204.3).

The Andalucía Statute of Autonomy also puts forward the notion of a consortium, although the deadline for its creation is not specified, nor is it anticipated that it become the Tax Administration in Andalucía. In particular, Art. 178.2, says that taxes other than own taxes and state-ceded taxes will be open to joint management when so required by the nature of the tax. To this end, a consortium will be formed, and participation will be equal between the state tax authority and Andalucía's tax administration. As in the case of Catalonia's Statute of Autonomy, the creation of an Andalucian tax agency is envisaged.

Last, the approved reform of Valencia's Statute of Autonomy may be described as less ambitious than the other two in relation to tax administration. In Art. 69.1, the new statute states that 'the application of the Generalitat's own taxes is entrusted to the Valencian Tax Service, under a system of functional decentralization'. In subpoint 3, it also states: 'When the application functions [over ceded taxes currently administered by the AEAT] were not attributed to the Generalitat, according to the previous section, measures will be taken to strengthen collaboration with the State Tax Administration in the application of the stated functions'. In other words, as in the case of Catalonia or Andalucía, a new entity is to be created to administer ceded taxes and own taxes. Administrative flexibility would probably be gained in its functioning. However, unlike either of the previous cases, it only expresses a wish to strengthen collaboration between the Generalitat of Valencia and the state in the application of taxes in Valencia. It does not envisage the creation of a consortium.[23]

3 ECONOMIC ANALYSIS OF THE PROPOSED REFORMS

This section sets out to analyze the basic characteristics of the previously cited institutional reforms, bearing in mind certain findings obtained in the economic literature. Unfortunately, the tax administration literature is not large, especially on the empirical side.[24] Nevertheless, from certain studies, interesting conclusions can be drawn concerning the Spanish case. Three aspects in particular are of interest: the level of tax compliance (Section 3.1), incentives for coordination and collaboration (Section 3.2), and the relationship between tax administration and tax autonomy (Section 3.3).

3.1 Level of Tax Compliance

Most of the institutional reforms mentioned in Section 2.4 propose integrating the tax administration and, in some cases, under a decentralized structure. For example, Catalonia's Statute of Autonomy would set up a sort of partnership between the AEAT and the Tax Agency of Catalonia. Thus, the first question to pose is whether decentralization would lead to a rise in tax compliance or a fall. Institutional reform can only be deemed positive if the answer is 'a rise'.

In a decentralized context, two features are often apparent in sub-central governments. First, if they have a degree of tax autonomy over mobile tax bases, a process of 'tax competition' may be seen. That is, attracting tax bases (i.e., financial resources) or avoiding their loss, which amounts to the same thing, will create an incentive for any sub-central government to reduce the tax burden. This behavior could lead to a 'race to the bottom', which is to say, to a smaller overall tax burden. Second, it is very likely that tax autonomy causes disparities in the level of per capita resources among sub-central governments. If, because of inter-territorial solidarity, it is desirable to avoid or mitigate this, the central government will implement a fiscal equalization system that eliminates or mitigate disparities. However, what is the relationship between the two factors – that is, tax competition and tax equalization – and the level of tax compliance?

On the one hand, addressing processes of tax competition, the literature has usually supposed that sub-central governments can modify statutory tax rates or other parameters affecting the nominal tax burden (e.g., tax credits and deductions). However, the greater or lesser effort made by a sub-central agency to ensure tax compliance within its territory, which the literature normally associates with a greater or lesser chance of being audited, will eventually affect the level of effective tax burden. Therefore, it can also change the incentives of tax bases to move (Cremer and Gahvari, 2000). As a result, the decentralization of tax control powers can lead to lower compliance and reduce incentives to fight against tax fraud.[25]

On the other hand, the effects of the equalization system on tax administration must also be viewed as potentially negative, involving less taxation control and, therefore, lower tax compliance. This has to do with the size of the equalization grant that a sub-central entity receives. The grant is calculated as the difference between the overall average tax capacity and that of the AC in question. If the difference is positive, the entity must receive a transfer calculated as the product of the difference and a standard rate. This means that the amount in question is a priori independent of AC decisions. This would not be the case, however, if the grant relied upon, for example, an AC's level of tax burden. However, when the sub-central entity is responsible for tax administration, it can indirectly modify its tax capacity depending on (as shall be seen further ahead) how the indicator of tax capacity is defined. So far, we are supposing that there is a direct relation between net collection (and, therefore, the level of tax compliance) and the indicator of tax capacity. In such case, tax capacity may fall because of greater tax fraud leniency or less onerous assessment levels, either of which may end up 'exporting' the tax burden to other sub-central entities that finance the equalization system. That is to say, collection shortfalls would automatically be compensated at the standard rate via horizontal equalization (that can be funded by the federal government, viz. Canada; or by the other sub-central bodies, as in the German case). Baretti, Huber and

Lichtblau (2002) used the German case to demonstrate two key character-istics of the present analysis: the decentralization of tax administration and a system of horizontal equalization.[26] The existence of such disincentives has helped to widen the fiscal gap. These authors called the effect a 'tax on tax revenue'.

A priori, the negative effects on tax administration arising from the equalization system could be solved using an indicator of tax capacity that was completely exogenous to the decisions of the sub-central entity. A macroeconomic indicator such as GDP, for example, could be used. When choosing an alternative, efficiency should be weighed up against the goal of not generating perverse tax incentives or being vague about when tax bases are to be measured. Should such imprecision be relatively significant, it would be advisable to use dedicated displays of the size of each tax base (under what is called a 'representative tax system', or RTS). In order to cal-culate this, it will be critical to have tax collection data to hand. For that reason, as argued earlier, any sub-central action generating greater tax col-lection for itself (e.g., exercising greater control over tax fraud) will be indi-rectly understood to have raised its tax capacity, because tax capacity will have to be recalculated on the basis of the new data collected. However, cal-culating the level of tax capacity also uses collection data from the other sub-central entities.[27] As a result, an increase in collection will not have a 100 per cent impact on tax capacity levels, but it will be directly propor-tional to the quantitative importance with respect to the other entities (i.e., if they all have the same importance, the impact would be of $1/n$, where n is the number of sub-central entities).[28] In the appendix to this chapter, this statement is demonstrated and a comparison is made of the effects of various tax capacity calculation approaches and their incentives or disin-centives to effective tax management.

Normally, the effects of tax competition and tax equalization have been treated independently in the literature.[29] However, Table 10.3 shows the consequences of dealing with them simultaneously.

According to Table 10.3, an increase in tax control always produces a positive effect, because it raises tax collection via the sanctions imposed on uncovered fraud. Some indirect effects may also arise, however, which might change the size of the net effect in various situations to be described shortly. The first column in the table reflects the effects of an increase in tax control exercised over a productive mobile factor (e.g., capital).

If the equalization transfer is a 'lump sum' (see first row), that is, a macroeconomic indicator of tax capacity is used or, in other words, tax control actions have a limited impact on the indicator of tax capacity (i.e., $1/n \rightarrow 0$), then a strict compliance policy may generate an outflow of tax bases without any change in the amount of the transfer.

Tax administration

Table 10.3   Effects of an increase in the efforts of the tax administration

	Mobile Tax Base	Immobile Tax Base
'Lump sum' equalization	At a given level of taxation, the amount to collect will increase due to established tax fraud punishment (+)	At a given level of taxation, the amount to collect will increase due to established tax fraud punishment (+)
	On the other hand, tax bases will tend to 'emigrate' to other jurisdictions where inspection actions are not as severe (−)	Furthermore, greater efforts will lead to a higher base value and thus to greater collection, given the effective tax burden (+)
Equalization dependent on the efforts of the tax administration	At a given level of taxation, the amount to collect will increase due to established tax fraud punishment (+)	At a given level of taxation, the amount to collect will increase due to established tax fraud punishment (+)
	Negative mobility effects are compensated (let us suppose completely) by the equalization system (so this is a positive effect of equalization in the case of mobility)	Greater taxation will produce lower transfers, which compensates (let us suppose completely) for additional tax revenue collected, given the level of tax rates (a negative effective of equalization, or a 'tax on tax revenue') (−)

Tax base 'flight' would not occur if the taxed productive factor were immobile (e.g., labor), as reflected in the second column. However, if the transfer depends on the efforts made by the tax administration (see second row) and the tax base is immobile, an increase in control efforts entails a negative effect. The tax administration would receive a lower equalization transfer. This negative effect contrasts with what happens when the taxed productive factor is mobile. In that case, increased tax control generates tax base flight, which is compensated by the equalization system. That is, unlike in the previous situation, the equalization system now benefits the entity that increases tax compliance efforts, since it is isolated in this case from the pernicious effects of tax competition.

Therefore, when the taxed productive factor is mobile, it is beneficial to set up an equalization system based (indirectly) on tax compliance efforts. However, the opposite happens when the productive factor is immobile. Nevertheless, if we start from the notion that the most efficient situation is the one in which equalization is based on 'lump sum' transfers and the tax base is immobile, any other situation entails a social cost. Now let us suppose the situation at issue was identical to a centralized system of the tax administration, where, by definition, equalization transfers do not play any role and the mobility of tax bases is not seen as a problem, since the centralized administrative unit's sphere of action covers the entire territory. In any case, the important thing to bear in mind is that a decentralized tax administration as envisaged in Catalonia's 2006 Statute of Autonomy avoids generating a social cost. In efficiency terms, the solution blocks any allocation other than 'lump sum' equalization regarding immobile tax bases, since direction is shared between the AEAT and the ATC, and the AEAT should counteract any incentive for the ATC to behave strategically. The AEAT's objectives are meant to fit overall standards of social well-being and not only those of the respective ACs.

3.2   Coordination and Collaboration

Section 2.4.1 showed how various proposals for institutional reform of Spain's tax administration have responded to the need to foster greater coordination and collaboration in the application of the Spanish tax system. Further, Section 2.1.1 identified several areas in which Spanish legislation has encouraged collaboration and coordination between tax administrations. But, is the matter really so important?

For example, Spain is one of the few countries that have a wealth tax (WT). One of the main reasons for the tax, as well-argued in the autonomic financing report of 2002 (Secretaría de Estado de Hacienda, 2002), is to serve as a reference instrument for income tax, given the limited amount of revenue it can generate.[30] However, the report adds that AC administration and the AEAT do not always work in a timely fashion (p. 87). In fact, Section 2.3.6 in this chapter gives certain practical examples of the failures that may take place when collecting wealth tax, which can end up diminishing its instrumental value in income tax collection.

Esteller (2004) uses a theoretical model to demonstrate the positive tax compliance effects of fostering collaboration and coordination between administrations in the cases of income tax and wealth tax. For example, the model identifies collaboration with situations in which the AEAT carries out an income tax inspection and simultaneously makes an effort to uncover possible WT fraud (as envisioned in Art. 46.3 of Law 21/2001). In addition, coordination means that the inspection policies for both taxes (income tax and WT) should be designed using the same audit scheme in order to be totally effective. Basically, coordination means avoiding a low audit probability in one tax when the effort for the other tax would be great.

Such asymmetry can have negative effects on compliance levels for the two taxes. If coordination and collaboration actually work – which is an open question, analyzing the 2002 report on the autonomic financing system (Secretaría de Estado de Hacienda, 2002) or reading various reports on the management of ceded taxes – the wealth tax becomes an interesting instrument for the tax system because it manages to fulfill the role of tax control. If, on the other hand, they do not work, it is worth asking, as the experts who compiled the 2002 report did, what sense it makes keeping Spain as one of the few EU (15) countries and OECD countries where the tax is still in force.[31]

The economic literature does not explain in much detail the conditions under which administrations will establish some type of collaboration/ coordination. The seminal article on these questions is the one by Bachetta and Paz Espinosa (1995), which demonstrated that, in certain cases, collaboration will arise spontaneously because it is strategically beneficial for the region/country to act that way. (Most typically this type of literature is framed internationally and, therefore, makes reference to countries.) In any case, it is a very particular situation.

Very recently, Keen and Ligthart (2006) have completed a very interesting review of the theoretical literature and of practical examples of collaboration (between countries). One of their more interesting conclusions is that it is not only important that countries exchange information, but that they truly make an effective use of the information. It matters whether taxpayers clearly perceive that any attempt at tax arbitrage (e.g., relocalization for tax reasons, or capital evasion) will be punished by the tax administration where the tax obligation is assessed.

In the Spanish case, the main conclusion concerning collaboration/ cooperation is that automatic channels must be established through the Joint Commission or the Territorial Councils on Taxation.[32,33] (The conditions for voluntary collaboration/coordination, since they only emerge from the literature, are not very admissible.) In any case, with respect to the reforms raised in Section 2.4, none of them would manage to fulfill the collaboration/coordination principle. Therefore, in no way would this question be subject to discussion when considering institutional reform of tax administration in Spain.

3.3   Tax Autonomy

There is no doubt that this issue is a controversial one. For example, the study group (Grupo de Estudio, 1995) is categorical when it states that political decisions made about public revenue are based almost exclusively on the volume of revenue to collect and its distributive pattern; to a lesser extent, the design of the legal framework for reaching these two objectives is also relevant, but it is merely a technical question. The group concludes by stating that any formula for institutional organization of the tax administration does not affect political decisions on tax autonomy. As a result, the institutional make-up of the tax administration would have to be chosen on grounds of efficiency, which leads it to raise the creation of a single, shared tax administration, as noted in Section 2.4.1.1.

Certainly, a priori, it is difficult to find administrative approaches that result in increased tax autonomy. However, it is possible. For example, on certain occasions to be noted shortly, the administration of taxes can affect political decisions previously taken on amounts to be collected and on the distributive pattern, potentially distorting the initial political criteria. Yet, it is necessary to have information on the results of the later process of tax administration ex ante in order to design the taxes correctly. In the second case, it would be necessary for sub-central entities to have access to tax information channels that were automatic and complete in order to design its taxes, even if there were a single tax administration and it were shared or even centralized. In the first case, however, sub-central entities must have an active role to play in the management of tax administration, both over 100 percent ceded taxes and over taxes shared with the central administration.

The economic literature has shown that there are certain situations in which relationships do arise between tax design and tax application:[34]

- Since acts of tax fraud and anti-fraud policies have an economic cost for the administration, it is inevitable that fraud is never completely eliminated.[35] As a result, how control policies are designed becomes fundamental, and efficiency is a possible design criterion. That is to say, efficiency would mean obtaining the highest possible level of tax compliance, using the budgetary resources assigned to the tax administration. Authors such as Reinganum and Wilde (1985) and Scotchmer (1987) analyze the problem through the design of deterministic audit policies (i.e., based on the information provided by the taxpayer returns). In that case, the result obtained is that the audit policies would have to be regressive. That is, from a certain threshold of declared base, the audit probability would have to be null, while below that threshold, all returns should be audited in order to maintain commitment to the policy. Therefore, they find that audit policies are regressive, similarly to the distribution of fraud.[36] Obviously, this is an extreme result, and it may not have direct practical application. However, it clearly raises a question. If the tax administration must govern itself only and exclusively by criteria of economic efficiency, the results in terms of 'distributive pattern' can nevertheless be different from the ones initially pursued by law-makers.[37]

- From the initial assumptions stated above, it is inevitable that voluntary compliance will be below 100 percent (especially with respect to income sources that are not subject to withholding). The resources that law-makers wield, therefore, will always be less than anticipated. This might not have any consequences if it were anticipated (see the following point) or if, in the end, expenditure needs were also below initial forecasts. However, when neither of these assumptions hold, having access to the tax administration can give the government an added degree of flexibility in balancing the budget. Esteller (2003, 2005a and 2005b) has demonstrated for the Spanish case that the ACs and the state make use of that power through their respective tax administrations. Obviously, on the one hand, this may involve greater efficiency in the sense that the public sector has more instruments to reach its spending objectives; but, on the other hand, it is totally uneven, because the conclusion is that, 'when the public finances are going well', efforts are less strenuous, which clearly ends up benefiting certain taxpayers (the ones that pay when the things are going well) and harms the rest (which could be the same ones, but in different time periods).

- Finally, the effects of tax autonomy do not only occur ex post, as we described in the two previous situations. Ex ante, it is also important that the government can simultaneously decide the nominal parameters of tax burden and establish the basic parameters of tax management. In the literature, various models appear, including some already mentioned and other more recent ones, such as the one offered by Richter and Boadway (2005), who demonstrate the need to address the two levels of tax autonomy – legal and management – at the same time in order to try to reach any political objectives pursued on the revenue side (either a certain level of revenue and/or a certain redistributive pattern).

Undoubtedly, the administrative application of taxes has political consequences, and the complete fulfillment of political objectives on the revenue side requires coordination of legal and management authority, preferably by the same agent (or, at least, jointly between two agents who both have interests in the same tax). If such premises are accepted, based on the theoretical and empirical literature, it seems that the consortium envisaged by Catalonia's Statute of Autonomy is the one that would be most effective. Any of the other reforms could also work, but it is difficult to imagine that that connection between legal and management powers could be so perfect.

4 CONCLUSIONS

Over time, while assuming legal power over income tax, some ACs have simultaneously begun to lay claim on a more important role in the administration of the taxes levied in their territory, at least over taxes shared with the state and administered by the AEAT. Their claim has been fulfilled in part by the creation of the Joint Commission on Tax Coordination and the corresponding Territorial Councils on Taxation in 1997, along with participation on the AEAT Board from 2002. Together, these steps have given ACs greater access to tax management information on the other taxes of interest, especially personal income tax. Nevertheless, institutional improvements of this sort are not entirely satisfactory for some ACs. They call for greater involvement in tax direction and management in cases where they have a right to a share of the tax revenues, especially, although not solely, income tax. That is, indeed, what Catalonia's 2006 Statute of Autonomy poses.

The Statute of Autonomy is of interest and ought to be analyzed because of its unique character and the formal specificity of its terms. First of all, the statute anticipates the creation of the Tax Agency of Catalonia (ATC; Agència Tributària de Catalunya). Such an administrative reform should encourage greater organizational flexibility and budgetary autonomy on the part of the present DGT with respect to other departments under the umbrella of the Ministry of Finance. In addition, the agency set up under the reform, administratively, has the same characteristics as the AEAT. Indeed, this is fundamental to implementing Art. 204.2 of the statute, namely setting up a consortium (or equivalent entity) in which the AEAT and ATC have an equal share of participation. The consortium would take on application of all taxes in Catalonia. In principle, however, it is most likely that the consortium will begin its work by focusing on personal income tax. Therefore, the not yet fully defined formula would involve decentralizing income tax administration in Catalonia, in collaboration with the AEAT. Obviously, for such reform to be genuinely innovative, the tasks entrusted to the consortium should include joint direction and joint management. If reform was limited to direction tasks, then it would be merely an improvement; the access to information would probably be more automatic and immediate. However, the reform would also improve representation because it envisages equal representation. Currently, there are four representatives of the Special Delegation of the AEAT and three from the AC on the Territorial Council in Catalonia.[38]

This reform should be viewed as very positive, because, on the one hand, it guarantees a degree of uniformity in the tax processes (with respect to citizens in other ACs), avoids the fragmentation of tax information generated in Catalonia that is of interest to other ACs and obviously to the AEAT, and, last, does away with any possible disincentives to efficient tax management, perhaps caused by questions of tax competence and/or horizontal equalization. This is all because membership on the consortium's board will be equally shared between the AEAT and the ATC. As long as any of the above questions remain unresolved, the AEAT – which has great interest in the fulfillment of all of them – could act through the direction board to fulfill them. However, the reform allows a degree of non-uniformity in the tax processes (e.g., permitting specific fraud detection filters and differing rules for taxpayer treatment). It allows for improvement to the income tax assessment procedure used locally and gives the Catalan administration much greater access to tax information. Last, it helps to set tax collection forecasts and assess the impact of envisaged tax reforms.

In all likelihood, the most serious issue to be raised by the consortium in Catalonia is the extent to which taxes may, in fact, become non-uniform because of decentralization. What would the limit be? Certainly, the drawbacks of non-uniformity should be contrasted with the benefits that decentralization may bring in effectiveness terms (see Art. 103.1 of the Constitution or Art. 3.2 of the General Tax Law). In any case, both factors seem difficult to quantify, especially more effective administration, in order to resolve the dilemma. As a result, the most reasonable assumption to make is that any factors causing non-uniformity in the application of taxes that are caused by decentralization will need to be lessened, especially with respect to income tax. Even so, as argued earlier, decentralization in the form of a consortium seems an improvement over the present institutional structure of tax administration in Spain.

APPENDIX A   EQUALIZATION AND INCENTIVES – CALCULATING TAX CAPACITY

This appendix puts forward a straightforward explanation of the disincentives to effective management of the tax system that can occur as a result of the way that tax capacity is calculated, where a horizontal equalization mechanism is in place.

To do so, we will focus on Autonomous Community i, which is part of a federation composed of n ACs. At the moment, to simplify, we will also assume that the nominal tax burden is identical in all regions and equal to 1. Finally, we establish a very simple relation between tax compliance and the level of tax compliance effort made by the tax administration: $\phi = \delta \times E$, for any tax administration, where ϕ is the level of tax compliance (between 0 and 1), and E is the effort level exerted by the corresponding region (between a minimum level of 0, and a maximum fixed at 1) and, finally, δ is a parameter that can vary among regions and represents the extent to which an increase in effort brings about a higher level of tax compliance. In principle, δ might vary among regions because of the nature of the tax bases in each region, or because of the intrinsic incentives of the taxpayers in each region to fulfill tax obligations.

Let us see what happens, then, if the equalization mechanism – expressed in a highly stylized way – is formulated in such a way that the index of tax capacity is calculated directly as the amount of taxes collected (e.g., the German case):

Case 1: Index of tax capacity calculated based on the amount of taxes collected (i.e., totally endogenous indicator of tax capacity)

$$T_i = (\delta \times \bar{E} \times \bar{B}) - (\delta_i \times E_i \times B_i) \qquad \text{(A.1)}$$

where T_i is the amount of the equalization transfer, calculated as the difference between a standard amount of tax revenue collected (identified by the multiplication of the variables with bars) and the effective amount of taxes collected in AC i. As with the standard amount, effective collection – recall that the tax rate is 1 and identical in all the regions – is obtained by multiplying three factors: two exogenous factors and one endogenous factor. The exogenous factors are those that affect tax compliance efforts in the territory (e.g., percentage of capital income versus labor income) and the objective indicators of tax capacity (e.g., in the case of property-based taxes, house prices and so on). The endogenous factor is the amount of effort spent in ensuring tax compliance (e.g., number of tax audits carried out).

Then, an increase in tax compliance efforts has the following impact on the amount of equalization transfers to be received:

$$\frac{\partial T_i}{\partial E_i} = -(\delta_i \times B_i) \leq 0 \qquad (A.2)$$

whose sign is clearly negative, unless $\delta_i = 0$. In addition, it is possible to demonstrate that the total amount of resources is exactly $(\delta \times \bar{E} \times \bar{B})$, irrespective of the level of tax compliance effort. This is the disincentive called a 'tax on tax revenue', identified and confirmed empirically in the German case.

Case 2: Totally exogenous index of tax capacity

Analysis of this case will make use of the current Spanish situation. The 'Sufficiency Fund' (FS; Fondo de Sufiencia), as it is known, is calculated for a given AC i in the following way:

$$FS_i = NG_i - (\delta_i \times \bar{E} \times B_i) \qquad (A.3)$$

where NG_i is the imputed expenditure requirement of that AC. From this is deducted the amount of taxes that the AC would collect under normal conditions (i.e., given a standard tax compliance effort). Shared taxes are not included, because they fall outside the scope of the current analysis as a result of being administered by the AEAT.

From here, the total amount of revenue of an AC, R_i, would be as follows:

$$R_i = FS_i + (\delta_i \times E_i \times B_i) = NG_i - (\delta_i \times \bar{E} \times B_i) + (\delta_i \times E_i \times B_i) \quad (A.4)$$

Then, from this expression, we can derive the following one:

$$R_i = NG_i + [(E_i) - (\bar{E})] \times \delta_i \times B_i \qquad (A.5)$$

Thus, if all ACs made the same legal and management effort, that is to say, $\bar{E} = E_i$, then the AC in question would end up having exactly the right level of resources required to cover its expenditure needs, neither more nor less.

However, in the Spanish case, is expression (A.5) actually in operation? The answer is clearly no. In theory, the variables that appear as standard values there and serve to calculate the amount of taxes to be collected under normal conditions are not updated annually because of any AC actions. As a result, neither a direct nor an indirect relationship exists (to be checked shortly) between an AC's indicator of tax capacity and its own efforts using legislative or management power. The reason is that legislative power in this case is associated with the normative or standard tax collection figure, whose basis is the effective amount of tax collected in 1984. Since then, the normative collection figures have been updated at a homogeneous rate of change for all the ACs, based on the state's revenue growth rate. Therefore, unlike Case 1,

$$\frac{\partial FS_i}{\partial E_i} = 0 \tag{A.6}$$

which implies that, despite the imperfect nature of calculations of normative collection levels in Spain, the imperfection itself has paradoxically contributed to the absence of negative incentives in the administration of ceded taxes.

Case 3: Partially exogenous indicator of tax capacity

Obviously, in spite of relatively efficient tax management under the current equalization system in Spain, it would be advisable to calculate the normative collection figures correctly for each AC. Otherwise, we would be sacrificing inter-territorial equity for the sake of administrative efficiency. (The beneficiaries in this case would be the ACs whose normative collection is far from reality.)

In order to see the effects of recomputing normative collection figures, we return to expression (A.3):

$$FS_i = NG_i - \left(\delta_i \times \left(\sum_{i=1}^{n} \alpha_i \times E_i \right) \times B_i \right) \tag{A.7}$$

where the average tax compliance effort, $\bar{E}$, is simply replaced by the formula that should give its value. In a simpler but sufficiently clear version, this would be the weighted average of the ACs' tax compliance efforts made, where the weight of an AC i is α_i. It is thus demonstrated that the value of $\bar{E}$ would indirectly affect the normative collection figures. That is, it would affect an AC's tax capacity indicator. However, unlike Case 1, the impact is clearly more limited. Specifically, the impact is as follows:

$$\frac{\partial FS_i}{\partial E_i} = -\delta_i \times \alpha_i \times B_i \leq 0 \tag{A.8}$$

Without a doubt, the impact is negative, as in Case 1. However, in absolute terms, it will tend to be relatively small when $\alpha_i \to 0$ and, in any case, it will be much smaller than the impact in Case 1.

In addition, unlike Case 1, the impact on the total amount of resources will continue to be positive. That can be verified by changing expression (4.2) slightly. In that case, the variation in total resources arising from an increase in management effort would be:

$$\frac{\partial R_i}{\partial E_i} = \delta_i \times B_i \times (t_i - (1 - \alpha_i)) \tag{A.9}$$

whose sign can be predicted to be positive, although less so than in Case 2 (which can easily be verified by setting $\alpha_i = 0$).

NOTES

1. The author wants to acknowledge helpful comments made by Josep Costa i Solà, Jorge Onrubia and Antoni Zabalza.
2. See García (2000), p. 60 onwards on the legal difference between collaboration and coordination.
3. See also Cayón and Bueno (2000), p. 44 onwards.
4. This procedure involves all AC representatives being simultaneously changed, an issue that the Joint Commission is thinking of reforming.
5. See http://www.aeat.es/AEAT/Contenidos_Comunas/La_Agencia_Tributoria/Informa cion_institucional/Memorias/MEMORIAS_DE_LA_AGENCIA_TRIBUTARIA/ 2006/Memoria2006_en.pdf which explains how real collaboration and coordination occurs.
6. Finally, as to the areas of collaboration identified in the legislation, it is necessary to mention the ones that are, in practice, actually occurring between the AC tax administrations and the AEAT, for example, the annual campaign for filing income tax returns.
7. In any case, one of the advantages of decentralizing management in the public sector is the increased likelihood of generating innovations that raise social well-being. This is due, basically, to the greater number of institutions that are responsible for delivering a certain good or public service. To the extent that an innovation is generated in a certain territory over the medium or long term, it is expected that it would eventually be implemented in the other territories. Consequently, this type of non-uniformity would, a priori, only generate inequality in the short term.
8. It also ought to be demonstrated that a centralized application of taxes is genuinely equal across the whole country.
9. This information has been obtained from the *Informe Sobre la Cesión de Tributos a las Comunidades Autónomas*, a report annually annexed to the General State Budgets. To be specific, the reports appear with a delay of two years. That is, the Budget Act of 2004 contains the AC reports for 2002.
10. For instance, some ACs have outsourced computing services or they are carried out by other bodies. I am grateful to Isabel Comas for this comment.
11. In no case can such information be used as an indicator of relative efficiency. For an analysis along those lines, see Esteller (2003).
12. See the annual report of the AEAT (2005) for details of the institutional relations between the AEAT and the ACs under the foral regime, p. 19.
13. For example, on 19 July 2006, the assessment corresponding to the 2004 fiscal year came into effect. See *El País*, 'The Communities Received 51.8% more Between 1999 and

2004'. Differences in the procedure of payments on account from FY 2005 are also made clear in the article, which will be discussed later on.

14. See Durán and Esteller (2005).
15. For example, in 2002, in the report on the management of ceded taxes, Valencia expressed its concerns regarding the AEAT's poor management of income tax credits.
16. For example, Costa i Solà (2006, p. 7) states, 'Coordinating action across the consortium [in Section 2.4.2, we will see that the consortium is an institutional form of decentralized tax administration], I am sure that important advances will be made in curtailing tax evasion, since the tax evader will feel the tax administration much nearer'.
17. Obviously, this situation should be compatible with few central sufficiently powerful services to control any tax evasion that goes beyond the borders of an individual AC, that is, a 'central pool of big taxpayers'. This pool now exists within the AEAT. In addition, the existence of central services would be coherent with achieving economies of scale in tax administration.
18. For example, in the province of Lleida, there is only one AEAT delegation (in the provincial capital, Lleida) and there is no other administration in the whole province. I am grateful to Josep Costa i Solà for this example.
19. Unlike the 1995 report, which did not address this question, the 2002 group of experts proposed that the ACs should take part in the economic and administrative review of ceded and shared taxes, which is currently an exclusive competence of the state exercised through the so-called Economic-Administrative Regional Courts.
20. The full text is available at: http://www.parlament-cat.net/porteso/estatut/estatut_angles_100506.pdf.
21. In fact, compared with the previous 1979 statute, the real innovation is the fixing of a temporary limit to initiate these joint administration tasks.
22. This tax would start to be jointly administered by the consortium.
23. In any case, it is necessary to note that the Second Additional Provision establishes the following: '1. Any modification to State law that expands the competences of the autonomous communities in general throughout the national territory, shall be applicable to the Comunitat Valenciana, whose competences shall be expanded on the same terms; 2. The Comunitat Valenciana shall ensure that the level of self-government established in the present Statute remains equal to the other autonomous communities; 3. To this effect, any expansion of the competences of the autonomous communities not stated in the present Statute and not previously assigned, transferred or delegated to the Comunitat Valenciana will require that the legitimate institutions of self-government take the necessary steps, where appropriate, to bring them up to date.' This provision can be interpreted to the effect that the creation of a consortium in any other AC, which would involve expanding AC competences, would therefore suppose the implementation of the same reform in Valencia.
24. See recent reviews by Andreoni, Erard and Feinstein (1998), or by Slemrod and Yitzhaki (2000). In a federal context, this treatment is even less common, for example, Mikesell (2001) and Esteller (2002), where pros and cons for a decentralized tax administration are given.
25. It is worth evaluating Spain's decentralization process in light of the tax competition hypothesis. Since 1997, and with increased emphasis since 2002, the ACs have undertaken a process of tax competition in the IGT, especially relating to transfers *mortis causa* from parents to children (Durán and Esteller, 2005). This could, in part, be caused by tax base mobility. To a greater extent, they could be expected to move to ACs adjacent to those under the statutory regime. Then, the question is whether, since the ACs under the common regime have legislative authority, they have become involved in competition. What was happening before 1997 when they only had management authority? The hypothesis put forward in the literature is that ACs that are more exposed to tax competition (i.e., closer to the Basque Country and Navarre) could only have used the instrument that they then possessed to forestall tax base flight. That being the case, paradoxically, and contrary to the opinion of many authors, the devolution of legislative power and an ongoing process of tax competition arising from legal reforms must be seen

as positive. Unlike the period before 1997, taxpayers can now see and, therefore, evaluate government action, which was not as visible to the public before, when hypothetically it could only be seen through actions taken by the tax administration.

26. In the German case, the equalization grant is calculated directly from the net collection obtained by every *Land*. The disincentives to effective administration are obvious. By contrast, the opinion given by the study group in 1995 (Grupo de Estudio, 1995) finds these types of disincentives unlikely. It stated that 'normative collection must, without a doubt, turn out to be equal to the actual one' (p. 85). If we applied this mechanism to the Spanish case, and the normative collection were recalculated annually, the disincentives found in the German case would be expected to appear.

27. They should use information from the other ACs in order to get an indirect measure of the average level of effort against tax evasion. This would mimic the way a standard tax type (or average one) is used to calculate the amount of transfers received.

28. In Spain, calculation of the equalization grant (Sufficiency Fund) involves use of an indicator of taxing power called 'standard collection'. This amount is taken to be what any AC, under normal circumstances, should obtain from ceded taxes, given tax authority. Both the initial figure (net collection for the year 1984) and its annual increase (as a function, basically, of the annual growth rate of the state's tax revenue) together cause the annually recalculated figure to bear no relation to any actions taken by the autonomic administrations. In this sense, paradoxically, we might say that this indicator of taxing power has turned out to be efficient in the sense that it does not distort the incentives to controlling the tax fraud. See the appendix at the end of the chapter for an analytic proof of this statement.

29. An exception is Stöwhase and Traxler (2005).

30. Kaldor (1956) was the first to make this argument to justify WT.

31. In Spain, other practical examples of the need for collaboration involve the application of contact points for ceded traditional taxes. This was solved in part through the report of the Joint Commission (July 2000): 'Establishment of specific control mechanisms and assurances that enable verification of the correct application of the procedures of functional and territorial competition'. Beyond the report's example of income tax vs. WT, vertical coordination is also needed when interpreting VAT or TCT on certain transactions. As already explained in Section 2.2.2, this issue is subject to the work of committees set up in each AC's Territorial Council on Taxation.

32. The use of automatic channels was meant to avoid excessive information-sharing costs. This was one of the reasons given by the 1995 study group (Grupo de Estudio, 1995) to justify the creation of an integrated tax administration.

33. Another conclusion to draw from the Spanish case is riskier or less rigorous, but identical to the findings of Keen and Ligthart (2006). Stable collaboration requires reciprocity between the involved countries/regions. For example, sharing taxpayer contact points between two (or more) ACs (see note 31) requires a certain degree of reciprocity between them. That is to say, an AC does not collaborate if another AC does not (e.g., the management report for ceded taxes in 2002 sets out the case of Castile-León vs. Madrid, in which Castile-León did not return wrongly paid revenue to Madrid until the latter reciprocated). Undoubtedly, the empirical analysis of the behavior of different administrations in the area of contact points would be interesting for the emerging literature on collaboration concerning tax information.

34. See Slemrod (1990) for a seminal contribution going beyond the analyses of optimal taxation theory and arguing in favor of addressing the administrative questions of taxation. For example, Marhuenda and Ortuño-Ortín (1997) put forward an optimal taxation model that builds in the costs of inspection and conclude that no politics can both ensure tax compliance and, simultaneously, be progressive.

35. Another option, which would not have any economic cost (at least, not directly), would be to establish a few sufficiently severe sanctions. The sanctions should be somewhat proportional to the level of tax evasion or, in other words, as Christiansen (1980) says: 'Nobody should be sent to prison for life for evading a few taxes' (p. 391).

36. Cremer and Gahvari (1996) obtain a very similar result using an optimal taxation model.

37. This might be avoided by establishing a 'contract' that clearly specified that the tax administration's criteria to take action cannot be incongruous with the criteria already set by law-makers. Even if this were possible, the doubt would remain whether a single contract would be sufficient (i.e., one for all the ACs). Or should as many contracts be designed as the number of ACs, given that they can have different political aims? In that case, the network of relationships would be more complicated, since it would give rise to a multi-principal situation (all the ACs and only one agent: a single tax administration).

38. We commented on this issue immediately after the news appeared in the press. The current AEAT director was quoted as saying that the consortium (or equivalent entity) will only undertake functions of direction and not properly those of management. In fact, management would be impossible in the context of the AEAT director's statement, since he does not foresee the joint AEAT-ATC body having its own legal standing. For more information, see *Expansion*, 'A Fiscal Consortium Without Executive Powers', 2 June 2006.

BIBLIOGRAPHY

Andreoni, J., B. Erard and J. Feinstein (1998), 'Tax compliance', *Journal of Economic Literature*, **36** (2), 818–60.

Bacchetta, P. and M. Paz Espinosa (1995), 'Information sharing and tax competition among governments', *Journal of International Economics*, **39** (1–2), 103–21.

Baretti, Ch., B. Huber and K. Lichtblau (2002), 'A tax on tax revenue. The incentive effects of equalizing transfers: evidence from Germany', *International Tax and Public Finance*, **9** (6), 631–49.

Cayón, M. and C. Bueno (2000), 'La gestión de los tributos cedidos a las Comunidades Autónomas', *Revista Aragonesa de Administración Pública*, **17**, 11–56.

Christiansen, V. (1980), 'Two comments on tax evasion', *Journal of Public Economics*, **13** (3), 389–93.

Costa i Solà, J. (2006), 'Descentralización Fiscal y Estatutos de Autonomía. La Futura Agencia Tributaria de Cataluña', Speech given at the state tax briefing *VI Encuentros Tributarios*, Universidad Pontificia Comillas, Madrid.

Cremer, H. and F. Gahvari (1996), 'Tax evasion and the optimum general revenue tax', *Journal of Public Economics*, **60** (2), 235–49.

Cremer, H. and F. Gahvari (2000), 'Tax evasion, fiscal competition and economic integration', *European Economic Review*, **44** (9), 1633–57.

Durán, J.M. and A. Esteller (2005), 'Descentralización Fiscal y Política Tributaria de las AC. Un Primera Evaluación a Través de los Tipos Impositivos Efectivos en el IT', in *La Financiación de las Comunidades Autónomas: Políticas Tributarias y Solidaridad Interterritorial*, N. Bosch and J.M. Durán (eds), Barcelona: University of Barcelona Press (Serie Transformacions 1.1), pp. 47–86.

El Pais, (2006), 'Las comunidades ingresaron un 51.8% más entre 1999 y 2004', http://www.elpais.com/articulo/economia/comunidades/ingresaron/518/1999/2004/elpepieco/20060720elpepieco_3/.

Esteller, A. (2002), 'La Administración Tributaria en un Contexto Federal. El Caso Español', Unpublished doctoral thesis, University of Barcelona.

Esteller, A. (2003), 'La eficiencia en la administración de los tributos cedidos: un análisis explicativo', *Papeles de Economía Española*, **95**, 320–34.

Esteller, A. (2004), 'Tax Evasion in Interrelated Taxes', Working Paper No. 2, Barcelona: IEB.

Esteller, A. (2005a), 'Is there a connection between the tax administration and the political power?', *International Tax and Public Finance*, **12** (5), 639–63.

Esteller, A. (2005b), 'Incumplimiento Fiscal en el IRPF (1993–2000): Un Análisis de Sus Factores Determinantes', Working Paper No. 227, Madrid: FUNACS.

Fiscal and Financial Policy Council (Consejo Nacional de Política Fiscal y Financiera) (2001), *Sistema de Financiación de las AC de Régimen Común*, Madrid.

García, A. (2000), *La Gestión de los Tributos Autonómicos*, Madrid: Civitas Ediciones.

García, J., P. Pérez and J. Zornoza (1998), *Constitución y Financiación Autonómica*, Valencia: Tirant lo Blanch.

Grady, P. (2004), *A Separate Personal Revenue Tax Collection System for Alberta: Advantages and Disadvantage*s, Edmonton, AL: The Alberta Finance Ministry.

Grupo de Estudio (1995), *Informe Sobre el Actual Sistema de Financiación Autonómica y sus Problemas*, Madrid: Institute for Fiscal Studies.

Joint Commission (Comisión Mixta de Coordinación de la Gestión Tributaria) (2004), *Relaciones de la Secretaría de Estado de Hacienda y Presupuestos y la Agencia Estatal de Administración Tributaria con las Administraciones Tributarias de las AC y las Ciudades con Estatuto de Autonomía*, Document approved by the Full Committee on 22 October, Madrid.

Kaldor, N. (1956), *Indian Tax Reform*, New Delhi: Government of India, Ministry of Finance.

Keen, M. and J. Ligthart (2006), 'Information sharing and international taxation: a primer', *International Tax and Public Finance*, **13** (1), 81–110.

Marhuenda, F. and I. Ortuño-Ortín (1997), 'Tax enforcement problems', *Scandinavian Journal of Economics*, **99** (1), 61–72.

Mikesell, J.L. (2003), 'International Experiences with Administration of Local Taxes: A Review of Practices and Issues', *Tax Policy and Administration Thematic Group*, The World Bank, http://www.worldbank.org/publicsector/decentralization/June2003Seminar/Administrationlocaltaxes.pdf.

Ortiz-Calle, E. (1998), *La Agencia Estatal de Administración Tributaria*, Official State Bulletin (*Boletín Oficial del Estado*), Madrid.

Ramallo, J.J. (1994), 'Las relaciones interadministrativas en la aplicación de los tributos', *Documentación Administrativa*, **240**, 165–96.

Ramallo, J. and J. Zornoza (1995), 'Sistema y modelos de financiación autonómica', *Perspectivas del Sistema Financiero*, **51**, Madrid: FIES Foundation.

Reinganum, J.F. and L.L. Wilde (1985), 'Income tax compliance in a principal–agent framework', *Journal of Public Economics*, **26** (1), 1–18.

Richter, W.F. and R.W. Boadway (2005), 'Trading off tax distortion and tax evasion', *Journal of Public Economic Theory*, **7**, 361–81.

Sánchez-Saché, M. (2006), *Administració Tributària i el Consorci entre l'ATCat i l'AEAT*, Directorate General for Economic Planning, Ministry of Economy and Finances, Generalitat of Catalonia (Direcció General de Programació Econòmica, Conselleria d'Economia i Finances, Generalitat de Cataluña).

Scotchmer, S. (1987), 'Audit classes and tax enforcement policy', *American Economic Review*, **77** (2), 229–33.

Secretaría de Estado de Hacienda (2002), *Informe sobre la Reforma del Sistema de Financiación Autonómica*, Madrid: Working Group of the Spanish Financial and Fiscal Policy Council, Ministry of Finance.

Slemrod, J. (1990), 'Optimal taxation and optimal tax systems', *Journal of Economic Perspectives*, **4** (1), 157–78.
Slemrod, J. and S. Yitzhaki (2000), 'Tax Avoidance, Evasion, and Administration', NBER, Working Paper No. 7473, Massachusetts.
Stöwhase, S. and Ch. Traxler (2005), 'Tax evasion and auditing in a federal economy', *International Tax and Public Finance*, **12** (4), 515–31.

Index

AC *see* Autonomous Communities (Spain)
administration problem 104
administrative decentralization 28
administrative effectiveness in tax system, Spain 214–15
Advisory Council on Fiscal Imbalance, Canada 133
affordability, and natural resources 127
Agencia Estatal de Administración (AEAT), Spain 213–14
income tax information 221–2
tax administration, Spain 215
wealth taxes 218
Agència Tributària de Catalunya (ATC) 237
air travel 42
Álava, Spain 219
Alberta, Canada 121
sales tax 180
alcohol tax 43, 96, 100
Allied High Commission, Germany 207
alternatives for using VAT 97
Andalucia 154
information technology use 216
Andalucia Statute of Autonomy 228, 229
anti-fraud policies 235
assets 130–31
Asturias, information technology use 216
Atlantic Canada, provinces 171
auditing 212, 217
structures, different 206
Auditor General of Canada 175
Australian Commonwealth Grants Commission 149
Austria, federal structure 86
autonomic competition 78
autonomic financing, Spain 74, 85
autonomic tax agency 104

Autonomous Communities (ACs), Spain 3, 74, 147
financing 7–15, 209
system, reform 224–6
powers 4
tax administration, Spain 215, 217
taxes 9–13
treasury offices 93–4
autonomous financing, weak points 15–21
autonomous taxes, ceded 82
autonomy of regions in Spain 4
autonomy to set tax rates 33, 34

balanced distribution of income 85
Balearic Islands 4, 91, 154, 156
information technology use 216
self-sufficiency 76
'basket of taxes' 85
Basque Country 7, 79, 160, 223
Bavaria 193, 197
tax administration 198–9
wages tax 203
'benefit taxes' 38, 39
Berlin 199
betterment levies 41
betting taxes 91
bonded taxes, Germany 196
border adjustment between countries 47, 86
Brazil, sub-national VAT 46
Budget (2006) of Government of Canada 187
budget for tax administration, Germany 201
Budget, *Restoring Fiscal Balance in Canada* 187
budget revenue 76
buoyancy potential of consumption tax 85
business taxation, Germany 139

business tax rate, weighted 140
business value tax (BVT) 43

Canada 92
  federal revenue 170
  and Quebec arrangement 179–80
  sub-national VAT 46
  'tax competence' 86
  and United States model 49
Canada Health Transfer (CHT) 110,
    112
Canada Revenue Agency (CRA) 174,
    175, 185
  tax coordination 187–9
Canada Social Transfer (CST) 110,
    112
Canadian Constitution 169
  major revision 114
Canadian equalization system 121
Canadian provinces 109
  direct taxation 169
Canadian Revenue Agency (CRA),
    federal 223
Canary Islands 4
  information technology use 216
Cantabria, information technology use
    216
capital transfer tax 99, 101, 216
car registration tax 96, 98, 100
Castile 92
Castilla-La Mancha
  information technology use 216
Catalan language 216, 223
Catalonia 21, 22, 23, 92, 229
  self-sufficiency 76
  tax administration authority 216
Catalonia, Statute of Autonomy 2002
    210, 224, 226, 229
ceded administration 96
centralization of tax information 226
centralized registration 96
central transfers 31
children 161
church tax 202–3
CHT *see* Canada Health Transfer
CITCA *see* Comprehensive Integrated
    Tax Coordination Agreement
clearing-house arrangement 47
cohabitation of tax bases 33
cohesion, lack of, Germany 206, 207

collaboration 211–14
  agreements 216
  and coordination 233–4
  among levels of government 94
Commission on Tax Coordination and
    Regulatory Evaluation 219
common responsibilities 8–9
common tax base 174, 177
common taxes, Germany 195
communities in Germany, taxes 194
compensating VAT (CVAT) 48
Comprehensive Integrated Tax
    Coordination Agreements
    (CITCAs) 179–86
computing procedure, mistrust 221
Comunidades Forales 7, 160
  of Basque Country and Navarre 219
Comunitat Valenciana 243
Consejo Superior de Dirección, Spain,
    functions 213–14
consortium board membership,
    sharing 238
consortium for decentralization 228,
    229
Constitutional Court 214
Constitution of Spain 3, 4
consumption patterns 88
consumption taxes 84–7
  Spain 148
  and territorial benefit 85
coordinating authority, Germany 207
coordination 211–14
  and collaboration 233–4
  of decentralized administration
    204–205
  incentives 229
  mechanisms, lack f 21
co-responsibility 76, 93
corporate income tax 68, 69
  Canada 121, 174
  Spain 16
  at sub-national level 45
corporation tax 99, 101
  income, Germany 195, 203–204, 207
  management of 219
Court of Luxembourg and freedoms
    78
CPFF (Spanish Fiscal and Financial
    Policy Council) 225–6
CRA *see* Canada Revenue Agency

cross-border trade 43
cross-state cases 205
CST *see* Canada Social Transfer
customs duties 99, 197
CVAT, compensating VAT 48

debts 130–31
decentralization areas 101
   in form of consortium 238
   in Germany 205–208
   levels of 84
   in Spain 3, 4, 5, 229
   of tax administration, Germany
      193–208
   variation of degree of 56
deconcentration in tax administration,
      Spain 214
deferred payment approach 47
delocalization of purchases 97, 99
demographic changes 19
demographic growth in Spain 148
Denmark 92
Department of Finance, Canada 175
destination-based tax 47
devolution process, Spain 147
DGT *see* Directorate General of Taxes
differentiation on regional level 91, 92
direct and indirect taxes 77
direct management control, shared
      taxes 223–4
Directorate General of Taxes (DGT)
   Galicia 221
   Spain 216–19
direct taxation 169
disaggregation of tax bases 124–6
discretionary approaches 112
discretionary charges 122
Disputación, Spain 4
drinking water, safe 38
dual administration 175
dysfunctions 220–24

East Germany, former 143
economic environment, stable 36
   downturns 64
economic principles, Canada 114
economies of scale 226
   Canada 175
educational services, Spain 161
education, as fundamental service 14

effectiveness versus equality 215
efficiency 205
   for tax compliance 235
efficiency-accountability trade-off 34
elderly groups 161
electricity tax 80, 96, 97,100
entitlements, volatility of 131–2
equality in tax system, Spain 214–15
equalization 22, 23
   adequacy of 111, 112
   affordability of 111
   design of system 115–21
   grants 23
   and incentives 239–42
equalization grants
   from central government 76
Equalization Grants (Asignaciones de
      Nivelación) 149
   Spain, reform of 154, 159
equalization system 230, 231
equalization transfers 109, 121–2
equalization transfer system, Spain
      148–53, 154–62
equitable income distribution 36
European Community Directive 91
European harmonization 88, 89, 95, 96
European Union 85, 99
evasion level 93
exchequer revenues 75
excise duties 80, 91, 96–103, 197
Excise Tax Act, Canada 184
excise taxes 9, 43–4
exclusionary approach 33
expenditure areas, Spain 8
expenditure equalization 120–21
expenditure requirement indicators
      23
Expert Panel on Equalization and
      Territorial Formula Financing
      133
Extremadura 156
   tax unfairness 223

fair treatment to provinces, Canada
      223
federal administration, Germany 197,
      198
federal government, Canada 177
federalism in North America, history
   of 29

Federal-Provincial Committee on
    Taxation, Canada 175
federal-provincial transfer system,
    Canada 109, 132–3
federal structures 86
federal tax 174, 184
    Germany 142
fees and user charges 39, 40
financial and adminstrative area,
    Canada 189
financial autonomy 24, 210
    of Autonomous Communities, Spain
        16
financing
    adequate levels of 30
    of Autonomous Communities 79, 84
First Nations (aboriginal peoples,
    Canada) 188
First World War, costs, Canada 172
Fiscal and Financial Policy Council
    (CPFF), Spain 8, 79, 212
fiscal autonomy 226
fiscal capacity 139, 141
fiscal decentralization
    Canada 109, 114, 115
    Germany 137–9
fiscal disparities, horizontal 30
fiscal equalization 12, 17–22
    Canada 109–35
    Germany 137–45
    Spain 147–64
fiscal federalism 109
    Germany 145
    Spain 74
fiscal imbalance 112
fiscal inequity 115
fiscal need 139
Fiscus GmbH 200
foral provinces, Spain 79, 219–20
foral regime regions, Spain 160
forecasts 220
formula-based approaches 112
fraud
    chance increased 88, 89
    detection filters 238
    leniency 230
free movement, Canada 177
freedoms, fundamental 78
fuel tax 43, 80, 96, 100
funds, specific 17, 18

Galicia 91
Galician language 223
gambling revenues 125
General Fund, Spain 151
General Tax Act 214, 222
geographic neutrality 37
German Constitution 193, 197
German Federal Republic 137
German Federation 193, 194
German Senate 149
German tax administration 194–205
Germany
    decentralization of tax
        administration 193–208
    federal structure 86
    fiscal equalization 137–45
    fiscal federalism 145
gift tax 9, 11, 16, 100
Goods and Services Tax (GST)
    administration by Quebec 185–6
    Canada 171, 184
    exceptions 182
governance issues 132
government policy objectives 36
government, intermediate levels, taxes
    13–14, 34
grants
    Europe and Australia 14
    Spain 12
Great Depression (1929-39), Canada
    172
Gross Domestic Product (GDP) 231
gross equalization 118, 159
GST *see* Goods and Services Tax
Guiopúzcoa, Spain 219

harmonization
    among foral provinces 219
    of tax base 174–5
harmonized sales tax (HST) 183–7
    revenues, sharing 185, 186
health
    Canada 110
    as fundamental service 14
health care 56
health costs 42
health responsibilities, resources 8, 9
health services 151, 161
horizontal equalization system 231
    Germany 142

horizontal equity, rupture of 19
horizontal imbalances 150
HST *see* harmonized sales tax
human resources area, Canada 189
hydroelectric utilities 125

immigrants 23
incentive effects of equalization 126–7
  and natural resources 128
incentives 94
  and disincentives 76
incidence and revenue yield 102
income tax 109, 113
  assessment procedure 238
  auditing 222
  flat-rate, piggyback 44
  Germany 195, 207
  law of 2007, Spain 221
  personal 9, 10
  withholding mechanism 221
India and Pakistan, VAT 33
  sub-national VAT 46
indirect taxation 81, 83, 85–6
inflation 172
information exchange 211, 216, 226
infrastructure 130–31
inheritance tax 9, 11, 16, 100
institutions, Spain 211
    insurance contracts 91
insurance premiums 96, 100
  tax on 97
intergovernmental transfers 31, 56, 57
international experience, tax
    assignments 48–9
international obligations, Canada 179
inter-provincial sales 184
inter-provincial tax policies 128–9
inter-regional distribution, Spain 149
inter-regional solidarity 79
inter-territorial Equalization Fund 80
inter-territorial equity, Spain 17
invoices, control of 94
Italy, regional business tax 43

Joint Commission on Tax
    Coordination, functions 212–13

La Rioja 156
  information technology use 216
Labrador 179, 183

Länder administration, Germany
  197–201
land tax, Germany 139
land values, taxing 41
languages, co-official, Spain 223
legal principles, Spain 210
legislative powers of state, Spain 4
liquidity problems 41
local administration, Spain 4, 5
local business taxes 42–3
local communities, Spain 5
local management, quality of 208
low-income tax reductions 176, 179
Low Population Density Fund, Spain
  151
lump-sum
  allowances 203
  payments 41
  transfers 231–3
Luxembourg 92

Maastricht criteria 208
MacEachen guidelines, Canada 176, 177
macroeconomic stability 30
Madrid
  self-sufficiency 76
  tax administration authority 216
management of services, pooling 225
mandatory collection 216
manufacture, taxes on 96
measurability, and natural resources
  128
measurement of 'tax autonomy' 58–9
Mecklenburg-Western Pomerania 199
Mill, John Stuart, on taxes 169
Minister of National Revenue, Canada
  188
mobile and immobile tax bases 232
modernization process, Germany 207
municipal fiscal equalization 139–42
municipal revenue sources 125
municipalities in Spain 4, 5
Murcia 154

national harmonization 178
natural resources, Canada, 121, 122,
  127–8
  geographic concentration 42
  revenues 111, 125
  taxes 42

Navarra 7, 79, 160
needs, estimated, of Autonomous
    Communities, Spain 79–80
net equalization 159
net fiscal benefits (NFBs) 115
    differentials 117, 118
New Brunswick 179, 183
Newfoundland 179, 183
non-residential property 40
non-uniformity in tax processes 238
non-university education 56
normative competences 104
North-Rhein-Westphalia 199
Novia Scotia 179, 183

OECD *see* Organization for Economic
    Cooperation and Development
oil and gas revenues, Atlantic provinces
    122
Ontario, tax on consumer goods 186
Organic Law 7/2001, Spain 79
Organic Law 8/1980, Spain 84
Organic Law on AC Financing, Spain
    211
Organization of Economic
    Cooperation and Development
    (OECD)
    countries, tax assignment 56–73

partnerships 229
payment for tax officers, Germany 202
payroll tax 109
Performance Comparison between
    Länder 205, 206
personal income taxes 68, 69
    Canada 121, 122, 170
    collaboration on 225
    Spain 48
    at sub-national level 44–5
piggyback taxes model 49
place of consumption, electricity 97
police, Spain 161
policies of provinces 117
political decentralization 27
political economy 29
pollution of environment 42
population 17
    groups 161
    low density 8
    and public services 130

post-secondary education, Canada 110
powers of Autonomous Communities,
    Spain 4
preferential treatment 179
profit tax 37, 64
    at sub-national level 45
property taxes 40–41
    British Columbia 122
    Canada 121
    equalization 129–30
property values 129
provinces in Canada 169
    above-average 118
    below-average 118
    differing needs 115
    disparities 133
    flexibility 178
    own-source revenue 171
    taxes 174, 180–82
province-specific tax credits 176, 179
provincial government in Spain 4, 5
provincial property rights 127
public expenditure distribution,
    Spanish 5–7
public services 75
    of provinces 117
    standard level 118
public utility services, taxation 44

quality control in Germany 207
Quebec 109, 171
    administration of harmonized sales
      tax (HST) 185–7
    consumption tax base 185
    corporation
    goods and services tax (GST)
      186
    own tax collection system 173,
      174
    personal income taxes 113
Quebec Sales Tax (QST) 46, 47, 48,
    185

rate tax-back 126, 127
redistribution of income 36
reform of equalization sytem 123
reform proposals
    Spain 210, 224
reform, positive 238
regime of surcharge 94

regions
  autonomy principle 226
  consumption 88
  expenditure needs 152, 153
  financing systems, Spain 7, 220
  government in Spain 4, 35
  interests 149
  population, Spain 161
  powers, annual inspection 212
  resources, and Sufficiency Fund 158
  shares, Spain 147
  tax differences 93, 97
regressivity of user charges 39, 40
Relative Income Fund, Spain 152
rents, taxing 41
*Report on Reform of Autonomic
  Financing System* 225
representative equalization 118
representative tax system (RTS) 119, 124
  approaches to equalization 111
  Canada 109
  Spain 231
resource allocation 36
responsibility for states, Germany 206
representative tax system (RTS)
retail sales tax 46, 182
  Quebec 185
  territorial 90–92
retail sector 93
retail VAT, transferring 88–9, 92–6
revenue
  assignments 27–52
  authorities of *Länder* 203
  autonomy 32
    at margin 38
  behavior 101
  decentralization 28
  equalization 119, 121
  evolution 19
  needs of sub-national governments 50
  participation 87–8
  potential of property taxes 40
revenue-producing taxes 37, 38
revenue sources
  Canada 124–6
  small 125
revenue-sharing 3, 35, 46
  Germany 142
revenues, structure of 12–14
reversibility, principle of 96

rich or poor communities 30
Rowell-Sirois Commission, Canada
  113
Royal Decree-Law 12/2005 220
RTS *see* representative tax system
rules of modulation 18

sales
  by post 95
  electronic 95
sales tax 109, 180
  Canada 121, 190
  coordination 179–87
sales tax reform options 183
sales tax systems, harmonization 183
Savings Fund for Temporary Disability
  (El Fondo de Ahorro en
  Incapacidad Temporal) 12
SCG *see* sub-central governments
Second World War 113
  Canada 172
segmentation tax office 204
self-assessment 170, 184
services
  differences in 120
  quality and quantity of 37
smuggling 43
social security 90
social services resources 8, 9
soft budget constraint 117
software sharing 205
solidarity among territories 210
Spain
  comparison with federal countries
    5–6
  fiscal decentralization 23, 27–52
  political decentralization 23
  regional co-responsibility 74–105
  shared governmental responsibilities
    4, 5
  tax administration, reform of
    209–245
Spanish Constitution 1978 3, 4, 214,
  222
  on taxes 210–11
Spanish Fiscal and Financial Policy
  Council 149, 224
Spanish regions 3–23
Spanish tax administration,
  dysfunctions 224

Special Delegation of AEAT, Spain 237
special taxes 100
spending power, abuse of 112
staff satisfaction 205
stamp duties 91, 101, 216
standard tax base, Canada 123–4
state exchequer 81, 82
state fiscal equalization transfers 143
state-level fiscal equalization, Germany 142–5
State Tax Administration, Spain 229
state tax authority (AEAT), Spain 215
State Treasury 210
states in Germany, *Länder* 193, 194
Statute of Autonomy 8, 21, 237
    Catalonia 103, 210
statutory reforms 226–9
structural change 64
students, enrolled 161
sub-central governments (SCGs) 56, 58
    and tax 58–9, 64
    and tax-sharing arrangements 68
sub-national governments 29–49
sub-national taxes 37
    autonomy 30, 34
    poor choices 44–6
sub-national VATs 46–8
subsidies 125
Sufficiency Fund (Fondo de Suficiencia) 12–13, 24, 80, 147–54
    adjustment mechanisms 19–20
    poor functioning 17, 18, 19
supplementary resource systems 76
surcharges 81, 90
    territorial, administration of 89–90
surtaxes 176

task completion 205
tax administration 22
    Catalonia 228
    centralized 34
    foral regime 219
    Germany 197, 198
    software, Germany 199–200
    Spain 215–16
    and tax autonomy 229
Tax Agency of Catalonia (ATC) 237
tax agency, shared 225–6
tax and public expenditure in ACs, Spain 15

tax assignment 29, 36, 79–84
    in OECD countries 56–73
Taxation Agency 22
    of Catalonia 226–9
taxation, extra-territorial 84
tax auditing 211
tax autonomy 1995–2002 31–5, 64–7
    good level 49, 50
    in OECD countries 56–73
    Spain, 209, 234–7
    sub-central governments 59, 60–63
    state level 143
    tax category 69–73
tax burden 77, 230
tax capacity, calculating 239–42
tax categories in Germany 194, 195
Tax Collection Agreement (TCAs), Canada 171, 173, 187
    from 1962 to 2001 176
tax collection, normative, Spain 157
tax competition 37, 92, 97, 139, 230, 231
tax compliance 230
    and decentralization 222
    level of 229–33
tax coordination 187
    Canada 169–91
Tax Coordination Agency of Basque Country 219
Tax Coordination Agreements, Canada 171
tax coordination agreements, integrated 183–5
tax co-responsibility 94
tax credits 16
    options 89
    and restrictions, provincial 178
tax equalization 205
taxes 7, 23
    and benefits 187, 188
    ceded 9, 10, 11, 12 ,16, 22, 79
    devolved, Spain 155
    normative capacity 22
    open or closed lists 32–3
    reassignment 64
tax evasion in Germany 206, 208
tax fraud 214, 230, 231, 235
tax harmonization 79
    in Canada 113, 189–90
tax helix, Germany 196

taxing power 59
  of sub-central governments 59, 60–62
tax instruments, kind of 32
tax liquidations 17
tax monopolies 197
tax officers, training system, Germany 201
tax offices and taxpayers, physical closeness 223
tax on capital transfers (TCT) 217
tax-on-income, Canada 181–2
tax-on-tax system 176
  Canada 180
taxpayer service 222, 226
  differing rules 238
Tax Policy Review Committee, Canada 183, 184
tax rates setting 33
  autonomy in 34
tax reliefs 63
Tax Rental Agreements, Canada 173
tax revenue
  and administration, Germany 196–7
  decentralization in OECD 138–9
  Spain 9–12
  and total resources 20, 21
tax-sharing 35
Tax Sharing Agreements 35, 63–4, 68, 69, 173
tax-sharing/transfer model 49
tax system, Spain 214–15
tax transfers 97
tax (VAT) 9, 10
TCA *see* tax collection agreements
TCT *see* tax on capital transfers
terminology, unclear, Spain 154
Territorial Council in Catalonia 237
Territorial Council on Taxation 216, 223
  Spain, functions 213
territorial financing 100
territorial inequalities 76
territorial tax, visibility 85
territories in Canada 169
tobacco tax 43, 80, 100, 101
top-province standard 118
trade and commerce, free movement 78
trade tax 204
  Germany 195
training on-the-job, Germany 201–202
transfer system 117

transparency, lack of 21
transportation taxes 41–2

uniform regulation 91, 96
unilateralism 112
United States 92
  and Canada model 49
  retail sales tax 86
user fees 124

Valencia, Autonomous Community 162–3
  information technology use 216
  tax unfairness 223
Valencian Tax Service 229
value-added tax (VAT) 43, 80, 86, 87, 182
  Autonomous Communities portion 87–90
  Canada 183
  Germany 68, 69, 195, 207
  Quebec 180
  Spain 16
  at sub-national level 45–6
vehicle taxes 41–2
vendor sales, exchange of information 186
vertical fiscal imbalance 111
vertical imbalances 150
viable integrated VAT (VIVAT) 48
victimhood 77
VIVAT, viable integrated VAT 48
Vizcaya, Spain 219
volatility of equalization 111
voluntary compliance 236

wage tax cards 202
  Germany 202–03
war financing 113
Wartime Tax Agreements, Canada 173
wealth tax 9, 11, 16
  administration 218
  audits 223
  compliance 223
  Spain 233
wealthy and poor areas 76
welfare, Canada 110
withholding mechanism 221

zero-rating approach 47